Islam in Tropical Africa

Islam in Tropical Africa

Second Edition

Edited by
I. M. Lewis

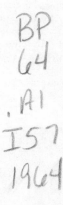

International African Institute
in association with
Indiana University Press
Bloomington and London

Manufactured in Great Britain

Library of Congress Cataloging in Publication Data

International African Seminar, 5th, Zaria, Nigeria, 1964.
   Islam in tropical Africa, Second Edition, 1980.
   Includes bibliographies and index.
    1. Islam—Africa—Congresses. 2. Africa—History—
Congresses. 3. Muslims—Africa—Congresses.
I. Lewis, I. M. II. Title.
BP64.A1I57 1964 297'.096   79-3292

ISBN 0-253-14956-8 (cloth)
ISBN 0-253-28514-3 (paper) 1 2 3 4 5 84 83 82 81 80

CONTENTS

PREFACE TO THE SECOND EDITION

Since this volume of papers from the Fifth International African Seminar, held at Zaria, was first published in 1966 there has been a healthy growth in research on Islam in sub-Saharan Africa. Some of the more important additions to the literature on themes discussed in the Introduction have been indicated in the footnotes to this edition and are included in the additional reference section on page 92 (which, however, makes no pretension to being exhaustive). This recent work includes monographic studies by social anthropologists and political historians on particular religious brotherhoods (e.g. Cohen, 1968; O'Brien, 1971), comparative works on the Islamic brotherhoods and the *jihads* associated with them (Martin, 1976), studies on the interaction between Islam and traditional African politics (e.g. Last, 1967; Levtzion, 1968; Paden, 1973), more general histories (e.g. Willis, 1979), and a valuable survey of the whole field by the distinguished Arabist, J. S. Trimingham (1968).

One of the more interesting theoretical developments is the debate between R. Horton (1971, 1975) and H. J. Fisher (1973) on the relationship between traditional African beliefs and infrastructures and conversion to Islam. Following our general argument (see e.g. pp. 59, 80 and 81), Horton contends that the expansion of socio-economic relations associated with the development of trade and colonization accentuated indigenous theistic concepts, thus facilitating conversion to Allah as a transcendent deity. Islam, as it were, did not invent God, but rather took advantage of trends in African cosmology which were already in train independently of Muslim prosyletization. Pursuing this line of argument, Horton adopts what he terms an 'intellectualist' (but it is also Durkheimian) view of conversion which seems too narrow to apply adequately in the case of Islam or other religions. For contrary to this mentalistic view, Islam is not simply or solely a way of explaining things intellectually at the conscious level: it is also a source of spiritual solace and pride and a set of rules for life. At the same time, the Muslim faith introduces, as we emphasize, a radically different eschatological evaluation of sin and moral dereliction, which adds a new dimension to most traditional religious concepts—a factor largely ignored in Horton's somewhat mechanistic model.

In common with most orientalists and theologians, Fisher in contrast overvalues the influence of Islam as a transcendental spiritual force and underestimates the significance in conversion of traditional religious beliefs and institutions. Like that of the Islamic proselytizer his approach is essentially diffusionist. In this vein Fisher follows the leading British authority on Islam in Africa, J. S. Trimingham, whose three-stage model of conversion (germination, crisis, and gradual re-orientation) he transcribes as 'quarantine', 'mixing', and 'reform'. These phases may indeed seem to characterize a gradual process of acculturation (or enculturation at the individual level) from the perspective of an external Muslim observer, or one applying the external standards of Islamic observance and belief. They do not necessarily, however, convey what the people (or person) so characterized consider themselves to be—Muslim or non-Muslim. Nor do they do full justice to the subtleties of a faith in which the most revered of saints are regularly exonerated from performing the daily Islamic observances. The limitations of this diffusionist approach and of Horton's intellectualist perspective are highlighted if we ask how they could possibly explain the contemporary Black Muslim movement in America. This example, by no means necessarily unique to its present period and setting, indicates the crucial importance of Islam as an *identity* as well as a religious faith. Both views again neglect what many people would take to be the typical conversion experience, where divine election manifests itself as a searing affliction which can only be cured by entering the new religion (cf. Lewis, 1971).

Although it seems unlikely to be resolved in terms of single cause explanations, the problem of conversion has clearly received considerable attention since the first edition of this book. Other issues have attracted less interest and discussion. It may be worthwhile to draw attention to topics which seem unjustifiably neglected and invite further research. It is still unfortunately true that there is a surprising dearth of research by sociologists or social anthropologists on the relationship between actual beliefs and ritual, in the sense of practical religion, in Muslim societies in sub-Saharan Africa. More specifically, there remains much to learn of the processes by which traditional African deities and spirits (including ancestors) are incorporated in Islam. Similarly, the interplay between indigenous jural institutions and the Shari'a which has been so extensively treated elsewhere, has been almost ignored by social scientists working in this region of the Islamic world. On a broader canvas, comparative historical research on the expansion of Islam under the different colonial regimes remains as unexplored as the important theme of the influence of Islam on the development of modern African nationalism. For those who seek promising research topics, Islam in sub-Saharan Africa offers an unusual abundance of un-exploited and exciting material. A new generation of African scholars is beginning, but only beginning, to turn its energies seriously to this rich heritage.

I. M. LEWIS

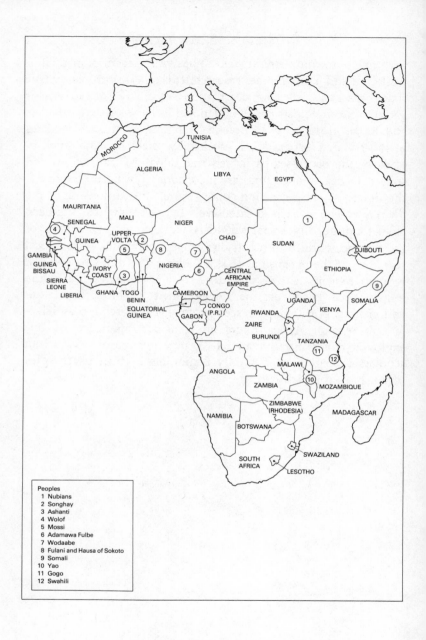

Peoples
1 Nubians
2 Songhay
3 Ashanti
4 Wolof
5 Mossi
6 Adamawa Fulbe
7 Wodaabe
8 Fulani and Hausa of Sokoto
9 Somali
10 Yao
11 Gogo
12 Swahili

I. Location of Peoples referred to in Special Studies

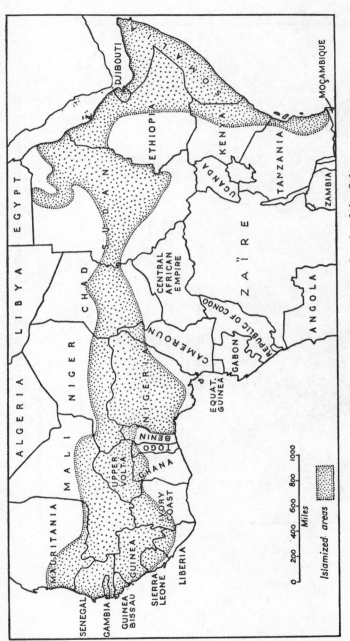

II. Contemporary Distribution of Islam South of the Sahara

Islamized areas

Miles
0   200 400 600 800 1000

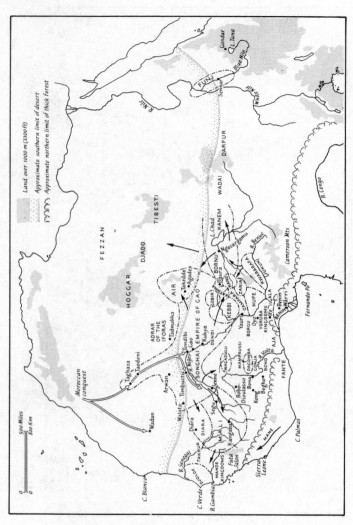

III. Principal Areas of Muslim Influence in the Sixteenth Century

Land over 1000 m (3300 ft)
Approximate southern limit of desert
Approximate northern limit of thick forest

500 Miles
800 Km

C. Blanco
Wadan
Arwan
Taghaza
Taodeni
Moroccan conquest
FEZZAN
HOGGAR
DJADO
TIBESTI
ADRAR OF THE IFORAS
Tadmakka
AIR
Takedda
Agades
Walata
Timbuktu
Tondibi
Gao
SONGHAI EMPIRE OF GAO
Kukiya
DENDI
R. Niger
Jenne
R. Senegal
Diara
DIARA
MALI
MANDE KINGDOMS
Kangaba
Futa Jalon
C. Verde
R. Gambia
TAKRUR
Sierra Leone
C. Palmas
MANE
Bobo Dioulasso
Kong
Bono
Begho
FANTE
WAGADUGU
MAMPRUSSI
DAGOMBA
GURMA
GONJA
R. Volta
Bond
Oyo
YORUBA KINGDOMS
AJA
Benin
IBO
ISHAN
Warri
Fernando Po
NUPE
BORGU
Yauri
KEBBI
GOBIR
KATSINA
KANO
ZAZZAU
ZARIA
DAURA
BORNU
KANEM
L. Chad
Ngazargamu
WADAI
DARFUR
HAUSALAND
MANDARA
MARGHI
Cameroon Mts
R. Benue
R. Congo
R. Nile
Blue Nile
Gondar
L. Tana
Sennar
FUNJ
JINJ
White Nile

1. INTRODUCTION

The Muslim population of tropical Africa[1] is more widely scattered and less continuous in its distribution than that of North Africa. In many instances its members form minority communities in states which have no national allegiance to Islam, and even when they live in countries which are predominantly Muslim, few of these are formally constituted as Islamic states.[2] Despite this, however, likely estimates place their total number at almost 60,000,000,[3] the same figure usually taken to represent the strength of the Muslim population of North Africa. Tropical Africa, therefore, notwithstanding the highly variegated character of its peoples' religious adherence and their wide cultural diversities, is thus nearly a quarter Muslim, and must be regarded as one of the major Islamic areas of the world.

The Special Studies which form the basis for this volume consider particular aspects of the Islamic life of a number of communities—widely separated in space and time—within this great Muslim belt. This introductory essay, which serves as a preface to these Studies, begins by reviewing the broad historical circumstances and salient characteristics of the penetration of Islam in the five regions into which tropical Africa may conveniently be divided. It then proceeds to consider the contribution made to the dissemination of Islam by such agencies as trade and

[1] I.e. Africa south of the Sahara, but excluding Southern Africa.

[2] Exceptions are the Somali and Sudan Republics.

[3] Approximately two-thirds of this total are concentrated in West Africa, and about 19,000,000 of these live in Nigeria. In Senegal, Guinea, Mali, and Niger, Muslims constitute the predominant element, while the proportionately smallest Muslim populations are found in Liberia, Ghana, and Togo. In North-East, East, and Central Africa, where the remaining third of the total Muslim population of tropical Africa is found, Muslims are in the majority in the Sudan Republic (c. 9,000,000), while Zanzibar and the Somali Republic have for all intents and purposes entirely Muslim populations. The Muslim element is also strong in Ethiopia (including Eritrea) and in Tanzania, representing perhaps a quarter to a third in each case. The smallest Muslim communities are found in Uganda, Malawi, Zambia, Zimbabwe (Rhodesia), and in Zaïre.

proselytization. This leads to consideration of the interaction between traditional local institutions and Islam in the political field, and that in turn to the wider problem of the impact of Islamic Law on customary law and practice. Discussion of the influence of Islam on traditional religious phenomenology and on beliefs and ritual follows; and in the final section attention centres on the more contemporary issues of the role of Islam in the colonial and post-colonial periods.

These themes are broadly those which were followed in our general discussions at Zaria, and many of the points made then are incorporated in the essay which follows.[4] Here the principal aim is to outline a sociological framework within which the inter-relations between African and Muslim beliefs and institutions can be meaningfully and profitably discussed.

Since there is in European languages, to say nothing of Arabic, already a substantial body of writing on Islam in Africa, it might be thought that the preparation of a short sociological essay such as this would be a light task. This, however, has not proved to be the case. For, on closer examination of much of this literature, it becomes abundantly clear that the sociological study of the connexions between beliefs and ritual among living Muslim peoples is still in its infancy. The present position is thus a frustrating one; and it is necessary to begin by challenging such misleading preconceptions as that only centralized states can readily adopt Islam, or that matrilineal societies are uniformly resistant to Muslim penetration, or that Islamic marriage rules are incompatible with clan exogamy, before proceeding to establish the real implications of the conversion of African societies to Islam.

If, therefore, many of the conclusions reached in the following pages seem negative this is largely a reflection of the superficiality and inadequacy of much of our present knowledge. It is also a demonstration of the fundamental fact that Islam can be analysed sociologically only within the social context of the actual life and folk beliefs of living Muslim communities. What is

[4] Here I should like to acknowledge my debt to all the discussants at Zaria. For comments on earlier drafts of this introduction I am particularly grateful to the painstaking comment and criticism of Dr. Abner Cohen, Professor Daryll Forde, Professor Spencer Trimingham, and Dr. Peter Ucko.

enshrined in the orthodox literary tradition of Islam and usually taken as this religion's essential character is often very differently represented in the concepts and practices which inform everyday Muslim life. Moreover, the method long established in Islamic Studies of tracing the origins and historical development of beliefs and institutions does not necessarily take one very far in understanding their contemporary significance in any given social context of living Islam. Of course, history, where it is known or discernible, cannot be ignored—to do so would be to limit the scope and depth of social analysis—but purely historical explanations of events in terms of their antecedents are no substitute for systematic analysis of the manner in which institutions are inter-related and mutually sustaining in a given social setting.[5]

Thus, in this province of Islamic Studies, as elsewhere in the subject, the final plea must be for more intensive field research on actual Muslim communities. And, for the social anthropologist and sociologist, there is the added challenge that the study of the interaction between traditional pre-Islamic and Muslim beliefs and institutions offers special opportunities for testing the validity of functional hypotheses. If a social anthropologist's analysis of the social significance or 'functions' of institutions and customs in a traditional Pre-Islamic community is correct it should have some predictive value in suggesting how Islam will be accommodated. New developments under the impact of Islam which do not support the previous analysis must inevitably cast doubt on its validity. Hence the study of Islam in Africa, particularly where Islam and Christianity are competing for new adherents, presents a field full of potentialities for the social scientist and deserves much more rigorous and concerted attention than it has so far received.

[5] See E. E. Evans–Pritchard, *Anthropology and History*, Manchester University Press, 1961.

I. REGIONAL REVIEW OF THE DISTRIBUTION AND SPREAD OF ISLAM

(a) THE EASTERN SUDAN

Of the regions of tropical Africa which are our concern in this book, Islam made its earliest, most concerted inroads in the Eastern Sudan and Horn of Africa. While the southern part of what is today the Sudan Republic, with its largely Nilotic and negroid populations remained until recently for the most part shielded from any intensive Muslim influence, the north was from early times subject to Islamic penetration along three main paths. From the seventh century Islam began to infiltrate with trade from the east, through the Red Sea ports of Badi, Aydhab, and Suakin (and from the Dahlak Archipelago after A.D. 702.) Later, a western stream of influence through Darfur assumed some importance. But these two distinct lines of Muslim contact pale into insignificance in comparison with the impact of the main channel of early Islamization from Egypt and the north.

Following the Arab invasions and conquest of Egypt, from the seventh century onwards Arab immigrants began to move south into the northern Sudan in an ever-increasing tide. This informal penetration was encouraged rather than hampered by the generally cordial relations which were established between Christian Nubia and the north after the failure of the initial Egyptian attempts at conquest in A.D. 641 and 651. Nevertheless, as Muslim Egypt grew in strength Nubian power gradually diminished over the centuries, and what is remarkable is its surprisingly long span of life rather than its eventual eclipse in 1317 when the Christian kingdom at last bowed to the might of Mamluk Egypt. By this time, the effect of the continuous process of population drift and infiltration was such that the northern Sudan had become extensively populated by Arabic-speaking peoples who had mixed in varying degrees with the indigenous Hamitic peoples giving rise in many cases to entirely new ethnic aggregations.[1] Later Muslim immigrants and proselytizers thus found that a broad framework of Islamic culture had already been established, and this was subsequently further built upon and consolidated, particularly in the Turco-Egyptian period, achieving its most dramatic political expression in the nineteenth-century Mahdia.

This prevailing current of Muslim influence has left an indelible mark on the character of Sudanese Islam. The Egyptian connexion accounts both for the prevalence of the Maliki School of Law introduced from Upper Egypt probably in the middle of the sixteenth century,[2] and for the establishment during the Turco-Egyptian conquest in the early nineteenth century of the Hanafi School as the official code of the courts. At the same time the direct experience, at first hand, of Arabian Islam (the acceptance of which would seem to have been facilitated by correspondences between Hamitic Sudanese and Muslim Arab social institutions) has had a profound effect which is readily apparent in the close association of Islam with Arab identity. More than for most of the other Muslim peoples of Africa, for the Sudanese to be a Muslim is to be an Arab. It is this deep assimilation of Islam and identification with Arab culture and society which is expressed in the universal claim to Arab ancestry[3] and the overwhelming currency of Arabic. Only the Nubians and Beja have preserved their own languages.

When, however, we turn to that other equally salient trait of Sudanese Islam, the emphasis placed on the cult of saints and the great proliferation of Sufi *tariqas* (lit. 'the way', i.e. path of devotion or religious discipline) or Religious Orders (often also called 'brotherhoods')[4], we have to look to the influence of the Hijaz

[1] For a fuller account of this process, see Fadl Hasan below, pp. 112–23.

[2] Holt, 1961, p. 29.

[3] See MacMichael, 1922.

[4] In addition to the various Schools of Law, these Orders form a basis for denominational divisions within orthodox Sunni Islam. The adherents of each Order believe that the religious exercises established by the Order's founder and the distinctive liturgies associated with him represent the ideal path to spiritual blessing. Rivalry between Orders thus centres on the respective powers of sanctity and ritual efficacy—as mediators with God through the Prophet—attributed to their founders. And where the followers of several Orders live together each Order tends to maintain and worship in its own exclusive mosque.

during the Fung period (1500-1800). Trimingham[5] has noted the existence of over twenty separate Orders, many of them locally based, of which the Shadiliyya is probably the earliest (*c.* 1445), and the Mirghaniyya (or Khatmiyya) the most popular today. To appreciate their significance in the recent history of the Sudan it is only necessary to recall that the Mahdi Muhammad Ahmad (1843–85) was himself an affiliate of the Sammaniyya Order, and indeed, *Khalifa* or head of one of its branches. His mission as Mahdi, of course, transcended sectarian *tariqa* loyalties, and his rule showed little tolerance of rival movements. But the division between those who look to the religious leadership of his descendants and are known as the Ansar, and those who adhere to the Khatmiyya Order, remains one of the most important factors in the religious and political life of the Sudan Republic today.

(b) NORTH-EASTERN AFRICA AND THE HORN

Whereas in the eastern Sudan the principal early bearers of Islam were the Arabic-speaking Semitic tribal invaders whose descendants, heavily mixed with Hamitic and negroid indigenous elements, make up so much of the present population, Ethiopia and the Horn of Africa were not subjected to any comparable Muslim Arab influx. Their early Semitic-speaking peoples—of whom the Christian Amhara must be regarded as the prototype—have, on the whole, rejected and resisted Islam, which, by contrast, has made its most notable gains among Hamitic- (or Cushitic-)`speaking populations such as the Saho, 'Afar (Danakil), and Somali, and more recently, and with less striking success, among the Oromo. Important Semitic-speaking peoples who have adopted the Muslim faith, however, are the Beni 'Amir (Beja) of the eastern Sudan and Eritrea, the Bait Asgade, the Marya and Mensa of Eritrea, and some of the Tigrina-speaking groups of Eritrea and north-west Ethiopia.[6]

In this region as a whole the main gateway for Muslim influence has been the Red Sea and Indian Ocean coasts. Along these shores Muslim Arab, and in some cases also Persian colonies,

---

[5] Trimingham, 1949.
[6] For a detailed account, see Trimingham, 1952, pp. 147 ff.

established—or continued—a string of trading posts from shortly after the *hijra*. The Dahlak Islands off the coast of Eritrea were occupied by a Muslim Arab garrison in A.D. 702, after a piratical Abyssinian attack on Jedda, but the most important coastal settlements were apparently at Zeila in the north and Mogadishu in the south. Al-Ya'qubi at the end of the ninth century supplies the first secure reference to Zeila, and later Arab writers describe the town and its political circumstances in increasing detail.[7] Similar evidence, as well as local inscriptions, the earliest dated A.D. 720, indicate that Mogadishu[8] and her sister towns (Merca and Brava), of what later became known to the Arabs as the 'Benadir' coast, had thriving immigrant Muslim communities by the tenth century, appreciably earlier than the date generally accepted for the foundation of Kilwa to the south.

In these small coastal mercantile centres Muslim Arab and Persian merchants and proselytizers settled, usually as local aristocracies with a superior technology, bringing the faith and marrying local women but rarely offering their own daughters in return. Despite thus seeking initially to maintain their own exclusiveness, however, these communities in due time blended in various degrees with the local inhabitants to form a mixed coastal culture. This, at any rate, is the record of the Zeila region, where the final hybrid 'Zeilawi' culture represents a blending of Arab, Somali, and 'Afar (Danakil) elements. With Mogadishu the case was much the same; but here the 'Afar were not represented and Persian influence seems to have been considerable. Farther to the south, at Brava, there was also apparently a Bantu component, the evidence for which is preserved in the town's distinctive Bravani dialect ('Chimbalazi').

As far as the spread of Islam to the peoples of the hinterland is concerned, it was the northern rather than the southern coastal sector which exercised the widest influence. In the north, and especially from the smaller ports to the east of Zeila, the carrying of Islam into the interior coincided with the great series of Somali movements of expansion which, from perhaps as early

[7] See article, 'Zeila', *Encyclopaedia of Islam*.
[8] Ibid., article 'Makdishu', Vol. III, pp. 165–6, and Cerulli, 1957.

as the tenth century and over nearly a thousand years, finally brought the extension of the Somali nation to its most southerly point in northern Kenya.[9] Throughout this large area, and over this long period, the Somali pastoral nomads were the main carriers of Islam and its principal local exponents.

To the north-west the position was different again. Here, from the port of Zeila, the main trade-routes lay towards the Ethiopian highlands by way of Harar,[10] and the expansion of Islam must have been intimately connected with the trade in which Arabs and Arabized Africans participated directly. Commercial expansion and political aggrandisement are probably inextricably mingled in the origins of the Muslim sultanate of Ifat, which arose in eastern Shoa about the end of the ninth century, and to which trade flowed along the caravan routes through the port of Zeila.[11] The same motives seem to explain the associated development of a loosely knit cluster of other Muslim principalities (Dawaro, Hadiya, and Bali) round the periphery of the expanding Christian kingdom of Abyssinia. These early hinterland centres of Islam were soon embroiled in a long and bitter struggle for political supremacy with the Abyssinians. Intermittent hostilities dragged on for almost five hundred years without any truly decisive result for either side until, in 1542 when under their prodigious champion Imam Ahmad Gran (the 'left-handed') the Muslims, although apparently on the point of final victory, were at last defeated utterly, and their states lost all political importance.[12]

In marked contrast to the collapse of Christian Nubia in the Sudan, the final failure of the Muslim holy wars (*jihads*) in Ethiopia in the sixteenth century led to the eclipse of Muslim power in the highlands, to a great efflorescence of Abyssinian and Christian influence—despite the Galla incursions—and to a tradition of religious antagonism between the Christian peoples

---

[9] See Lewis, 1960.   [10] See Cerulli, 1936.
[11] On the history of the state of Ifat, see Cerulli, 1941, and Trimingham, 1952.
[12] For this period there is an unusual wealth of documentation in both the Ethiopian and Muslim chronicles, of which the *Futuh al-Habasha*, written about 1540 by Shihab al-Din, who was present at many of the battles, is quite outstanding.

of the highlands and the Muslims of the lowlands and coast. The *jihad*, so forcibly led at the beginning of this century by the Somali Shaikh Muhammad 'Abdille Hassan, was a latter-day attempt at Muslim resistance in the era of Christian colonization and Abyssinian encroachment in the Muslim Somali lowlands.[13]

Although in those parts of the area in contact with the eastern Sudan both the Maliki and Hanafi Schools of Law are represented, the proximity to and constant social and cultural interchange with most of the area and the Arabian peninsula have ensured that the dominant School is that of al-Shafi'i. Otherwise the Horn of Africa shares with the Sudan that marked emphasis on the cult of saints and Sufi Orders which is a characteristic feature of traditional Islam. Although fewer *tariqas* are represented, their hold is such that the profession of the faith is virtually synonymous with attachment to, if not formal membership of, an Order. The most important in its following is probably the earliest, the Qadiriyya,[14] reputedly introduced to the ancient centre of Muslim learning of Harar by Sharif Abu Bakr ibn 'Abdallah al-'Aydarus, who died in Aden at the beginning of the sixteenth century. In the nineteenth century, however, the Ahmadiyya *tariqa* of the great Meccan reformer Ahmad ibn Idris al-Fasi (1670–1837) and its derivatives—notably the Salihiyya to which Muhammad 'Abdille Hassan belonged—assumed prominence. Although, as in the Eastern Sudan, modernist opinion today is often strongly opposed to the excessive veneration of saints and the exaggerated regard in which some holy men are traditionally held, the Orders continue to play an important role in the lives of the majority.

(c) EAST AFRICA

If authentic sources for retracing the early history of Islam in North-East Africa leave much to be desired there is little improvement as we move farther south into the East African coastal zone proper. Here the earliest known local inscription is the dedication of the mosque in Kizimkazi in southern Zanzibar,

[13] See Lewis, 1965(*a*), pp. 63–91.
[14] The Qadiriyya is the oldest Order in Islam. It was founded by Sayyid 'Abd al-Qadir al-Jilani, who died in Baghdad in A.D. 1166 and whose name is celebrated throughout the Muslim world.

which dates as late as A.D. 1107. Moreover, there is some conflict
between such documentary evidence as may be gleaned from the
early Arab geographers[15] and the results of recent archaeological
excavation; Ibn Battuta, for example, describing the chief mosque
of Kilwa as a wooden structure in 1332, whereas archaeologists
conclude that it must have been made of stone at this time.[16]
Equally, although the local Swahili chronicles appear at first
sight to promise much, it must not be forgotten that their composition cannot generally be securely dated before the nineteenth
century. Nevertheless, it is commonly accepted that the Kilwa
Chronicle giving the date of Kilwa's foundation as A.D. 957 is
probably the most reliable.

Yet although much is thus left in obscurity and doubt, certain
broad trends can be distinguished. In the first place, in contrast
to the circumstances of the implanting of Islam in the Eastern
Sudan and Horn, where the tides of population movement seem
generally to have favoured the advance of the faith, in East
Africa the case is very different. Here, as a whole, the trend of
population movement seems mostly to have been from the non-
Muslim hinterland—as with the mysterious Zimba incursions
of the sixteenth century, and with the predatory movements of
the Galla in the northern sector of the area a little later. These
and the ultimately paralysing effect of the Portuguese presence
dealt a severe blow to the Shirazi and largely Persian-inspired
coastal culture. Henceforth the dominant Muslim influence was
from the Hadramaut, and this ensured the overwhelming prevalence of the Shafi'i School of Law.

Secondly, as the Kilwa Chronicle and other sources seem to
emphasize, the centre of gravity of early Muslim settlement was
not so much on the coast itself as on the offshore islands, the
Comores, Zanzibar, and Pemba. And despite the exploitation
by Arab traders of the resources in gold, ivory, and slaves of
the interior, there seems until recent times little evidence of any
powerful politico-economic Muslim centres in the distant
hinterland. Indeed, apart from the connexions of Sofala with the

---

[15] For a recent examination of these sources see Trimingham, 1964, pp. 1–18.
[16] Kirkman, 1954. See also Chittick, 1963.

Rhodesian mines, only apparently towards the end of the eighteenth century did Muslim traders regularly frequent the far interior.

From early times until the nineteenth century, therefore, Islam seems to have remained an important force only on the islands and along the coast. Its diffusion along such inland trade-routes as existed must be assumed to have been discouraged both by the nature of the terrain and its lack of large centres of population and resources sufficient to attract the serious attention of the Arab merchant. For, unlike West and North-East Africa, there were few large-scale centralized kingdoms in the far interior to serve as foci of economic interest, and the diffusion of Islam by other means was hampered by the prevailing currents of population movement. Moreover, such traffic as there was seems to have been directed mainly towards the satisfaction of outside markets, and carried out largely by slavers in a manner which was hardly conducive to the reciprocal flow of goods characteristic of trade elsewhere.

The impact of the hinterland on the coast, rather than the opposite trend, is reflected in the structure of the Swahili language with its rich store of Bantu roots. This is also apparent in the distinctive character of Swahili culture as a whole, with its unique synthesis of Bantu and Perso-Arab elements in no sense a pale replica of Arabian civilization. In East Africa, consequently, the prototype of the local Muslim is not the Arab, but the Swahili, and new Arab settlers, as much as Africans from the interior, have to adopt Swahili culture before they can gain acceptance as members of this coastal society.[17]

Originally, the Shirazi–Swahili area probably extended northwards at least as far as Brava, which, with its Swahili dialect 'Chimbalazi', thus formed a bridge between the Islam of North-East Africa and that of the East African coast. From the twelfth to the fourteenth centuries Mogadishu and Kilwa seem to have shared the distinction of being the most important towns on the coast, Kilwa exerting a fitful control over the

[17] For a recent examination of the character of Swahili culture see Lyndon Harries, 1964, and also Arens, 1975.

lucrative gold trade through Sofala to the south. Thereafter, Pate assumed prominence; and by the fifteenth century there were at least thirty-seven towns established along the littoral from Kilwa in the south to Mogadishu in the north.[18]

Notwithstanding the obscurity which still surrounds their detailed political history, it is now clear that the many different circles of alliance which these towns assumed at different times scarcely approached the mythical 'Zanj Empire', based on Kilwa, of nineteenth-century tradition.[19] Moreover, the arrival of the Portuguese in the fifteenth century appears to have coincided with the period of greatest local turbulence and disorganization, the combined effect of which was to reduce the coastal centres to isolated outposts or deserted ruins.[20] It was only after this devastation, probably in the seventeenth century, that the fusion of various ethnic elements, with their strong Bantu component, took place in the new synthesis of Swahili culture and society. By this time, Mombasa had become the strategic centre for the entire Swahili coast and continued to enjoy this position until the Omani conquests. Finally, after the Portuguese withdrawal, from the middle of the eighteenth century Mombasa's fortunes again began to improve until the rise of Zanzibar in the nineteenth century.

Throughout this long era of Muslim influence, essentially restricted to the coast and islands, the whole area's history is fundamentally maritime, with occasional eruptions from the hinterland inimical to Islam. All this has naturally left its mark on East African Islam, which, besides its Swahili setting, remains largely town-based, poly-ethnic in spirit, and directed towards the formation and development of urban commercial enterprise rather than profoundly embedded in the exclusivistic social structures of the peoples of the interior. In conformity with this, the main local shrines of saint veneration are on the coast, as for example at Lamu; but in any case the cult of saints does not seem to have achieved an importance comparable to that in North-East Africa. Nor has the assimilation of lineage ancestors to Sufi

[18] See Mathew, 1963.   [19] See Freeman–Grenville, 1962.
[20] Prins, 1961, pp. 44 ff.

saints, typical of that region, occurred here on the same scale.[21] The *tariqas*, of which the Qadiriyya has the largest following, are also largely limited to the coast, and do not seem to figure as prominently in local Islam as in the Eastern Sudan and Horn.[22]

Finally, as has already been indicated, the principal Law School is undoubtedly that of Shafi'i; but the Ibadi code is important in Zanzibar, where it was introduced with the ruling Arab class from Oman. Alone of the regions dealt with in this book, East Africa has also a substantial Shi'a community composed almost exclusively of relatively recent Indian and Pakistani immigrants.

(d) CENTRAL AFRICA AND THE CONGO

With central Africa we enter a more peripheral zone in which Muslim influence today is slight, but where there is some vestigial indication of a once larger Islamic presence brought chiefly by Arab and Swahili traders. It has been claimed, for instance, that Muslim influence in the form of 'Bantuized Perso-Arabs or Indo-Arabs' made itself felt in the Karanga kingdom of what is today Zimbabwe (Rhodesia) as early as the tenth century, and that by the sixteenth, when the Portuguese dislodged the Arab settlement at Sena on the Zambezi there were several thousand Arabs settled in the Karanga provinces.[23] While it is not improbable that further discoveries may corroborate these indications and reveal other evidence of early Muslim penetration of these areas, there seems little doubt that such importance as it had was checked decisively by the Portuguese.

What remained of Arab influence after this time lay dormant until the nineteenth century, when the stimulus of Zanzibari interest and the new demand for slaves on the coast inaugurated a new expansion of Muslim trading ventures. Thus, by the 1830s, as Dr. Cunnison has shown,[24] Arab traders from Zanzibar were firmly ensconced among the Lunda. Indeed, by 1882/3 these merchants seeking ivory and slaves, having occupied the

[21] This, of course, is partly to be expected in view of differences in social structure between the regions.

[22] For a recent survey of the main Orders, see Trimingham, 1964, pp. 93–103.

[23] Abraham, 1961, p. 212.   [24] Cunnison, 1963.

Maniema region in North East Zaïre, had opened a post at Stanley Falls, and by 1889 had reached the neighbourhood of Lake Albert.[25] Their most westerly post was at Isangi, across the Lomami from Stanley Falls. While their interests were evidently primarily commercial, these Muslim traders found it convenient to build up a loose-knit organizational network which did, incipiently at least, exert some wider religious and political effect. Leopold II's colonizing action in the Congo, as Fr. Ceulemans shows,[26] at first took advantage of this Arab presence and thus temporarily strengthened its impact.

The nineteenth-century renewal of Muslim activity was not only centred on Zanzibar, nor was it merely commercial. In the same period this region was also subjected to pressure aiming at Muslim conquest from the north. This came first from the Egyptians pushing southwards towards Lake Victoria; and then from the Sudanese Mahdists, who in 1894 briefly established themselves on the Upper Uele; and finally, also from the Muslim ruler of Ndele to the north-west. This latter-day resurgence of Muslim interest, however, was too long delayed and came at a most unpropitious time for successful consummation. The collapse of the Mahdists, and the strong measures taken by the European powers, of whom the British particularly were at this time naturally enough obsessed by fears of Islamic dominion and Mahdism, nipped the new efflorescence in the bud. Islam's advance was sharply arrested; and many tribes proceeded to relinquish those elements of Muslim dress and accoutrement which, in emulation of the Arabs and Sudanese, they had begun to adopt. Only in parts of Tanzania and among the Yao of Malawi was the influence of Islam sustained on any substantial scale.

Subsequently, Islam seems to have made little notable advance. Partly, no doubt, this is to be ascribed to the association of the Christian missions in Malawi with African nationalism and to the unfavourable political circumstances of the immigrant Asian communities who have been Islam's chief recent protagonists. More fundamentally, however, account must also be taken

[25] See Ceulemans, in *Islam*, 1st ed., pp. 174–176.   [26] Ibid., pp. 180–187.

of the fact that the area is one in which matrilineal descent is strongly entrenched, as the prevailing traditional system followed in the inheritance of property and in succession to office. For while, as will be discussed more fully presently, matrilineal descent favours rather than hinders the initial establishment of immigrant Muslim dynasties, it can scarcely be said to facilitate the wider diffusion of the principles of Muslim inheritance which emphasize patrilineal kinship ties at the expense of matrilineal connexions. Consequently, although in Central Africa Islam has certainly gained a foothold, it can scarcely be said to have penetrated very deeply, despite the considerable extension of Swahili as a lingua franca. In so far as it was introduced mainly from the East African coast, its features are similar to those of Swahili Islam, the local element distinguishing Muslim ritual in Tanzania being the *jando* circumcision ceremonies.[27] *Tariqa* affiliation is hardly widely significant, although among the Yao denominational cleavages are of some significance.[28]

(e) WEST AFRICA

Islam entered this region mainly from the northern Sahara, its southward advance being facilitated by traffic and movements of population in the same general direction. Thus, as in the North-East, in West Africa also there was a wide early proliferation of Muslim influence in the interior of the region which was directly connected with the foundation and expansion of trading states, and eventually produced a series of local distinctive Muslim cultures. Unlike the Horn and Eastern Sudan, however, Islam was not spread mainly by Arabs, even initially, but rather by other Muslim and only partly Arabized peoples. Unquestionably the most influential of these were the Berbers, whose prominent role ensured the dominance of Maghribi influence throughout most of Muslim West Africa.

Despite certain important lacunae, a broad chronological framework for the history of the spread of Islam in the later medieval empires of Ghana, Mali, and Songhay has now been

---

[27] See Trimingham, 1964, pp. 129 ff., and below, p. 111.
[28] See Mitchell, 1956, pp. 51–2.

proposed.[29] While it is evident that Muslim traders of Berber and Arab affiliation had earlier opened considerable settlements, such as the merchants' quarter associated with the capital of Ghana described in the travellers' reports compiled by the Moorish geographer Al-Bakri in 1067, it was apparently not until the eleventh century that the ruling dynasties came to adopt Islam.[30] This striking advance in the political domain must be ascribed to the far-reaching effects of the rise of the Almoravid sect, which, particularly through its adherence to the Maliki School of Law predominant throughout West Africa, has left a firm imprint. The zealous followers of this early messianic movement conquered Ghana in 1076, and perhaps also won the Mali dynasty for Islam, and finally left evidence of their presence in Songhay in the tombs at Gao.[31] In the same crucial period also, the rulers of Kanem-Bornu seem to have accepted Islam, although in this case the predominant Muslim stimulus came across the central Sahara and derived ultimately from Arabia rather than from the Maghrib.

While much remains to be discovered of the internal Muslim history of these great Niger states, the general outline of their subsequent fortunes is well established. In the first half of the thirteenth century Mali began to replace Ghana after that state's decline and eclipse at the hands of the Almoravids.[32] The rise to renown of the Songhay empire under Sunni 'Ali in the fifteenth century was even more directly at the expense of the predecessor power, Mali. Songhay and its sphere of Muslim influence was in turn largely destroyed by the abortive Moroccan attempt to gain direct control of the Western Sudan in the sixteenth century.[33] This fierce intrusion, however, though it overwhelmed Songhay, developed in time into a new local centre for the spread of Islam.

[29] For a recent appraisal, see Trimingham, 1962; Mauny, 1961; and also Pageard, 1962.

[30] Although as far as Songhay is concerned Al-Muhallabi, quoted in Yaqut (*Mu'jam al-buldan*), describes its rulers as Muslim at the end of the tenth century

[31] See Sauvaget, 1950, and Vire, 1959.

[32] The Arab traveller Ibn Battuta spent about eight months in Mali and a month at Gao in the middle of the fourteenth century. His direct observations are reported in his *Tuhfat al-nuẓẓar*.

[33] And it is in this and the following century that the two most important local chronicles were composed—Mahmud Kati's, *Ta'rikh al-fattash* (sixteenth century) and Al-Sa'di's, *Ta'rikh al-Sudan* (seventeenth century).

Already, probably in the fourteenth century, both Kanem and Mali had contributed significantly to the introduction of Islam in the Hausa chiefdoms. And about the same time groups of largely non-Muslim Fulani nomads seem to have begun their gradual penetration of Hausaland, although the full import of their presence was not dramatically realized until the *jihads* of the eighteenth and nineteenth centuries.

In the regions peripheral to the great states of Senegal, the Middle Niger, and Chad the importance of the Islamic factor prior to the nineteenth century may have been underestimated, although a final assessment will have to be postponed until further evidence has been uncovered. In Senegambia on the Atlantic coast the records of the Portuguese explorers Ca da Mosto in the mid-fifteenth century and Pacheco Pereira in the sixteenth suggest that already Islam had secured some hold on the Tokolor, Wolof, and Malinke, and not only among the ruling dynasties— although clerics were still largely foreigners (Arabs and Sanhaja). Among the Yoruba in the seventeenth century too, as Bivar and Hiskett have recently shown,[34] Muslim communities were apparently established. In Mossi the settlement of Muslim Yarse was deliberately encouraged, a number of Mossi kings themselves adopting Islam in the eighteenth century.[35]

Such influence also extended into the regions comprehended in modern Ghana, where from the fourteenth century the activities of Muslim Dyula traders played a major role in disseminating Islam. A century later certain of these intrepid entrepreneurs reached the Guinea coast itself. It was their influence which secured the late-sixteenth-century conversion of the Gonja aristocracy, where Muslims came to constitute one of the estates of the realm, and a century later those of Dagomba and Mamprussi. Finally, in Ashanti itself, although traditional opposition prevented the Muslim faith gaining acceptance as the state religion, the King Osei Kwame was converted about 1780.[36]

Although some Dyula communities, as in Kotokoli and no

[34] BSOAS, 1962.
[35] See E. P. Skinner, 'Islam in Mossi Society', below pp. 173ff.
[36] See Ivor Wilks, 'The Position of Muslims in Metropolitan Ashanti in the early 19th Century', below, pp. 144ff.

doubt elsewhere, shed their faith, their significance as a vital
factor in the continuity of Muslim influence from the late medieval
Niger empires to the *jihads* of the eighteenth and nineteenth
centuries cannot be ignored. Of the great surge of Muslim energy
and expansion promoted by the eighteenth- and nineteenth-
century reformers, all that need be stressed here is the connexion
which seems to have existed between the Fulani *jihads* of Futas
Toro and Jallon, Masina, and Sokoto and the Sudanese Mahdia,[37]
and through this movement with the Somali *jihad* of 1900–20.[38]
While in no way questioning the extent to which each of these
'protest' movements must be seen as rooted in its own local
circumstances, there can be no more impressive demonstration
of the effectiveness of the vital network of communication and
sentiment which Islam had succeeded in establishing by the end
of the nineteenth century.

As far as the character of West African Islam is concerned,
it is important to note the strong emphasis placed on the law
(here Maliki) as the basis of Islam, its connexion with the rise of
centralized states, and its eventual fulfilment in theocratic rule.
The cult of Muslim saints which is so strongly engrained in the
Eastern Sudan and North-East Africa is not generally widespread
or important. Instead, the local West African emphasis is on
indigenous spirit-possession cults such as that of the Hausa
bori, rather than as elsewhere on the co-existence of both phenomena. Nevertheless, although their esoteric content is generally
not strongly developed, the *tariqas* have made some impact, their
most significant representatives being the Qadiriyya and Tijaniyya. The first of these was brought to Timbuktu by an Arab
Kunta shaikh in the sixteenth century, while the second was
introduced some two centuries later in the lifetime of its founder,
Ahmad al-Tijani of Fez (*d.* 1815). Of particular interest also is
the more recent, locally based, Senegal Muridiyya Order founded
by Ahmad Bamba (d. 1927) with Qadiriyya associations. This
has acquired remarkable popularity.[39] Elsewhere, the Tijaniyya

[37] See Saburi Biobaku and Muhammad al-Hajj, below, pp. 226ff.
[38] See Lewis, 1965(*a*), pp. 63–91.
[39] See Gouilly, 1952, pp. 116–25; and Bourlon, 1962, pp. 53–74; Monteil, 1962;
O'Brien, 1971.

has rapidly eclipsed the Qadiriyya in the strength of its following, although the latter retains considerable influence in Northern Nigeria through the teaching of 'Uthman dan Fodio. The Hamallist reformist derivative of the Tijaniyya, named after its founder's successor Shaikh Hamallah, whose turbulent career ended with his death in exile in 1943, has been much less successful.[40] Finally, the Indian Ahmadiyya movement, with its strong missionary emphasis, has introduced a new element of religious controversy.[41]

[40] Gouilly, op. cit., pp. 134–61; and Moreau, 1964.
[41] See Fisher, 1963.

II. AGENTS OF ISLAMIZATION

(a) TRADE-ROUTES AND THE SPREAD OF ISLAM

In the previous section we emphasized some of the fortuitous factors which seem to have aided or impeded the spread of Islam in different parts of tropical Africa and noted the apparently crucial significance of the prevailing currents of population movement and migration. In East Africa the overall pressure of population shifts ran contrary to the direction in which Islam was spreading; in the Eastern Sudan, North-East Africa, and West Africa, by contrast, the tides of population movement and Muslim influence broadly coincided—with the results we have seen. We also saw the importance of nomadism as a factor in the dissemination of Islam. We now turn to consider the significance of trade and proselytization as more direct agencies in the spread of Islam through much of tropical Africa.

It is not always easy to distinguish between the Islamizing role of Muslim traders, on the one hand, and of teachers and holy men, on the other, since these two activities are often associated in Muslim communities and regularly combined in the same person. Nevertheless, it is useful to begin consideration of the means by which Islam has penetrated into and spread in tropical Africa by examining the direction and character of long-distance trade, which, in some areas certainly, only made its appearance with the faith. Here, at the outset, it is important to appreciate that, despite the Islamic prescriptions on usury (which in any case are not difficult to circumvent), the Muslim ethic as a whole is markedly favourable to trade, commerce, and industry. These indeed are all regarded as eminently respectable activities, and their practice in Africa has been favoured by the supra-ethnic ethos of Islam, its common procedures and values, and the use of Arabic as a means of commercial communication and account-keeping.

The main routes followed in the expansion of Muslim trade were often those which already linked tropical Africa with the

Mediterranean and Arabia, and which in previous ages had carried some Mediterranean influence as far as the Gulf of Guinea. Thus, by the tenth century the interior of the continent lay exposed to trade and to Islam along three principal axes: through North Africa, through the Red Sea coast, and through the ports of the Indian Ocean. From North Africa the caravan routes fanned out in three main directions. In the west of the desert tracks ran from southern Morocco to Mauritanian Adrar, from the present Algerian–Morocco confines to Wagadu and Ghana by way of Taodeni, and from southern Algeria to Timbuktu via Tuat. In the centre, Tunisia was connected with Gao by way of Ghadames and Air, and from this route subsidiary tracks led towards Tripoli, and in the south towards Chad. To the east, the Nile valley was connected with Darfur through Assiut, and through Darfur with Kanem, while another route led from Cyrenaica through Kufra to Darfur.

Along these well-worn though often hazardous paths passed the more readily transportable riches of the West African hinterland: gold from the deposits along the Upper Niger and Senegal valleys, slaves from most of the area, and ivory, and kola nuts, and in later periods also ostrich feathers and hides. These largely luxury exports were exchanged for the more utilitarian imports of horses, salt, cloth, copper, some metal weapons, as well as of cowrie shells, beads, and trinkets.[1]

Although much of its traffic passed northwards through Egypt, the eastern Sudan had also more direct trading outlets on the Red Sea coast at Suakin, Badi, and Aydhab. Following the routes towards these ports, large caravans crossed the eastern desert to the gold-mines in the Beja country; and particularly at the time of the Crusades this path, with its western connexions through Darfur, was favoured by pilgrims from West Africa and from Egypt on their dangerous and wearisome journey to Mecca, in the course of which many sought to defray their expenses by engaging in trade on the way and some found a permanent home in the Sudan.

[1] On the trade and trade-routes of the Western Sudan, see Bovill, 1933; and Mauny, op. cit., pp. 228–441.

Towards the south, through the port of Zeila on the Somali coast, the line of trade led first to the ancient walled city of Harar in the Ethiopian highlands, the 'Timbuktu of East Africa' as Burton described it in the nineteenth century, and thence along two main paths, one leading westwards towards Shoa and the Sidamo kingdoms, the other ranging farther south through part of the Somali Ogaden to the sacred settlement of Shaikh Hussayn Baliale (dating from at least the sixteenth century) on the Upper Shebelle valley.[2] Besides a host of subsidiary caravan tracks, other important routes ran from Mogadishu and the other ports of the Benadir coast up the valley of the Juba River and its tributaries into south-eastern Ethiopia. Here the traffic in slaves, ivory, and coffee, as well as in rarer commodities such as civet, from the Ethiopian highlands—augmented by hides and skins, ghee, ostrich feathers, and myrrh and frankincense from the torrid pastoral lowlands—passed chiefly through Zeila to the markets of the East. The goods entering in return included cloth, dates, tea, iron, weapons, and chinaware, pottery, and glass vessels, although as in West Africa some of these commodities were also manufactured locally. Grain from the highlands also descended along the same routes to the coastal plains, while salt from Lake Assal was carried far into Ethiopia.[3]

Finally, farther still to the south from the East African coast exports consisted chiefly of ivory, timber, tortoise-shell, skins, ambergris, and gold, as well as the ubiquitous slaves. Here, until the track from the port of Bagamoyo through Wagogo and Tabora to Ujiji on Lake Tanganyika was opened up in the nineteenth century, only in the gold trade from the Rhodesian mines through Sofala did any regular trade-routes reach into the far interior. This line of commerce and Muslim penetration lay far to the south of the much more widely ramifying reticula of trade-routes in the north and west, and the attempts made on the eve of European colonization by the Muslim slavers and merchant chiefs to bring this route firmly into the main channel of Muslim enterprise came too late to alter the general East African picture of coastal concentration.

[2] See Cerulli, 1959, p. 135.   [3] See Pankhurst, 1961.

This brief survey is sufficient to indicate the early association of long-distance trade and the march of Islam, with the consequent implanting of nuclei of Muslim influence, both in the dispersed centres of wealth and political power and in their intermediary staging posts. From Mali, Songhay, and Kanem-Bornu through Darfur and Sennar to the Muslim states of the north-east, all the main centres of trade were strongly influenced by Islam. In the Eastern Sudan, however, where Islam came initially with the Arab tribal migrations from Egypt, trade was a less crucial though by no means negligible vehicle for the dissemination of the faith. And finally, the vital general significance of the trading factor in the spread of Islam is especially apparent in the case of the East African interior, where, prior to the nineteenth century, there was to all intents and purposes neither trade nor Islam.

(b) TRADERS AND THEIR ORGANIZATION

The next step in tracing the concurrent extension of trade and Islam is to distinguish the particular ethnic groups principally involved, the character of their commercial interests, and their internal social organization, as well as their relations with the non-Muslim communities in which they settled and with which they did business. While in North Africa and on the East African coast especially, Persians and Arabs (and much later Indians; and in West Africa particularly, Syrians and Lebanese, etc.), and the medley of mixed communities to which they gave rise by intermarriage with local peoples, played an important part, due attention must also be paid to the crucial role, above all through the caravan trade, of the great camel-owning non-Arab nomads such as the Berbers in North-West Africa and the Somali and 'Afar in the North-East. It was these latter who provided the main link in the chain of trade connexions over vast areas of the continent. And despite the lack, over much of the distances covered by the major routes, of any single uniform rule of peace and order, a system of safe-passage and commercial patronage existed which, though by no means free from extortion, enabled the traffic to flow and ensured its carriers some measure of protection from the dangers of brigandage and banditry.

By these means the territories customarily occupied by independent and frequently mutually hostile peoples, however uncentralized their political organization and free-ranging their movements, could be regularly traversed. At each stage in the journey as the caravan left one sphere of political influence to move into another, agents were hired, preferably from the most influential groups, whose patronage ensured the support of their kinsmen and provided the members of the caravan with temporary rights of citizenship in the area concerned. This system of safe-conduct was paralleled in the arrangements applied to foreign Arab and Persian merchants in the ports of the Red Sea and Indian Ocean coast, where, at least in the Somali area, prominent local figures were engaged to act as patrons and protectors (*abbans*) to ensure their employers the co-operation and support of their clansmen in case of need.[4]

As well as these nomads converted to Islam who found in long-distance trade an attractive and profitable supplement to pastoralism, a number of other indigenous peoples in West Africa developed highly specialized commercial organizations associated with Islam which, though operating often on a smaller scale, also contributed much to the promotion of the new religion. Of special significance here were the Hausa and the Karimiya (of Kanem) in the east, and the Dyula on the marches of the Mande empire farther to the west. Although little is yet known of the details of their early trading organization and of their part in the extension of Islam at different periods, some conception of their significance may be indicated by a brief consideration of the Dyula.

The name Dyula, which in Malinke means 'trader', is a generic term used today to refer to a number of Malinke-speaking Muslim named and highly dispersed corporations (such as the Watara, Turay, Kulibali, Bamba, etc.), specializing in commerce.

---

[4] This system, which is still in operation in some Somali centres, is described at Mogadishu by Yaqut (twelfth century) and by Ibn Battuta (fourteenth century). For further information see Lewis, 1961, pp. 186–9.

Membership of these groups is generally acquired by birth, a son following his father; although descent is not usually traced to a common ancestor nor are the groups exogamous. While in many cases cherishing Arab and sometimes Meccan pedigrees, the Dyula today seem to trace their origins and early dispersal centre to the medieval empire of Mali,[5] from which their outwards spread apparently gathered momentum from the fourteenth century. By establishing trading colonies, and sometimes later states, these Muslim merchants created a wide-flung supra-ethnic network of trade which, according to the evidence of the Arab historian Ibn Battuta, had spread widely by the middle of the fourteenth century, and extended to Hausaland (the Kano Chronicle), Senegambia, and the Guinea Coast (Portuguese records) a century later. Through their organization in dispersed corporations, or guilds, they were able to wield considerable economic influence within the various states and communities in which they operated. Thus, an eighteenth-century Dyula merchant in Timbuktu might well employ agents buying gold in Ashanti in the south, and others selling it in Fez in North Africa. In central West Africa, where they met with the Hausa, the latter similarly enjoyed a virtual monopoly of trade to the east, working through what are today the states of Nigeria, Benin (Dahomey), Togo, and Ghana.[6]

With their large extension and scope, these wide-ranging Muslim trading communities inevitably command attention. But we must also take due account of the smaller, more diversified, and technically specialized communities of Muslim craftsmen,[7] of various origin and provenance, who made themselves indispensable in the main centres of the West African states and elsewhere as blacksmiths, leather-workers, dyers, and jewellers (working gold and silver), and in later periods as gunsmiths and

[5] Delafosse, 1912, and others have regarded the Dyula as of Soninke origin, suggesting Masina as their point of dispersion. The view expressed here is based on Professor Ivor Wilks' studies on the Dyula in Ghana, the Ivory Coast, and Upper Volta. See also Levtzion, 1968; Person, 1968.

[6] Dr. A. Cohen has recently made an extensive study of contemporary Hausa trading activities in Southern Nigeria, the results of which should throw new light on this important topic. See Cohen, 1965, 1968, and Yusuf, 1975.

[7] As distinct from indigenous non-Muslim artisans and specialists.

artificers. Characteristic examples of these economically specialized Muslim nuclei are to be found in the Kotokoli of Togo,
the Bauba of Benin, and in the *kalmashubbe* goldsmiths of
such ancient centres at Harar and Mogadishu in North-East
Africa. Being less mobile, these small immigrant craft communities
tended to settle more permanently among non-Muslim populations, and marrying with their hosts, or certain classes of them at
least, must often have produced a more enduring impression.
They and those other Muslim immigrants who lived as permanent
residents in their adopted communities often acted as agents and
retailers, and as brokers and bankers for their more mobile co-
religionists, fulfilling a vital service in the collection and dissemination of market intelligence. Where the majority of their
hosts remained attached to traditional religious beliefs, such
Muslim minorities with the women they had married locally
occupied a distinctive and relatively self-contained quarter of a
town; or, if their numbers warranted it, formed their own urban
aggregation separate from the traditional political capital.

Throughout much of tropical Africa these ethnically diverse
Muslim traders and craftsmen seem often to have been the first
bearers of Islam and to have at least prepared the ground for a
later expansion of their faith, even where they made no efforts
at direct proselytization. Although all too little is yet known of
the initial impact made by them in particular areas and circumstances, or of their social relations with their hosts, the attention
attracted by their practice of the outward Muslim devotions and
the effect of their confidence in the superior spiritual power of
Islam in healing the sick, in ensuring the fertility of women and
crops, and in averting the dangers of witchcraft and sorcery can
be gauged from the regard in which they are held in those regions
in which Islam is spreading today. At the same time, we know
how in many cases such immigrant Muslim commercial colonies
sought, for the most part successfully, to gain the benevolent
protection and patronage of their local rulers. However damaging
to the position of traditional ritual experts and cult-leaders who
naturally sought to preserve their authority, such support
inevitably enhanced the standing of the new religion and culture

of which these Muslim immigrants were the bearers. It did not, of course, ensure its success. There are many examples of the strong traditional reaction which this provoked, sweeping away with it in some cases rulers who, with miscalculated enthusiasm, had too warmly espoused the cause of Islam.[8]

(c) TEACHERS AND HOLY MEN

If for so many parts of tropical Africa Muslim traders must be regarded as those who first blazed the trail for the eventual extension of Islam, it was the holymen and teachers who accompanied and followed them, or they themselves in this guise, who were left with the task of consolidating the process of religious conversion. Widely separated in space and time, by teaching and practice, by their mystical powers (*baraka*) claimed for and attributed to them, as mediators in secular as well as religious affairs, and with their additional advantage as participators in a written culture whose mysteries were only available directly to the literate, these sturdy protagonists of Islam came to exercise a remarkable effect in the communities upon which they impinged and into which they often married. Wherever trade or migration established new Muslim communities, teachers were required to train the young and to direct the religious life of the faithful. This was all the more necessary where commercial infiltration had sewn the seed of Islam more widely, and those turning towards the new religion sought advice and guidance, and not merely in the religious and ritual spheres.

On this basis the celebrated 'Abdallah ibn Yassin, founder of the Moravids, launched his mission, at first unsuccessful, among the Sanhaja in the eleventh century; similarly, the Fung kings encouraged holy men from the Hijaz to settle among them as teachers from the fourteenth century; and Mansa Musa imported sharifs to teach Islam in Mali a century later. The same century witnessed a wholesale influx of Fulani clerics into Hausaland; and the Qadiriyya Order made its first appearance in West Africa, where it was introduced at Timbuktu by the Moorish teacher 'Umar al-Bakka'i (d. 1553) of the Kunta tribe. About the same

[8] See, e.g., below, pp. 37–8.

this time Order was also apparently established from Aden by Sharif Abu Bakr ibn ʿAbdallah al-ʿAydarus (d. 1503) at Harar in North-East Africa, where the thrusting Muslim states led by Ifat had already attracted considerable numbers of teachers from Arabia, as well as producing their own.

The arrival of such foreign proselytizers as these, usually in the wake of trade, and many others with a less-widespread impact, such, for example, as Sharif Yusuf ibn Ahmad al-Kawneyn, who probably in the twelfth century gave a new impetus to Islam among the Somali nomads,[9] or Muhammad al-Jaʿali, who brought the faith to the Nuba Hills about 1530,[10] soon gave rise to thriving local centres of Muslim learning and scholarship, of which the best known were Djenne and Timbuktu in the west and Harar in the east. This gave a self-perpetuating character to the new religion; for each great shaikh produced scores of teachers, each of whom in turn, as his reputation grew, built up a large following of local pupils. Lacking any formal hierarchy beyond the loose organizations of clergy associated with the Religious Orders and with no exclusivistic tradition of expatriate appointment, there was little or no barrier to the recruitment and training of local teachers to spread the faith.

Whether or not this growth of an indigenous clergy necessarily introduced an entirely new occupational category—for the analogies perceived in many regions between Muslim holy-men and traditional ritual experts must not be overlooked—it often provided in societies where Islam was expanding successfully a new line of social advancement, especially for those of traditionally low status. In other more deliberate ways, too, many of these early fathers of African Islam made great efforts to make their message readily comprehensible, explaining the Quran, *hadiths*, and Shariʿa in the local vernacular, and often encouraging the transcription of the vernacular in the Arabic script, as, for example, among the Wolof,[11] Hausa, Swahili, and Somali. Not every great teacher, perhaps, went as far as Sharif Yusuf ibn Ahmad al-Kawneyn in Somaliland, who, eight centuries ago,

---

[9] See below.   [10] See R. C. Stevenson, in *Islam*, 1st ed., p. 209.
[11] See V. Monteil, below, pp. 166–72.

developed a Somali notation for the Arabic short vowels which considerably aided the teaching of Arabic, and is still in use today. Nevertheless, whatever the methods used, there soon developed throughout tropical Africa an extensive indigenous cadre of clergy and a religious literary tradition which, whether in Arabic or in a written or oral vernacular is in many regions as yet far from being adequately recorded, far less systematically studied. Such records, as well as revealing the local bias of religious interest—hagiologies clearly occupying a central place in the Eastern Sudan and Horn of Africa—also offer a unique source of information on a wide range of historical topics.[12]

Whatever the ethnic affiliation of clerics, however, their contemporary image in the popular mind as custodians of Muslim charisma, through their access to the mystically charged symbols of Islam, particularly the Quran, and their ritual functions widely applied to healing the sick and preventing or assuaging misfortune, as well as soothsaying, by means of Quranic charms, talismans, and prophylactics, indicates without doubt one range of their activities which has made a singular impression and attracted followers. Examples of this well-known aspect of the role of the Muslim cleric will be found in many of the papers in this book. We need only pause here to refer to the unusual situation among the partially Muslim Mossi, where traditional diviners would seem to be undermining their own position by attributing cases of barrenness in pagan women to the refusal of children to be born except as Muslims.[13] Elsewhere, the ritual aspects of Islam as a source of mystical power, and the activities of clerics as its principal agents, have, of course, at many times and in many places led to bitter conflict with traditional ritual experts. And it is only where other factors have been favourable that the resulting tension and conflict have been resolved in a new extension of Islam.

Probably the most militantly proselytizing achievements of teachers and clerics have been those associated with the Sufi

[12] See T. Hodgkin, in *Islam*, 1st ed., pp. 443ff.
[13] See E. P. Skinner, below, pp. 183ff. Cf. the production of 'therapeutic Muslims' among the Giriama where certain spirit-caused illnesses can only be cured by conversion to Islam. See Parkin, 1972.

Orders. As we have seen, the earliest and most deep-rooted development of Sufism in Muslim tropical Africa occurred in the eastern Sudan and in North-East Africa, while in West Africa the two most popular Orders—the Qadiriyya and Tijaniyya—only seem to have become widely significant towards the end of the eighteenth century on the eve of the Fulani *jihads*. This contrast and the accompanying disparity in the importance and popularity of Muslim saint cults must be regarded, in part at least, as the outcome of the adaptation of Islam to differing local circumstances in the three areas. In West Africa the early association of Islam with centralized states, and the continuity of Muslim state power, appear to have favoured an emphasis on the legalistic elements of Islam. But in the less-centralized conditions of much of North-East Africa and the eastern Sudan, at least over long periods of time, the Sufistic aspects have achieved a greater prominence and elaboration. This is a question of considerable theoretical interest, to which we shall return at a later stage in this introduction, when we consider the interaction of traditional and Muslim beliefs in a wider context.

Although the arresting impact of the more obvious ritual and magico-religious activities of holymen should not be minimized, it is equally important not to lose sight of the other more secular roles which clerics soon came to exercise as they began to penetrate non-Muslim communities. For the authority which they frequently gained here was no less significant in the consolidation and entrenchment of Islam. Many instances are on record of malams and shaikhs acting as negotiators and mediators, both internally—particularly in uncentralized societies—and externally, where in kingdoms and chiefdoms their knowledge of Arabic and participation in the para-ethnic culture of Islam made them especially valuable as agents and emissaries in external affairs. Such mediation clearly tended to foster some wider application of the Shari'a and helped to enhance the value in local eyes of the sources of Muslim Law. As scribes too, in centralized societies, we find such men performing accounting and other administrative functions, including the recording of court cases; and also acting more generally as advisers, where their far-flung connexions and contacts were evidently of great practical value. And, at least in the early stage of Islamization, as a neutral element in local affairs, the small group of Muslims under a ruler's patronage were eminently suitable for recruitment as members of his personal bodyguard. These are some of the more secular positions for which their special status as members of a minority group with its own distinctive culture made Muslim clerics and their followers peculiarly appropriate. Sometimes, of course, the original motive which set this process in train may have amounted to little more than the attraction of appointing a Muslim man of letters to adorn a non-Muslim court.

Despite tantalizing glimpses of the circumstances in which these early Muslim clerics sought to enlarge the hold of their faith, whether in centralized or uncentralized societies, there are few cases recorded in sufficient detail to permit thorough analysis and understanding of the full interplay of traditional and Muslim interests, which led in some cases to the furthering of Islam and in others to its frustration. In this volume something of the shifting character of the relations between Muslim minority and traditional communities, or partly converted established authorities, is revealed in Mr. Hunwick's study of the reign of the Songhay King Askia Muhammad;[14] and with a correspondingly greater wealth of detail, in Dr. Wilks' reconstruction of the more recent relations between Shaikh Baba and the Ashanti King and court in the nineteenth century,[15] a situation strongly reminiscent of the position of Shaikh Ahmad ibn Ibrahim at the Court of the Baganda Kabaka in the same period.[16] These instances suggest that it was the utilitarian and organizational aspects of Muslim expertise as much as the religious and ritual qualities of Muslim holymen and teachers which appealed to traditional rulers. If present conditions among peoples such as the Oromo[17] and Somali[18] are anything to go by, it may be presumed that in uncentralized societies it was often the ritual activities and arbitrating and mediatory role of Muslim clerics which attracted most attention and interest.

[14] See below, pp. 132–42.   [15] See below, pp. 144–63.   [16] See Gray, 1947.
[17] See P. T. W. Baxter, in *Islam*, 1st ed., pp. 233–50.   [18] See below, pp. 240–52.

III. ISLAM AND POLITICAL SYSTEMS

(a) ISLAM IN UNCENTRALIZED SOCIETIES

At first sight it might seem that uncentralized political systems, lacking any single focus of power, would be more likely to lie open to the influence of external cultural forces and innovations—whether in response to Islam or to other new stimuli—than politically centralized states shielded from penetration by a tightly woven structure of government and administration. From a different standpoint, however, it might be argued with equal cogency, as indeed it has often been assumed, that centralized states with a single authority to mediate the impact of foreign cultural influence, would be in a better position to accept and apply novel ideas and practices. This latter presumption would seem all the more plausible in the present context in view of the elaborate character of Islamic Law as a theocratic system, originating in urban conditions, and particularly appropriate to the needs and requirements of centralized administration. Certainly, in uncentralized societies it would be difficult to envisage the ready comprehension and general application of the Shari'a as a legal system, without the introduction of radical and far-reaching modifications. This, in turn, would suggest that centralized polities would assimilate the legal ordinances of Islam more readily, and with less dislocation, than traditional societies without chiefs and centralized authority. At the very least, therefore, we should expect to find different patterns of accommodation in the two contrasting types of political system.

What, however, are the facts? In West Africa, notwithstanding the equivocal role of the Fulani—once resistant to Islam and later its most vigorous and radical proselytizers—the history of Muslim penetration and expansion is, by and large, the story of the actions and attitudes towards Islam assumed by the rulers of centralized or relatively centralized states. To some extent, no doubt, this reflects the high incidence of centralized political organizations in traditional West Africa. But the significance of chiefs in the spread of Islam is also strongly suggested by the marked lack of response to Muslim influence evinced by uncentralized agricultural peoples in the interior of Guinea and the Ivory Coast, and more familiar to English readers, by the Tallensi, notwithstanding the close proximity of strong centres of Muslim radiation. When, moreover, circumstances in East Africa are included in the discussion the ineffectual Muslim penetration of its hinterland prior to the nineteenth century seems to lend additional substance to the argument linking the presence of chiefs with Islamization. For unlike West Africa, few of this region's traditional societies were organized in powerful states.

Yet, despite this not inconsiderable weight of evidence, even within the parts of Africa dealt with in this book, we cannot ignore the completely contrary reactions of the acephalous Muslim Somali, those of the Oromo who are Muslim, and a host of other uncentralized Muslim peoples in Eritrea and the eastern Sudan. If, moreover, we go beyond these limits and also take into account the pastoral nomads of North Africa and Arabia we find a further range of uncentralized societies whose acceptance of Islam is not in dispute.

From these examples it is abundantly evident that the distinction between centralized and uncentralized traditional political systems is not one which is crucial for the diffusion of Islam. Nor, indeed, can we make any broad generalizations as to the readiness or ease with which societies in either category will accept Islam. Once trade or migration has brought Islam into contact with traditional societies, whatever their political type, the subsequent trend of events would seem to depend in large measure on the effect of such other attendant variables as demographic factors—particularly those associated with population pressure and expansion; prevailing patterns of economic interest; and community ethos and values in the widest sense.

In pointing to the significance of these factors, we are prompted by what is known of the circumstances in which such uncentralized peoples as the Arab Bedouin, Berbers, and Somali and other Hamites have come to adopt Islam. Among such egalitarian and habitually warring pastoral nomads, especially in conditions of acute pressure of population on resources, and consequent expansion and migration, Islam, acquaintance with which is rapidly diffused by the high degree of geographical mobility and interaction characteristic of these societies, has been warmly embraced as an enhancement to a people's solidarity and exclusiveness. And with its appealing summons to the *jihad*, the new faith had readily been accepted as both a spur to, and a justification for, further expansion and conquest. Thus, ethnic congeries, such as the Somali, lacking any single fount of political authority but possessing a strong diffuse sense of cultural identity, have found in Islam new support for their traditional sentiments of ethnic exclusiveness and superiority. Nor is it merely in such cases that cultural identity is buttressed by Islam. More tangibly, and at least as significantly, through the adoption of the Shari'a system of blood-compensation payments these societies have acquired a novel method of compounding delicts and settling disputes which both permits and encourages the formation of wider political cohesion.

The influence of such provisions of the Shari'a as are applied in other spheres of customary law will be discussed in a later section of this introduction.[1] Here we need only note in passing that such acephalous societies as the Somali, and particularly those with a strongly delineated clan and lineage organization, have found it possible to adopt more than the minimal criteria of Muslim identity—the 'five pillars of the faith'[2]—while rejecting or disregarding many of the more detailed prescriptions of Islamic Law. Indeed, as will be argued later, it is here that the Sufistic (i.e. mystical) interpretation of Islam often affords an attractive avenue for Islamization where much of the apparatus of the state ordinances of the Shari'a would be inappropriate. In more centralized conditions, on the contrary, we should expect to find that as the process of Islamization gathers force and momentum there should develop a selective bias towards the application of the more

[1] See below, pp. 45–57.
[2] I.e. the profession of the faith; the daily prayers; fasting; the giving of alms; and pilgrimage to Mecca.

formally legalistic elements of Muslim Law. That there is indeed good evidence for this kind of adaptive selection we shall soon see. It is in this sense, and this sense only, that it becomes meaningful to take into account variations in political centralization, as in other institutions, in tracing the response of traditional social structures to Islam. Structural factors alone do not explain why particular peoples become Muslims while others do not. Rather they are of crucial importance in understanding the course followed once Islam has gained a foothold.

(b) ISLAM IN CENTRALIZED SOCIETIES

A number of the studies presented in this book afford revealing insights into the sorts of recurrent situations which have arisen with the introduction and expansion of Islam in states and centralized societies. As with other aspects of the various reactions and adjustments which occur in these circumstances, the influence of traditional structural forms and cultural features is always strongly marked. In contact with Muslim influence, either through trade or migration, the rulers of traditional states have shown themselves to be generally receptive to those elements of Islam and Muslim culture and organization which could be applied to reinforce and extend their established authority. Hence, as has been seen, we find traditional rulers in various stages of conversion to Islam utilizing Muslim functionaries, as the colonial administrations were to do after them, in a wide range of roles. At the same time, where in traditional values kingship has a strong ritual component—and there are few cases where it does not—Muslim regalia and ritual elements are often adopted for added lustre and support.

In this way we find Muslim rites adopted in their royal installation ceremony by the Kayor Wolof in the sixteenth century,[3] and spread widely in other West African kingdoms whose courts were as yet often far from being fully Muslim at this time. Such initial steps towards a fuller adoption of Islam are likely to be facilitated in local circumstances where Islam appears as the most obvious factor which distinguishes a thrusting and successful

[3] See V. Monteil, below, pp. 166ff.

kingdom from its less-dynamic rivals. Equally, of course, though perhaps not so often as might be anticipated, the advance of Islam may be retarded or arrested where the new faith, or such of its ritual elements as have been adopted by a warrior monarch, is identified with failure and defeat.

Whatever the external circumstances, however, one important structural principle which might be expected to militate against the establishment of Islam as the court religion, but seems in fact generally to have facilitated it, is matriliny. This is particularly so where Islam has been introduced by a migrant group who, once married into the ruling matrilineage, have by the local principle of succession secured dynastic rights in the throne. The importance of this convenient accession to power is particularly evident in the eastern Sudan, where the foundation of immigrant Muslim dynasties by marriage with the reigning chief's daughter in matrilineal societies is a theme which occurs frequently in traditional history.[4]

Whether, as in Nubia, by this structural juxtaposition or by a much slower and more long-drawn-out process of adoption and adaptation of Muslim ritual elements, a stage is eventually reached where the ruling stratum of society becomes increasingly Muslim, and, as with the rulers of Mali, and later Songhay, Islam is established as the apanage of aristocracy. Here the acceptance of Islam as in some sense a royal prerogative necessarily militates against its unfettered extension throughout the king's domains. Thus, we find the Songhay monarch Sunni 'Ali (1465–92) seeking to monopolize those Muslim elements with which he sought to embellish his ritual authority; and his successor Askia Muhammad (d. 1528) throwing overboard most of the old ritual panoply of kingship in favour of the *baraka*, which, like Mansa Musa of Mali, he had acquired through his pilgrimage to Mecca.[5] An extreme though perhaps fortuitous case of this Muslim ritualization of monarchy is seen in nineteenth-century Adamawa, where in some areas non-Muslim subjects regarded their Fulani rulers as sacred kings, 'praying and fasting for all their slaves'.[6]

[4] See below, p. 118.   [5] See J. O. Hunwick, below, pp. 124ff.
[6] See P. F. Lacroix, below, p. 209.

There is, however, an important distinction to be made between rituals of kingship in the old and new sense. Unlike pre-Islamic royal cults, those elements of Muslim ritual and myth which are applied to strengthen traditional authority do so only in a manner which is at once vicarious and accidental, and which is far from being their sole, or even principal, *raison d'être*.[7] By its very nature, Islam cannot in the long run be constrained to serve the interests, or be applied to the exclusive benefit, of particular kings, aristocracies, or peoples.

From the point of view of the ruler, of course, who sees in Islam an added vindication of his traditional authority, this universalistic current points towards the extension of his dominions. And although the dynamic qualities of traditional African political and ritual ideologies are often underestimated by the Arabist, Islam unquestionably presents special advantages for the extension of frontiers, particularly where there is cultural and linguistic confusion. As Gouilly has expressively put it, Islam offered those ambitious of power 'a doctrine, a flag, and an arm'.[8] But if the challenge was accepted, and the conquests which followed were successful, the new conversions which resulted from the extension of Muslim power might be little more than nominal. For the mass of the new subjects little more might be involved than acts of submission, vassalage, and clientage.[9]

But in the march of Islam all was not to the benefit of established authority. If Islam could be applied to enhance the legitimacy and to strengthen the arm of traditional sovereigns its universalistic message also inevitably pointed to a wider egalitarian fraternity which, in appropriate circumstances, was likely to encourage subject peoples to rise against their rulers under the inspiration of popular reformist leaders. Nor was it only in Muslim ideology that such protests might be phrased. Particularly in the early stages of the importation of Islamic ritual by kings, authority might be challenged in the idiom of pagan reaction against Muslim intrusion. Hence, as Mr. Hunwick observes in his study of Songhay,[10] those rulers who turned to Islam for

[7] Cf. Nadel, 1954, p. 233.
[9] Nadel, op. cit., p. 235.

[8] 1952, p. 42.
[10] See below, p. 142.

support and applied the faith to expand their dominions must always have found it necessary to steer a delicate course between the forces of Muslim innovation, traditional conservatism, and the fluctuating attachments of their subjects. This equivocal position of the innovating Muslim ruler, seeking to mediate between two partly opposed cultural systems, is, in some respects akin to that of the administrative chief or headmen under colonial rule.[11]

Thus, Islamic innovation provided—as the examples of Sunni 'Ali and the Baganda Kabaka Kalema show—as ready a target for revolution against a ruler, or ruling class, unpopular on other grounds, as in other circumstances imputed back-sliding afforded the motive and rallying-cry applied by the Fulani in the over-throw of their Habe masters. This latter instance, and the peasant revolts in Adamawa against the Fulbe aristocracy and Muslim clergy,[12] illustrate as much as need be said here of the final levelling effect of Islam and the politically crucial opportunities which it creates for social mobility. For once a tradition of reformist revelation had been created, the legitimacy of the established Muslim ruler was subject to scrutiny not merely by the clerical establishment but also, and ultimately more critically, by those who claimed a new, directly revealed dispensation from God.

(c) THEOCRATIZATION AND MAHDISM

It is, no doubt, a significant indication of the comparatively superficial character of early West African Islam in comparison with Islam in the eastern Sudan and North-East Africa that, notwithstanding the high incidence of centralized states and the corresponding bias towards a legalistic interpretation of the faith, true theocracies (or as Trimingham calls them 'divine nomo-cracies')[13] only made their appearance in the eighteenth and nineteenth centuries. In tropical Africa as a whole the earliest instance of a centralized Islamic state seems to have been ninth-century Ifat, shortly after which the coastal sultanates of Zeila, Mogadishu, and later Kilwa were developing—all utilizing to

[11] Cf. Barnes, Mitchell, and Gluckman, 1949.
[12] See P. F. Lacroix, below, pp. 206–12.   [13] 1959, p. 161.

some degree Muslim patterns of government and administration. In the eastern Sudan itself parallel developments seem to be later, the Fung sultanate of Sennar rising apparently in the sixteenth century and applying Islamic administrative and legal procedures shortly after.[14]

Although little or nothing is yet known of the pre-Islamic political institutions which preceded the foundation of these Muslim dynasties, their initial formation at least does not appear to have been the direct consequence of Mahdist revelation or holy wars of conquest. However, in North-East Africa particularly, Muslim expansion later acquired this character in the long cycle of conflict with Christian Abyssinia.[15] In West Africa, although *qadis* are recorded as having been appointed by those rulers who adopted Islam in earlier periods, and some limited degree of Muslim jurisdiction may be presumed to have existed among minority Muslim communities in still largely traditionalist states, more intensive forms of Muslim government inspired by the model of the Caliphate had to await the great reformist movements of recent centuries. The first manifestation of this tide of Islamic revival occurred in Futa Jallon in 1725, leading to the creation of the Imamate there with the capital at Timbo. This was followed by the foundation of the Imamate of Futa Toro in 1775, and led to the celebrated conquests of 'Uthman dan Fodio in Hausaland, of Sheku Hamada in Masina, and al-Hajj 'Umar in the Bambara states of Nyoro and Segu.[16] The new Muslim states which arose with their Fulani aristocracies out of the old Habe kingdoms are seen at their apogee in the Sokoto Empire of the mid-nineteenth century, which in the legalistic form characteristic of West Africa represents the area's fullest political realization of Islam in the pre-colonial era.[17]

'Uthman dan Fodio's model of government which he and his

---

[14] See Crawford, 1951; Holt, 1963.   [15] See above, p. 8.

[16] For an evaluation of this period as a whole, see H. F. C. Smith, 1961.

[17] The role of the Fulani in these movements, both as religious leaders and warrior followers, whether or not as Trimingham argues it has often been exaggerated, certainly merits further study. It would seem to have strong analogies with that of the Berbers and of the Arab Bedouin in similar circumstances.

followers sought to reproduce was that of the 'Abbasid Caliphate. Consequently, in nineteenth-century Sokoto under the Sultan or *Khalifa* ('the Commander of the Faithful', *amir al-mu'minin*) we find large political units, such as Kano and Zazzau, administered by locally elected emirs—but confirmed and deposed by the Sultan; and 'Uthman's principal assistants from the 1804–10 *jihad*, given offices as agents to supervise the various emirs. The most important of these was the Sultan's cross-cousin, the *waziri*, who held the position of executive head of the Fulani Sokoto states.

The internal organization of these component emirates varied to some extent, as we should expect, according to their former structures prior to the *jihads*.[18] Typically, however, in each the emir exercised authority in foreign relations, in tribute, in appointments to office, movements of population, the establishment of new towns, and the regulation of trade. The army, consisting of horsed noblemen and commoner and slave infantry, was entrusted by the ruler to the command of senior nobles— Fulani title-holders recruited hereditarily (the *tirikai*). In fiscal matters a theoretical distinction was maintained between the state treasury administered by the treasurer (*ma'aji al-mutwali*), a non-hereditary office, and the throne treasury containing royal insignia and palace wealth administered by eunuch officials separately from that of the State as a whole. State resources were freely applied to advance political ends and to reward loyal service. The police force in each state consisted mainly of palace slaves acting with the courts to apprehend and imprison offenders under the direction of the civil administration. Capital sentences could only be passed by the emir's judicial court, which also dealt with land disputes, redress of administrative wrongs, and relations between Muslims and non-Muslims. Here, in framing his judgements, the emir was guided by malams. Other legal matters were the responsibility of subsidiary *qadis'* courts, from whose decisions appeal ran to the chief *qadi* in each emirate, and ultimately to Sokoto. Tax records were maintained by mainly Fulani scribes.

[18] See M. G. Smith, 1960; Paden, 1973; Willis, 1979.

Territorial organization varied considerably. Apart from hereditary vassal chiefs living in their dominions and nominated by local electoral councils—these rendering military service and paying tribute rather than taxes—scattered fiefs were administered indirectly through titled functionaries recruited by kinship, clientage, and slavery for the fief-holders who lived in the capital. Locally resident chiefs, mainly Fulani, administered their communities under the supervision and control of the fief-holder, who could appoint as well as depose them. Between the various emirates there was considerable variation in the extent to which these fief-holding offices were hereditary, or allocated to members of different social strata. In the main, however, they tended to be held by Fulani nobles.

Each emirate had its electoral council composed of senior clerical officials and administrators (though not royals), to select candidates for succession to the office of emir. The Sultan at Sokoto, through his vizier, however, exercised final control. Emirs bearing tribute paid annual homage to the Sultan in the early dry season, and discussed affairs of imperial concern with him and his Court. Land taxes were levied on Muslims, poll tax (*jizya*) on non-Muslims, and cattle-tithes (*jangali*) on nomadic Fulani. Market vendors and craft specialists paid a variety of taxes; other revenue consisted of vassal tribute, court fines, and commissions—such as death duty and war booty.

The extent to which the elaborate Islamic governmental organization of this loosely knit Fulani Empire represented real innovations established by the Fulani conquerors, or merely continued earlier Habe practice, remains in many respects obscure. We may anticipate, however, that further light on this important question will result from the detailed comparative studies which Professor M. G. Smith is now conducting on the basis of his earlier work in Zazzau. But what is already abundantly clear is the degree to which the Fulani reformers based their claim to renovate and rule on a fundamentalist interpretation of Islam, and the Shari'a, inaugurating forms of government which however many institutions of the old régime they included, were essentially theocratic in spirit.

Assessment of the legitimacy of the various *jihads* launched
by the Fulani reformers is, of course, another matter and not
one which is easily settled in any absolute sense. For as with
other conflicting schismatic positions and movements in Islam,
as in other religions and philosophies, this question raises
complicated problems of interpretation for which it is by no
means easy to find a completely neutral basis of judgement.
This, as M. G. Smith rightly points out,[19] is especially true in
Islam, where the legitimacy of men's actions is largely decided,
according to the interpretation of the Quran, *hadiths*, and the
Shari'a and its numerous commentaries, by the ambiguous
notion of the consensus of the community. Here, in matters of
dispute, the ultimate problem is to decide who, precisely, constitute the 'rightly guided community'. Nowhere is this probem
more acute than when the legitimacy of messianic claims is in
question.

Whether these West African *jihads* are to be regarded as
religiously inspired eruptions of reformist zeal, as secular conquests won in the name of Islam, or as Fulani reactions to Hausa
domination, or more plausibly as a mixture of these and other
motives, it was in the Mahdia of the Eastern Sudan for which, as
Drs. Biobaku and Muhammad al-Hajj show,[20] they helped to
prepare the way, that the closest approximation to the ideal
Muslim theocratic state was attained. It was here too, perhaps,
that the striking potentialities which Islam affords for the political
unification of diverse peoples and cultures were most dramatically
realized. The Mahdi[21] Muhammad Ahmad ibn 'Abdallah (1844–85)
issued his governmental decrees on the authority of a visionary
meeting (*hadra*) with the Prophet, describing in one of his
letters how on a number of occasions the Prophet had conferred
the title upon him and 'girded him with his sword'.

The Mahdi's chief disciples, the commanders of divisions of

[19] See below, pp. 213–25.
[20] See below, pp. 226–39, and Hiskett, 1973.
[21] It is important to notice here that despite frequent European misconcep-
tions, although some of those associated with the eighteenth and nineteenth-
century reformers claimed the title of Mahdi, its main adherents did not actually
go so far as this.

the army of his followers (the Ansar), were invested with *Khalifa* titles linking them with the Companions of the Prophet, of whom the *Khalifa* 'Abdullahi (of Baggara origin) acted as vizier and head of the Mahdi's administration. Beneath these, officers of state were appointed from the ranks of those who had been the Mahdi's staunchest early adherents. These were generally given the title of emir, and later of *'amil* (agent). During his lifetime the State also contained a national treasury and a chief judge. Tax, levied at a lower rate than that applied under the Turco-Egyptian régime, was paid into the central treasury (the *bayt al-mal*), of which the chief source of wealth, however, remained the spoils of war. The Mahdi also maintained his own mint, from which the Ansar struck their coinage.

Legal cases were heard not only by the judges and chief judge (the *qadi al-Islam*) but also by other officers of state, and even the *Khalifas* and the Mahdi himself, who, indeed, while in theory ruling on the basis of the Shari'a, also exercised extensive legislative powers through his proclamations and decrees on points of law. This personal theocratic rule, with its proto-bureaucratic elements, hardened under his successor, the *Khalifa* 'Abdullahi, into a more highly centralized system of rule with more elaborate administrative, judicial, and fiscal organs, and a markedly bureaucratic structure,[22] akin to that of the Fulani-Hausa states.

Yet, however much power was in such circumstances concentrated in the hands of the ruler, the possibility of rebellious movements with new mahdist claims to legitimacy was not, and could not be, excluded. If, therefore, in tropical Africa the most highly centralized and theocratic systems of Muslim rule (with such exceptions as Ifat) have been established under the impetus of reformist *jihads*, these have also been those in which the question of the legitimacy of the rulers has been most acutely raised. Those states which owed their origin to, and drew their inspiration most directly from, the Muslim reformers were particularly susceptible to new messianic challenge. Islam, indeed, had now become so deeply rooted in the political life of these states that competition for power assumed the character

[22] See Holt, 1958.

of rebellion rather than revolution. The *jihad* had become institutionalized as the main instrument of usurpation and dynastic rivalry. In the present volume this effect is well illustrated in Professor Lacroix's analysis of the more recent history of Islam in Adamawa.[23]

[23] Below, pp. 206–12.

IV. ISLAMIC LAW AND CUSTOMARY PRACTICE

(a) GENERAL CONSIDERATIONS

Although it is still among the least systematically studied,[1] one of the most interesting and significant facets of the introduction and assimilation of Islam in tropical Africa is that of the interaction in the field of social organization and personal relations between the provisions of the Shari'a and the canons of customary legal procedure. Disregarding differences between the two major Law Schools—Maliki in West Africa and the eastern Sudan, and Shafi'i in North-East and East Africa, it can at once be said that those ordinances of the Shari'a which refer to secular rather than to purely religious matters have achieved their widest and most rigorous application in theocratic states. But, as in the history of Islam generally, even in such congenial conditions the theoretical regulations of the Shari'a are in their actual application much modified by the recognition accorded to local custom ('ado, or 'urf), as an auxiliary source of law. In less theocratic circumstances, as in most modern Muslim states, the scope of Islamic Law is often confined largely to matters of personal status administered by qadis (in West Africa, alkalis [H.]), other legal issues being decided by the courts of the secular authority. At the same time it should be remembered that in any case the Shari'a regards only a restricted range of offences as crimes in a formal legal sense. In the main, this category is limited to such matters as illicit sexual relations, theft, brigandage, drinking alcohol, and sometimes apostasy. Homicide and physical injury are not included, since they are treated as torts rather than as crimes. Moreover, the emphasis in the Shari'a on the principle of restitution in the settlement of such torts corresponds well with the spirit of much, perhaps most, traditional African law. This

[1] These remarks apply particularly to social anthropologists who have shown a disappointing tendency to shy away from this important topic, leaving the field almost entirely to Arabists—of whom Trimingham, and Anderson (1954) have unquestionably made the most valuable contributions to date.

coincidence consequently favours the, at least partial, application
of many Muslim legal categories and procedures in the settlement
of disputes, even when, in their actual operation, these are modified by the imperatives of traditional custom and social structure.] ✳

There is also much evidence to suggest that where traditional
and Shari'a courts exist side by side in a community in which
Islam is spreading and enjoys high prestige from its association
with (or opposition to) authority, litigants who are offered the
choice of being treated as non-Muslims or as Muslims tend to
prefer the latter. This trend towards the extension of Shari'a
influence, and consequent consolidation of Islam, is further
encouraged in all situations where access to a Shari'a court can
be applied to strengthen his legal position by the stronger of the
parties to a dispute. Furthermore, to the extent that changing
social conditions and exposure to new cultural ideals create
disputes and offences which involve dissension from traditional
rules of conduct, it becomes increasingly advantageous for
litigants and offenders to dissociate themselves from traditional
justice and to appeal to the new source of law and judgement
which the Shari'a offers.[2] This, of course, is particularly so where
the provisions of the Shari'a recognize the legitimacy of new
types of claim and interest and protect them against the demands
of custom. Thus, as we have seen with politics, attitudes towards
Islam as a source of law are also strongly coloured by utilitarian
considerations. As in other fields, in the accommodation of Muslim to traditional values and institutions, pragmatic considerations are of the utmost importance.

(b) THE TREATMENT OF DELICTS AND TORTS

In the treatment of wrongs and offences the most important
contribution brought by Islam to the traditional procedures for
settling disputes was either the introduction of a system of
compensation for injury and death or, where this already existed,
the establishment of a regular tariff of indemnifications for such
torts and its investment with Islamic authority. The sociological
significance of this innovation in providing a ready index of

[2] Cf. Nadel, 1942, p. 170.

status, and in the proportions of damages contributed and distributed by the various groups and categories of persons involved a quantitative evaluation of the jural content of their relationships, has seldom been fully appreciated by social anthropologists.

With both the Maliki and Shafi'i Schools of Law full blood-wealth (*diya*) for a freeborn Muslim male is set at a standard value of one hundred camels (or their local equivalent) and half that amount in the case of a woman. Compensation for less-serious injury usually varies similarly according to whether the victim is a man or a woman. These are the theoretical standards. In practice, however, great variation prevails in the values which are given locally to the different categories of compensation, and in the manner in which they are contributed and distributed.[3] In Kanem, for instance, in cases of male homicide fifty animals were paid by the chief, the *alifa* of Mao, and fifty by the kinsmen of the murderer, although the chief's contribution was later returned to him as his fee for settling the case.[4] Usually, the lives of slaves and people of servile or low status generally were valued at a lower rate than that payable in the case of free Muslims; and non-Muslims at lower rates still. Not infrequently, the recognition of these distinctions was further elaborated into a differential scale in which the actual amounts of damages claimed and paid varied not only with the sex and status but also with the age of the victim.

Where in traditional society the solidarity of corporate groups, typically lineages, was mobilized in such cases—and this applied in many kingdoms as well as in less-centralized communities—this collective responsibility found immediate justification in the Shari'a. For the Shari'a recognizes the legitimate involvement of the patrilineal kin (and sometimes of neighbours and guild members) of the parties in such issues. Yet, ideally, this extension of responsibility to the kinsmen of the victim and his assailant properly applies only in cases of accidental killing. In deliberate homicide the murderer alone should make

---

[3] For the modern position in Northern Nigeria generally, see Anderson op. cit., pp. 195–204.   [4] See Boullié, 1937, p. 211; Lebeuf, 1959.

reparation without the support of his kin. This, however, is a distinction which must often have seemed more academic than material; and in societies like the Somali, whatever the circumstances of a killing, such limitations to collective involvement are generally ignored, although they are known to be enjoined by the Law.[5] Where, on the contrary, these provisions are respected, and this is particularly the case where new social circumstances make their honouring advantageous, they encourage the curtailment of collective loyalties and the intensification of individual independence.

(c) KINSHIP AND SHARIʻA ATTITUDES TOWARDS PROPERTY RIGHTS

The effects of the patrilineal emphasis in Islam, particularly evident in Muslim rules of inheritance, where paternal ties are stressed rather than those traced through women, are seen most strikingly when matrilineal societies come to adopt the new religion. Here, as with Christian and Western influence generally (which are also assumed to present a patrilineal ideology and emphasis), the eventual effect is to weaken extended matrilineal bonds and to promote a more bilateral recognition of descent.

On the whole, matrilineal societies do not seem to have proved as uniformly resistant to Islam as these implications might suggest. Not only have immigrant Muslims frequently been able to acquire political influence through intermarriage, as we have seen, but also in a wider sense, particularly when in contact with patrilineal peoples, or where new economic conditions have afforded new opportunities for the formation of personal wealth and status, Muslim legal provisions have often been gradually adopted with a corresponding shift in the traditional pattern of descent in the direction of increased patrilineal emphasis.[6] This is seen, at least incipiently, among such traditionally matrilineal peoples as those of Western Guinea, and to a lesser extent among the Yao.[7]

[5] See Lewis, 1961, pp. 161–95.
[6] This may also be facilitated, as with the influence of Western Christianity generally, by the use of Muslim testamentary provisions and written wills, cf. Colson, 1950.   [7] See Mitchell, 1956.

On the other hand, strongly patrilineal societies where lineage members traditionally exercise corporate interests in livestock or land, or both, have shown themselves to be generally reluctant to adopt the full provisions of the Shari'a in matters of inheritance, transfer, and disposal. This is evident particularly with land tenure in Northern Nigeria,[8] the Kenya coast, Zanzibar, Southern Somalia, and Eritrea; and in relation to livestock among such Muslim pastoralists as the Somali and Fulani. In almost every case here, except where new economic and other innovating pressures are at work, the full application of the Shari'a inheritance rules is the exception rather than the rule. It is to the impact of these other imperatives as much as to that of Islam that we must attribute such radical changes, including the introduction of individual freehold, as those described in parts of Zanzibar by Middleton,[9] and in Nupe by Nadel.[10]

The same trend towards change can be seen where Islamic Law may be applied to circumvent onerous traditional obligations towards kinsfolk, converts to Islam taking advantage of their new legal position to deny specific kinsmen a share in newly acquired wealth. In this fashion, when new economic conditions favour individual enterprise and effort and at the same time reduce the need for collective solidarity in the old sense, those aspects of Islamic Law which stress the economic independence of the individual are readily seized upon. And such conflict of laws as may ensue is likely to lead to a further entrenchment of the Shari'a. This process is apparent, for example, in the changing character of the relations between Somali pastoral nomads and their urbanized merchant kin. The latter, living in conditions of relative security and progressively investing their wealth in urban property, can afford to neglect their traditional blood-compensation ties with their nomadic clansmen, and seek justification for their position in a strict interpretation of the Shari'a.

In such cases the final outcome in the tussle between opposed customary and Muslim rulings depends upon the extent to which

---

[8] See Cole, 1949; and Smith, 1955.   [9] Middleton, 1961.
[10] 1942, pp. 242–3. On the question in Futa Toro see Gueye, 1957.

those who see in Islamic Law an escape from irksome traditional obligations, and a rationale for increased individual independence, can in fact safely dispense with traditional loyalties; or manipulate them selectively to their own private advantage. Wealth and other new means of gaining adherents and support are clearly critical factors here. Those who refuse to reciprocate on a traditional basis will have to find other means of gaining the services of others when they require them.

(d) THE POSITION OF WOMEN AND SUBJECT GROUPS

Much the same range of factors emerges in relation to the position of women. Although the entitlement of female heirs to inherit property under the Shari'a is likely to be interpreted according to traditional patterns of property interest, especially where corporate patrilineal wealth in land or livestock is in question (as, e.g., among the Fulani[11] or Somali), the possibility of a new dispensation is at least given, and may be such as to change the general position of women advantageously.

And while in traditional Islam women are generally treated as minors, where Muslim affiliation enables people to claim a privileged status outside the reach of customary obligations, women may apply this to their own profit. Here the case of Kotokoli prostitutes in Northern Togo is not without interest. Those of these women who return home with a considerable personal fortune after plying their trade successfully in Ghana often profess Islam as a means of escaping from paternal authority and the burdensome demands of their kin.[12] On the other hand, while all traditional societies which accept Islam do not necessarily adopt the full rigours of Muslim purdah—and particularly not where, as among Somali and Fulani nomads, such constriction is seen as hampering women's pastoral duties—others do so, even in rare cases to the extent of re-assigning formerly degrading female tasks to men.[13]

---

[11] See Hopen, 1958; Stenning, 1959; and Dupire, 1962.

[12] See Alexandre, 1963, p. 54.

[13] Thus, in some Hausa areas women have discontinued their traditional farming duties on the conversion of their men-folk to Islam. See Greenberg, 1947.

In this respect the position of slaves and other dependent categories of persons and groups, traditionally subject to discrimination, is somewhat different. For while the Shari'a recognizes, and therefore might be applied to legalize, slavery and various forms of bondage, as, for example, in Zanzibar, it also permits upward mobility through the conversion of the most debased positions to those of client. Equally, it presents the possibility of complete enfranchisement (by manumission and the purchase of freedom), which may not have existed in the traditional system.[14]

This liberalizing effect was probably more significant in the case of captives or slaves proper (Hausa, *bayi*) than in the case of domestic slaves or serfs, who seem often to have enjoyed a traditionally more favoured status than that offered by Islam.[15] Muslim slaves (unlike women), moreover, were readily accepted into the clergy, and could also rise to hold political and military positions of power and eminence.

Certainly, while wide status differences and elaborate social stratification can scarcely be said to be of rare occurrence in the history of Islam, there is still present the ideal notion of Muslim equality. And this, as we have already suggested, has played an important part in the spread of Islam in tropical Africa. It is not surprising, therefore, that in such disparate cases as the relations between Fulani and Habe, or between the Fulani reformist clergy and their untutored nomadic kinsmen, or again between Somali nomads and their artisan dependants, such social differences should be rationalized and justified in terms of the imputed religious ignorance and negligence of those who are despised. If they were regarded as exemplary Muslims it would be less easy to treat them as inferiors.

(e) MARRIAGE PATTERNS

In marriage we find as diverse accommodations between traditional and Muslim practice as those already noted in other

---

[14] The position varies somewhat among the various Schools, the Maliki code being among the most generous in its views on the rights of slaves.

[15] See Trimingham, 1959, pp. 132 ff.; Smith, 1959; Sanneh, 1976.

fields. We must begin, however, by emphasizing that the pattern of preferential marriage between a man and his father's brother's daughter is not specifically enjoined in Muslim Law and cannot therefore be taken as an infallible index of the degree of Islamization of traditional societies. At the same time it should also be recognized that the practice of this form of marriage by the Bedouin and other Arabized peoples has given it a distinct lustre in the eyes of many Muslims who do consequently tend to regard it as a specifically Islamic feature. Hence although, like circumcision,[16] it is not properly an inherent Muslim trait, this type of marriage is widely distributed in Islamic tropical Africa, and particularly, but not only, in societies which lack deep, well-developed lineage organization.

Where such patrilateral parallel cousin marriage (with real or classificatory cousins) is practised extensively and where women are allowed some of their inheritance rights according to the Shari'a, this form of marriage is commonly regarded as a means of ensuring that property which passes to women remains within the extended family. Where women do not effectively inherit valued property, the practice may be justified on other grounds. Moreover, whatever the position in regard to inheritance, where this form of cousin marriage occurs, its actual incidence in relation to all other forms of marriage is not necessarily very high, and may even be surpassed by other patterns of cousin marriage, as, for example, with father's sister's daughter, and mother's brother's daughter. This is in fact what happens among some of the Fulani,[17] in some Swahili communities,[18] and has also been recorded in the Muslim Sudan.[19] Elsewhere, in some parts of the region surveyed in this book, as with the northern pastoral Somali nomads and the Wolof, the practice has made no obvious inroads at all.[20] For the reasons previously

[16] See below, p. 68.
[17] See Hopen, op. cit., pp. 71–83; Stenning, op. cit., pp. 111 ff.
[18] Tanner, 1964.   [19] Barclay, 1964, pp. 118 ff.
[20] But among the Wolof in the urban situation of Dakar patrilateral parallel cousin marriage has made some inroads, see Thore, 1964. And among the 'Afar (Danakil) of French Somaliland and Ethiopia, who adhere strongly to Islam, marriage is preferentially with the father's sister's daughter. See Chedeville, 1966.

given, these and other instances of failure to conform to this
pattern of preferential marriage, or for that matter of failure to
observe lineage endogamy in general, must not be taken as defi-
ciencies in Muslim devotion.

Next, we need to note the effect of the Islamic tolerance of
polygyny to the extent of four legitimate wives. As far as traditional plural marriage in tropical Africa is concerned, this
limitation is less formidable than it might at first appear. It is
in any case only likely to conflict with traditional marriage
practice in the case of extensively polygynous chiefs. Such
restrictions as it imposes are, moreover, mitigated both by the
ease of divorce in Islam, and by the discretion granted to husbands
in recognizing as legitimate heirs and successors their children
by concubines.

A more crucial issue is that of the way in which the Muslim
conception of matrimony, and the rights and duties created by it,
impinge upon the character of traditional marriage. Despite the
control over a woman vested in her guardian (*wali*), the Shari'a
conceives of marriage as in essence a voluntary contract between
individual spouses. The fundamental transaction is the explicit
agreement of the bride (subject only to the constraint, *jabr*, of
her guardian), and her acceptance of the personal marriage
payment (*mahr* or *sadaq*) proposed by the husband. This, of
course, has to be appropriately solemnized by witnesses and also
requires the presence of a cleric, or shaikh, to perform the marriage
ceremony.

The fulfilment of these requirements confers upon the husband
full rights over his spouse as a sexual and domestic partner,
and entitles him to claim as his all children born to his wife during
their union. Although marriage also gives the husband almost
complete authority over his wife, who, as a legal minor, is now
subject to his control rather than as formerly to that of her
father and brothers, it imposes corresponding obligations and
duties upon the male partner. At the very least these make the
husband responsible for the general well-being of his wife and
children. Yet the husband is not necessarily fully answerable at
law for the legal person of his wife. Nor, similarly, are her

jural links with her own natal kin (or guardian) completely severed by marriage. The husband's position is additionally strengthened by the ease with which he can terminate the union conditionally, or finally, by established divorce procedures, while still retaining his rights over the children. And his enviable prerogatives here are little weakened by the fact that, in such circumstances, the divorced wife is entitled to maintenance for a stipulated period; or by the consideration that, with greater ease in theory than in practice, she also may obtain the annulment of the marriage. This, indeed, only applies when the husband maltreats her 'unreasonably',[21] fails to provide for her, deserts her without adequate provision, or if he can be shown to be impotent, or suffering from certain other physical or mental defects. It need scarcely be added that in Muslim communities the degree of elaboration of the various Law Schools on these and cognate points is rivalled only by the extent of actual litigation on such issues.

As far as the adoption of Islamic marriage rules by matrilineal peoples is concerned, the most crucial effect is upon the position of the children, who, if their mother remains outside Islam, acquire dual affiliation—in their mother's group through their maternal ties, and in their father's group through their paternal ties. This may be seen as a source of conflict; or it may be utilized to advantage to extend the range of effective ties of the children of such unions. If the wife also adopts Islam the affiliation of the children is unambiguously with the father and his kin, thus reinforcing the impact of the Shari'a rules of inheritance.

In the initial stages of Islamization, as among the matrilineal Digo of Tanzania, conflicts are likely to arise over succession as well as inheritance, with divergent rulings being given by customary and Shari'a courts.[22] Here, again, individuals will take advantage, where they can, of the Shari'a to get round traditional rules which are against their interest. Thus, Yao chiefs utilize Islamic marriage with payment of *mahr* to give them more substantial control over their wives and, in particular, to by-pass the

---

[21] Evaluations of reasonable and unreasonable ill-treatment vary enormously, as may be imagined.   [22] See Trimingham, 1964, pp. 150–1.

traditional system of uxorilocal residence, under which the couple should continue to live in the wife's matrilineal settlement.[23]

It is something of a paradox, that while this conflict over affiliation, succession, and residence after marriage (where uxorilocality has previously prevailed) necessarily arises when Islam makes inroads into matrilineal societies, matrilineal marriage itself like marriage in (patrilineal) Islam is easily dissolved and often unstable.

Wider problems are raised by the normally corporate nature of African marriage relations, and the corresponding system of traditional marriage payments and prestations. To take the latter first, the essential Islamic marriage gift (*mahr* or *sadaq*) is usually adopted into the traditional system of payments as a personal and often conditional—indeed, sometimes entirely nominal—present to the bride which is payable principally upon the divorce or death of the husband. This is the general position among such diverse Muslim peoples as the Mandinka, Tokolor, Kanuri, Hausa, Fulani, and Somali.[24] Among the West African Dyula trading communities, with their more dispersed and fragmented organization, and generally in more urbanized conditions where corporate groups have shed many of their traditional functions,[25] usually only the bride's personal dower is paid.

Although the position in other cases does not seem to be very clear, there is some indication in Stenning's descriptions of pastoral Fulani 'contract' marriage[26] that here the Islamic part of the marriage prestations and ceremonial is interpreted as referring to that aspect of matrimony which concerns the relations between the spouses as individuals, rather than as members of affinally related groups. This distinction is especially clear among the Somali pastoral nomads, where the performance of the Muslim marriage ceremony and *mahr* contract, as in marriage by elopement, when no other marriage payments are made, establish a full marital union between the couple and give the husband complete control over his wife's fertility (during their union).

[23] See Mitchell, 1956, pp. 130ff.; cf. Islam among the Zaramo, in Swantz, 1970.
[24] See Trimingham, 1959, pp. 165–8; and for the Hausa, Smith, 1953, pp. 321 ff.; for the Fulani, see Hopen, Stenning, and Dupire; for the Somali, Lewis, 1962.   [25] See, e.g., Barclay, op. cit., pp. 246–7.   [26] Pp. 132 ff., 1959.

They do not, however, create an affinal relationship between the lineages of the spouses; nor do they entitle the husband to claim a sororatic replacement in the event of his wife's death, or allow his kin to automatically inherit his widow.

Thus, in the case of the Somali the *mahr* ceremony transfers to the husband full rights to any children borne to his wife during their union—whoever actually fathers them. From the present literature, however, it seems difficult to determine the extent to which this applies in other parts of tropical Africa, where the Islamic *mahr* has been incorporated into the traditional system of marriage payments. This is a point which requires more detailed and careful examination by anthropologists.

Leviratic marriage, widow inheritance, and sororatic replacement, which, in their wider group aspects, are disapproved of, if not disallowed by the Shari'a, have already been touched on.[27] Here the general position seems to be that where corporate kin groups continue to play an important part in social relations, and where marriage establishes an affinal relationship between groups, these traditional marital replacement rights are retained. Nevertheless, widows who, for personal reasons, wish to sever their connexion with their deceased husband's lineage, may generally do so by applying to the Shari'a courts.[28] Here, of course, the Islamic rules respecting the observance of the obligatory period of continence ('*idda*) (during which the widow may not remarry), which stress the rights of a deceased (or divorced) husband in his former partner's fertility, agree well with customary requirements in many patrilineal systems of descent.

Finally, a highly significant point which merits further study, and is likely to have a direct bearing on the influence of Islam on the stability of the marriage, concerns the nature of a married woman's jural relations with her own kin. While in patrilineal societies the Shari'a strengthens, or at any rate does nothing to

---

[27] The effect of Islamic Law on other traditional forms of marriage, such, for example, as Fulani 'cicisbean' marriage, is also worthy of mention. See Stenning, op. cit., pp. 140–6.

[28] Trimingham, 1959, pp. 169–70. In Nupe a conflict between traditional and Muslim practice arises here, since customarily only a junior brother may succeed to his deceased brother's widow. See Nadel, p. 280, 1954.

weaken, a man's rights in the child-bearing capacity of his wife, at the same time it also requires a married woman to retain strong *jural* ties with her own natal kin. In Islam it is indeed the woman's own paternal kin, rather than the husband and his relatives, who are legally involved in all serious torts concerning or committed by her. They, for example, rather than the husband, pay and receive blood-wealth (*diya*) on behalf of their married daughter. Thus, among the Somali a husband has no claim to blood-money if his wife is killed; his only entitlement is to a sororatic replacement from her own kin.

In many other traditional patrilineal societies, however, marriage involves not only the complete transfer of the wife's fertility to her husband (and his kin) but also the acquisition by him of full responsibility for her person at law.[29] It is in this type of patrilineal society that marriage is usually most stable, so that the introduction and application of the Shari'a here might be expected to have the double effect of altering the traditional distribution of rights over a married woman between her own and her husband's kin, and of weakening the strength of the marital ties as such. Changes of this kind are likely to be most striking in the case of peoples such as the Galla, where traditional marriage is indissoluble.

An analagous issue of interest here concerns the effect of these Shari'a principles regarding men's paternity rights in patrilineal societies, where (as with the Baganda) traditionally marriage does not confer on the husband monopolistic rights in his wife's fertility, and children born of irregular liaisons belong to the man who fathers them rather than necessarily to the legal husband.

If much has been said here of marriage and its associated rights and obligations, this is because it is in this area of personal status, as well as in inheritance, that the legal ordinances of the Shari'a tend to make their greatest impact. This trend has continued under colonial rule and into the present era of independence, where other aspects of law increasingly fall within the purview of the secular administration.

[29] These issues are discussed in some detail in Lewis, 1962; and in Lewis in Banton (ed.), 1965, pp. 87–112.

V. ISLAM AND TRADITIONAL BELIEF
AND RITUAL

(a) DOCTRINE AND BELIEF

Seldom in the first phases of its penetration in tropical Africa can Islam have been taught as a comprehensive theology. Indeed, in the purely religious field all that was required of its early converts was that they should acknowledge the fundamental doctrine—there is no God but Allah, and Muhammad is his Prophet—and a handful of related ritual injunctions and prescriptions.[1] Nevertheless, once introduced in however schematic a form, the question how much of the traditional religion (and not merely of its ritual) could be accommodated in Islamic practice, soon became an issue of importance. Here therefore, as in the other areas of social life already dealt with, we have to begin by examining such conformities as may exist between pre-Islamic and Islamic concepts and rites, and consider how far the resulting interaction, or 'dialogue', shapes the local character of Muslim worship.

Before examining how traditional religious phenomena affect and are affected by the profession of Islam, a general characteristic of most African religion may be noted. This is not the distinction so often drawn between animist religious systems and Islam as a 'revealed religion'; for, although it must be admitted

---

[1] Theoretically, the minimum definition of the practising Muslim is in terms of the observance of the five 'Pillars of the faith'. But in all Muslim communities it is recognized that these represent ideals of conduct which are often perfunctorily and imperfectly realized. They are therefore best regarded as ideals to which all professing Muslims subscribe and seek to honour with varying degrees of determination and success. Even such zealous spiritual leaders as the nineteenth-century West African reformers, including Muhammad Bello, showed in their treatment of captives that for them the profession of the faith and a correct knowledge of the statutory ritual ablutions were sufficient to determine Muslim adherence. Thus, ultimately, it becomes necessary to adopt the operational (and tautological) definition that those are Muslims who call and regard themselves such.

that this seems to have some force,[2] traditional spirit-cults are also often 'revealed' in one context or another. But what appears to be of much wider significance is the special character of *immediacy* which is such a striking feature of indigenous religions. Traditional religious powers are normally believed to sustain a moral order in which the just prosper and the good are rewarded, not so much in some nebulous afterlife as within society itself. The notions of heaven and hell thus seem not to be strongly emphasized, or to be absent altogether; and particular misfortunes and illnesses, and often death itself, are regarded, at least in part, as a reflection or epiphenomenon of the processes of moral life in society. For all their rich complexity and wealth of cosmological elaboration, therefore, this gives to most African religions an involute, enclosed, and highly ethnocentric character which corresponds well with the particularity of traditional society.

All this is evidently antithetical to the universalistic spirit of Islam, its concern with eternity rather than today, and in a religious context opposed to Muslim eschatology, with its fatalistic acceptance of divine reward and retribution in the after life rather than in this. Nevertheless, as we have repeatedly noticed, it is especially in circumstances of the expansion of cultural and social frontiers, with new possibilities of social interaction and interest, that the impetus towards the acceptance of Islam as a new cultural model is most strongly sustained. In such favourable conditions, where the scale of economic and social relations is widening, the contrasts noted above have not halted the march of Islam, but with other not easily compounded differences they have certainly contributed to the dynamic tension between the old and new religion. This tension, it should be remarked, is of a different character from that produced by other cultural interactions of the past. For the written heritage of Islam, however inadequately represented in the sparse libraries of local clergy, preserves a standard divinely inspired code of ideals which lays bare the inconsistencies and imperfections of

[2] Thus the tendency in West Africa not to accentuate the special role of the Prophet may perhaps be interpreted as evidence for the foreignness of this conception. See below, p. 61.

actual practice far more effectively than the orally conserved canons of custom.

In the ensuing process of the Islamization of traditional belief the most important aspect of Muslim religious phenomenology which has greatly facilitated its initial impact and appeal—often at the cost of a more thorough penetration—is its truly catholic recognition of the multiplicity of mystical power. Of course, Islam insists on the uniqueness of God as a single omnipotent creator deity, and rigorously excludes all conflicting sources of power which could in any way impair His absolute dominion. But once this is said, and as long as God's lofty pre-eminence is not compromised, the Quran itself provides scriptural warrant for the existence of a host of subsidiary powers and spirits. These may not all be equally legitimate, but their existence and effectiveness, whether as malign or beneficial agencies, is not disputed.

Consequently, as long as traditional beliefs can be adjusted in such a way that they fall into place within a Muslim schema in which the absoluteness of Allah remains unquestioned, Islam does not ask its new adherents to abandon their accustomed confidence in all their mystical forces. Far from it. In the voluminous Quranic store-house of angels, jinns, and devils, whose number is legion,[3] many of these traditional powers find a hospitable home; and passages from the Quran are cited to justify their existence as real phenomena. Moreover, pre-Islamic figures which can be assimilated without too great distortion to the Muslim concept of saints, especially in the mystical (Sufi) interpretation of Islam, can be readily absorbed into the chain of intermediaries along which men's humble petitions flow to the Prophet and through him to God.

Muslim theology is equally tolerant in its attitude towards divination, magic, witchcraft, and sorcery. It condemns the illegitimate use of the last two; but it does not question their efficacy. And these related mystical activities, known by a variety of names in Arabic but most generally perhaps as *sihr*,[4] have come

---

[3] See articles '*djinn*' and '*shaitan*' in *Encyclopaedia of Islam*, Vol. I, pp. 1045–6, and Vol IV, pp. 286–7.

[4] See article 'sihr', *Encyclopaedia of Islam*, Vol. IV, pp. 409–17.

to occupy a prominent and secure place in the popular heritage of Islam.

How successfully do these Muslim categories in fact provide for the assimilation of traditional beliefs and cults? Traditional concepts of a supreme power or spirit (a 'High God') seem generally to be readily identified with Allah. This is especially the case where the traditional power is essentially otiose or remote from the more specific concerns of men. Thus, we find the assimilation of the Cushitic god *waq* to Allah among both Muslim Galla and Somali, and the use among some of the latter of his name in a common expression for sacrifice (*waq da'in:* lit. 'Offering to God').[5] In the same way, the Mossi apply the name of their otiose deity *winam* to Allah; and the Nupe equate their traditional supreme deity *soko* with Him also.[6] Again, among the Swahili in East Africa the traditional creator God *mungu* is identified with Allah: and the Arabic term itself is reserved principally for use in poetry and in stock Arabic expressions, while *mungu* is invoked in informal prayer.[7] Similarly, those Yoruba who have adopted Islam identify their traditional High God *Olorin* or *Olodumare* with Allah. With the Hausa and Songhay, however, there is apparently no distinct pre-Islamic name for a supreme deity, if the concept is entertained at all, and vernacular terms equivalent to the English Master or Lord are applied to Allah.

For the Prophet Muhammad it is usually less easy to find a vernacular term expressive of his unique position, although in Swahili and Hausa he is described accurately enough as God's 'messenger'. In West Africa, particularly among the least Islamized, there is a tendency to play down the role of the Prophet. And in some areas the Muslim taboo on the pig has been inverted, this animal being regarded as sacred and associated in a special way with Muhammad.[8]

---

[5] There is in fact in Somali a wide range of vernacular equivalents for the ninety-nine praise-names of God. See Lewis, 1959.

[6] Nadel, 1954, p. 235, suggests, not entirely convincingly, that this equation may account for the Nupe failure to stress that part of the profession of faith which acclaims the uniqueness of Allah.

[7] See Trimingham, 1964, p. 78; Grottanelli, 1955, p. 306.

[8] See Trimingham, 1959, p, 67.

In the field of spirit activity of more direct concern to man traditional ancestor cults may be accommodated effectively and persist in a Muslim guise. In contrast to the identification of pre-existing 'High Gods' with Allah, however, ancestors can no longer remain if they ever were sources of power in their own right. Their role in Islam is that of intercessors in the chain of supplication which begins with man and ends in God. The transition point which, if achieved, ensures them an honoured place in the local practice of Islam is thus when they cease to be prayed to, but are rather prayed for, or through.

This complete incorporation is well illustrated among some Eastern Sudanese and Eritrean peoples; among the Somali, where clan and lineage ancestors are in effect canonized as Muslim saints and classed with the saints of Islam generally;[9] to some extent also among the Swahili;[10] and in parts of West Africa. In the last region, however, it must be admitted that the position is often far from clear, and evidently requires further study. The equation is reported among the Mende and Temne, where the dead, those who have 'crossed the river', are associated with the saints and the Prophet as intercessors with God;[11] and, more definitely on the North-East African pattern, among the Diakhanke of eastern Senegal.[12] In the case of the Songhay the position seems to be somewhat different. Here some ancestors are assimilated to angels (Ar. *mala'ika*) in the Muslim mystical hierarchy, while others, and it seems the majority, are classed as jinns (*ʒin*).[13]

Whether these instances of successful positive assimilation between pre- and Islamic categories of religious phenomena are in the long run likely to survive depends upon a variety of factors. Among the most important of these are probably: whether such cults are of ancestors proper, or merely of the undifferentiated dead;[14] whether the social groups which they represent (clans

[9] Here the channel of communication is explicitly stated to be as follows: the saint (whether an ancestor or otherwise) stands in the gateway of the Prophet, who, in turn, stands in the door of God.
[10] See Prins, 1961, p. 113.
[11] Little, 1951, p. 273.
[12] Pierre Smith, Musée de l'Homme, personal communication.
[13] Rouch, 1954, pp. 60 ff., and the same author's more detailed study, 1960.
[14] Cf. Fortes, 1965, pp. 122–44; and Bradbury, 1965, pp. 96–115.

and lineages) persist as viable entities; and, finally, the extent to which the Sufistic cult of saints as a whole receives local encouragement and support. Where a rigid fundamentalist interpretation of the Shari'a, or modernist contempt for 'venal' holy men condemns the veneration of saints and inhibits the local development of Sufism, this assimilation is likely to disappear, or to be consigned to a barely tolerated clandestine existence.

By the same token, strongly developed indigenous ancestor cults would seem to offer conditions propitious to the development of a Sufistic interpretation of Islam, with emphasis on saints as mediators between man and the Prophet. And this suggests that any consideration of the relative unimportance of saints and Sufism in West African Islam must take account not only of the way in which the region's kings and chiefs sought to appropriate mystical blessing (*baraka*) for their own use but also of the fact that the Fulani reformist leaders belonged to a society in which traditionally there was no ancestor cult.

Nature-spirits and powers associated directly with the fertility of particular localities (and this may include some ancestors)[15] are usually treated with less consideration by orthodox Muslims. Unlike lineage ancestors, they are generally not assimilated positively; their veneration is usually condemned, and they become negatively incorporated into the world of non-Muslim jinns.

Despite this, however, such phenomena are sometimes integrated indirectly in a manner which both emphasizes the superior power of Islam and maintains religious continuity. Thus, Trimingham reports that in some Temne villages mosques have been built in what were formerly the sacred groves of the local secret society, the mosque here deriving its sanctity from a conjunction of the old with the new power and symbolizing the pre-eminence of Islam.[16] Similarly, the tomb of Sharif Yusuf al-Kawneyn, one of the principal founding fathers of Islam in Somaliland,[17] lies beside a small hill which is said to contain the mortal remains of the pagan magician chief whose rule the

---

[15] This, for instance, is the case with localized ancestors in Songhay whom Muslims regard as jinns.   [16] Trimingham, 1959, p. 109.

[17] See above, p. 28, and Lewis, 1963a, pp. 113–15.

shaikh overturned, and whom, by his superior mystical power, he incarcerated in the mountain as a permanent memorial to the glory of Islam. Other attempts at this sort of association are often less successful and frequently give rise to serious religious controversy. Professor Skinner reports such an instance among the Mossi later in this volume.[18]

With spirit-possession cults which, under the impress of Islam, are likely to develop into voluminous repositories for other displaced traditional cults, the position is equally ambiguous. At best, as with many cults of nature spirits, the mystical forces at play here are classed as jinns on whose precise identification as good or evil, and on the degree of tolerance which should be shown towards them, there is often much debate among the clergy. Typical examples here are the spirit cults of the West African secret societies generally, and the Songhay *holey*, Mossi *kinkirsi*, and Hausa *bori* in particular;[19] the Swahili *pepo*-possession cults; and the *ẓar* cult in Ethiopia, Eritrea, the Somali Republic, and the Sudan. Despite the distaste with which they are almost universally regarded by the pious, these cults, particularly those which do not employ physical images and masks, have not only shown considerable powers of survival in their own local situation but have also sometimes succeeded in spreading to other Muslim countries. Thus, the cult of *ẓar*-spirits has been carried from its place of origin in Ethiopia into the Sudan Republic and Egypt, and even into the Arabian Peninsula itself.[20]

The continuing vitality of these spirit-possession cults, notwithstanding their official disfavour, is only partly explicable in terms of the fact that Islam does not deny the existence of the powers, however malignant, upon which they depend. Of at least equal significance is the positive attraction which they have for all those who are excluded from full participation in the public rituals of orthodox Islam. Hence their popularity with women, and through women their association in many cases with prostitution. Their appeal, however, is not limited merely to those

[18] See below, p. 188.

[19] See (Hausa) Greenberg, 1946, and Raulin, 1962; (Songhay) Rouch, 1954, pp. 61 ff., and 1960, pp. 45–77.

[20] See Leiris, 1958; Lewis, 1961, pp. 261 ff.

who are subject to regular discrimination and for whom they offer some sort of compensation. They also attract those who seek relief from afflictions which the orthodox rituals and prophylactics of Islam have failed to remedy. As is to be expected, conditions of rapid social change which bring in their train fresh conflicts and anxieties provide additional scope for the operation of these cults. And where in traditional life witchcraft and sorcery occupied a prominent place, these spirit-possession cults may fulfil some of the functions of anti-witchcraft movements. Certainly no one who has witnessed them can deny their cathartic function.

Finally, in witchcraft, oracles, and magic (all forms of *sihr*) Islamic ideas share a large measure of agreement with those of traditional religion. And, as long as they depend upon techniques which derive their validity from a Muslim source, Islam fully approves and sanctions magical procedures which are directed towards such legitimate ends as the cure of disease, the prevention and curtailment of misfortune, and the assurance of prosperity and success. For the fulfilment of all these hopes lies ultimately, of course, with God. Only modernist opinion condemns such attitudes as superstitious. The case is much the same with divination, on which a large number of Arabic compendia enjoy a wide circulation throughout Muslim Africa. And, as is to be expected, Muslim proselytizers are not above using divinatory techniques in their efforts to impress unbelievers with the power of Islam.[21]

As in traditional ethics, witchcraft and sorcery are regarded as evil, indeed amoral; and their use can only be justified when it is applied to protect the rights of the just and to trap wrongdoers. Thus, it is perfectly appropriate to employ a cleric to perform a spell upon the footprints of a thief. Similarly, wanton attack on a holyman is usually believed to evoke divine retribution, with or without the direct intervention of the victim. Indeed, clerics and holymen generally are thought to share something of the mystical blessing (*baraka*) of saints, which in itself safeguards them from danger. Again, as in traditional society, circumstances

[21] Cf. Little, 1947.

sometimes arise where the same mystical action is not regarded by all those concerned as equally justified or legitimate. Holymen, for example, may be considered to abuse their divine power by seeking to advance their own personal advantage, harming others in the process.

Yet, although their moral evaluation is thus not always unambiguous, these types of supernatural activity represent well-established themes in Muslim culture, to such an extent indeed that in some areas the presence of magic and divination must be attributed to Islam rather than to indigenous sources. This consideration and the formidable proliferation of cabbalistic works in Arabic on geomancy,[22] astrology, and divination make it essential to exercise some caution in regarding such 'animistic' beliefs where they occur in Muslim cultures as necessarily pre-Islamic, or as evidence of only a weak degree of Islamization.

On a more abstract plane, the continuing vitality in Muslim communities of these various mystical and spiritual forces seems to stem from their concern with those aspects of the immediacy of human intercourse which are largely excluded, or stifled in the orthodox cult of God and the Prophet. To this extent, all these peripheral cults, whether condemned or condoned, may be seen as attempts to bridge the gap between the moral intensity of traditional personal and social interaction and aspirations— with their customary mystical overtones—and the lofty and fatalistic conceptions of Muslim eschatology. With this in mind, the accommodations which have been discussed in the foregoing may now be summarized as follows:

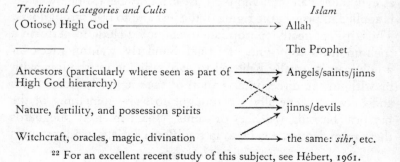

Traditional Categories and Cults	*Islam*
(Otiose) High God ——————————→	Allah
————	The Prophet
Ancestors (particularly where seen as part of High God hierarchy) ——→	Angels/saints/jinns
Nature, fertility, and possession spirits ——→	jinns/devils
Witchcraft, oracles, magic, divination ——→	the same: *sihr*, etc.

[22] For an excellent recent study of this subject, see Hébert, 1961.

Finally, when the adoption of Muslim theological and cosmological elements is considered from the point of view of the old religion in terms of a dynamic process of adjustment and adaptation, it is appropriate, at least in some phases of religious change, to refer to a 'syncretism' between Muslim and traditional concepts and ritual. From the point of view of Islam, however (and, *a fortiori* of the Arabist), this new syncretism is to be regarded merely as a temporary stage in the long journey towards a more perfect comprehension of the faith. For such inharmonious traditional beliefs and values as continue to be respected cannot blend fully with Islam to produce a new syncretic entity without changing the very nature of this religion. Whatever the practice, if the faith is to survive as an ideal it must retain its rigid doctrinal core unshaken and immutable.

Where therefore novel ideas and rites from traditional religion are incorporated, to the extent of modifying these basic doctrines, inevitably new schismatic movements arise which the majority of orthodox believers must regard as heretical. Nevertheless, between these two poles lies a vast territory in which the sorts of accommodations we have noted in the field of religious phenomenology provide ample ground for controversy.

(b) RITUAL AND CEREMONIAL

As we have seen, it is in the sphere of personal relations that the provisions of the Shari'a tend to make their readiest and most profound impact. So, too, with ritual. Along with the at least nominal observance of the daily prayers, those rites which pertain to the life cycle of the individual are usually those which are most quickly absorbed. Thus, often in cultures which in other respects are as yet little affected by Islam, those statutory Muslim rituals which cluster round the three main turning-points in life—birth, marriage, and death—are normally speedily taken up.[23] They may, of course, undergo considerable modification and reinterpretation in the process. Such accommodation is probably

[23] Thus, among the Fulani, of the internal rituals which refer to their pastoral existence, only those which are concerned with transitions in personal status bear the firm imprint of Islam. Those which relate to rights in cattle retain their traditional non-Muslim character. See Stenning, below, pp. 199ff.

best seen with the Muslim rite of circumcision which, though it is not explicitly mentioned in the Quran, is regarded alike by Muslims and non-Muslims as an indispensable mark of adherence to the faith.

Coinciding with the long-term trend in all regions subject to major social change, the emphasis in Islam is on the conception of male circumcision (and female clitoridectomy) as an individual rite. But where the traditional social structure includes an age-set organization and circumcision is a novelty introduced by Islam, the rite tends to be incorporated as a collective *rite de passage* in the cycle of age ceremonies. This assimilation, which normally fixes circumcision as an initiation rite into manhood and at a later age than is prescribed by Islam, is well calculated to provoke controversy among the clergy. It may also require the services of both traditional and Muslim ritual experts.

The sort of dualism which results in such cases is well illustrated by the Swahili *jando* circumcision rites. Here the actual circumcision is frequently performed by a local Muslim cleric, but the initiation retreat rituals which are part of the age-set ceremonies are controlled by traditional officiants. At the end of the novices' retreat the coming-out ceremonies include such Muslim rituals as the reading of the Prophet's birthday service (*mawlid*) and a sacrificial feast (*sadaqa*). Where, however, the Islamic circumcision ceremony is performed in early childhood, as is required on the orthodox view, and is thus detached from rituals of transition to adult status, the latter are celebrated separately. This is the position in some Swahili communities;[24] and often elsewhere when there is no traditional age-set organization and circumcision is performed as an individual act within the bosom of the family.

To those for whom bodily mutilations represent tribal identity marks, but who do not themselves traditionally practice it, circumcision regularly appears as one of the most striking Islamic traits. But the part must not be taken for the whole: as with such

[24] See Prins, 1961, pp. 108–9. For an excellent description of the *jando* rites in Tanganyika, see Cory, 1951, pp. 77, 78, 81–94, 159–68, and among the Yao, where it has made some slight headway, see Mitchell, 1956, pp. 81–2.

other superficial elements of Muslim culture as styles of dress and accoutrement, the spread of circumcision has often far out-distanced the faith with which it is associated. Thus, the Azande of the Sudan and Congo seem to have adopted it from an Islamic source without becoming Muslims:[25] moreover, not-withstanding such well-documented cases where a Muslim source is indicated, circumcision cannot always be attributed with certainty to Islamic influence.

It should also be noted that where Islam introduces, or reinforces, the practice of female excision or clitoridectomy among a people who traditionally carry out such other genital mutilations as infibulation, this conjunction may serve to add new weight, though quite without warrant, to the latter. To some degree this is apparently the case in those parts of the Sudan Republic, Ethiopia, and the Somali Republic where women are regularly infibulated.[26] Here, just as an uncircumcised man is incomplete and unclean, the purpose of clitoridectomy is to make a woman clean and wholesome in a religious sense. Infibulation, on the other hand, is concerned to exaggerate virginity and to ensure its preservation until the time of marriage.

With regard to marriage itself, the jural aspects of which have already been discussed, we need only note here the ready and widespread adoption of the appropriate Islamic ceremonial (especially the wedding feast, *walima* [Sw.]) and its various combinations with traditional rituals. Islam even sets the pattern for the length of the wedding festivities, which, particularly in the case of a man's first marriage, or the marriage of a virgin, usually continue over seven days.

The position is much the same with funeral ritual, which, wherever Islam has spread, shows a remarkable underlying uni-formity, despite the presence of an assortment of traditional elements. The distinctive Muslim traits are: the ritual washing of the corpse to the accompaniment of prayer; the incensing of the body; the use of a bier to carry the corpse to the grave; the

[25] See Evans–Pritchard, 1965.
[26] For a recent comprehensive examination of this subject see, C. G. Widstrand, 1964.

standard type and orientation of the grave towards Mecca;[27] the ritual funeral service conducted by clerics; the sprinkling of earth over the grave; the ritual mourning of the bereaved (washing, seclusion, and purification); and the observance of the subsequent ceremonies for the dead on the first, third, seventh, and fortieth days. All these elements, or the majority of them, are widely distributed—sometimes extending into areas where Islam has as yet made little other impression—and are variously combined with indigenous burial ritual. But, whereas most traditional religions share Islam's belief in the survival of the soul, generally the accompanying Muslim eschatology strikes a new note.

(c) CALENDAR FEASTS

The Muslim lunar calendar is everywhere adopted with Islam, and tends to displace other systems of time-reckoning, except where these are very firmly embedded in an unchanging seasonal cycle of economic interests. To the extent that pre-Islamic systems (e.g. solar calendars) continue to exist in parallel with the Muslim calendar, earlier non-Muslim ceremonies marking transition points in the year also tend to be observed.

Generally, however, the Arabic names for the Muslim months are adopted, although alternative local names based on an earlier calendar may also be utilized, as well as direct vernacular translations expressive of the social and religious content of the month in question. Thus, the month of Ramadan is known to the Mende as the 'moon of deprivation', and more generally throughout Muslim West Africa as simply the 'fasting month', a usage which is also found among the Somali[28] and in the Swahili area as well as elsewhere. This month of abnegation with its jubilant closing ceremony, the *'id al-fitr*, is everywhere celebrated and acquires a special measure of holiness, so that, for example, many evil spirits and malignant powers are believed to be largely incapacitated during it.

---

[27] There is, however, frequent controversy on the question of tombstones and the degree of their elaboration and conspicuousness. The fundamentalists, who oppose the cult of saints, also look askance at over-elaborate burials and grave markings.
[28] Where the following month is known as 'fast-opening' (*soonfur*).

Paradoxically, despite its name, the 'Great Feast' or *'id al-kabir*, which falls on the 12th day of the Muslim month of pilgrimage (Dhu'l-hijja), tends to be the lesser of these two important festive occasions. Known generally in the Western Sudan as *tabaske*, in centralized states such as those of the Wolof this feast provides the opportunity for public payment of homage to kings and chiefs.[29] This motif is strongly marked in Nupe, where Nadel has drawn attention to the manifestations of social solidarity and interdependence which the celebrations include, thus serving as a 'display of kingship' and a 'confirmation of political allegiance'.[30] The extent to which these important public political rituals of Islam may also include elements of symbolic rebellion and opposition, expressive of the tension in authority, has yet to be determined.

In contrast to the popularity of these festivals, the anniversary of the Prophet's birthday (*mawlid*) itself tends to receive less attention, especially in West Africa: in Nupe it is identified with the *gani* age-grade ceremonies.[31] In the eastern Sudan, North-East Africa, and East Africa, however, this feast is more regularly celebrated, and it is perhaps not too far-fetched to suggest that, like pilgrimage,[32] it may to some extent be regarded as an extension or sublimation of ancestor cults.

The Muslim new year falling on the 10th day of Muharram is also generally the occasion for festivity. The emphasis given to this feast seems to vary more or less directly with the extent to which earlier fertility cults, where they existed, have become detached from a pre-Islamic calendar regulating the productive divisions of the year. When the latter system of time-reckoning continues to play an important part through its connexion with seasonal economic interests and activities, traditional new-year ceremonies persist and are likely to eclipse Muharram in importance.

Thus, among the Swahili, where the old solar calendar, which is probably of Persian origin, is tied to sea-faring and cultivation,

---

[29] See Monteil, below, p. 167.   [30] Nadel, 1954, p. 240.
[31] Nadel, op. cit., p. 217.
[32] It seems significant in this context that the Swahili hold ceremonial feasts commemorating the dead during the pilgrimage festivities of Dhu'l-hijja.

the new-year feast of *Nayrus* is widely celebrated with elaborate feasting and sacrifice, while Muharram is largely ignored.[33] This feast continues to enjoy prominence all the way up the Somali[34] coast; and among the southern agricultural Somali is also regularly celebrated, particularly in the elaborate 'feast of beating' (*iskutun*) at Afgoi near Mogadishu. Among the nomads, however, who lay greater emphasis on the Muslim new year, this traditional feast is no longer regularly observed, and has become little more than a superstition. Finally, in Nupe the reverse process has occurred. Here the traditional and Muslim new-year festivals have fused and the *navu* feast of torches is celebrated in Muharram. This new hybrid ceremony has spread into non-Muslim areas to be incorporated in other calendrical cycles.[35]

Everywhere the persistence of such traditional rituals, whether as part of the Muslim cycle of feasts, or as part of a separate calendar, or as elements variously blended with those of the Islamic heritage, provides fertile soil for religious debate in the increasingly Muslim community. In this book a very characteristic example of such disputation on the question of the legitimacy of traditional rites is that described in a Swahili community by Dr. Peter Lienhardt.[36]

(d) ALMS AND SACRIFICE

Having already made brief passing reference to the assimilation of Muslim elements in traditional kingship rituals,[37] we must now turn to consider the meaning given in the local African context to the two principal categories of Muslim alms (*sadaqa*) and tithes (*zakat*). While in the Islamic theocracies of West Africa (and in the Mahdist state of the Eastern Sudan) *zakat* formed part of the state taxes, under the colonial régimes it ceased to be levied in this form and is generally everywhere confused today with *sadaqa*, voluntary alms. Such distinction as remains is that usually the term *zakat* is applied to contributions made to prominent shaikhs and the clergy, generally by way of charity,[38] while *sadaqa* de-

---

[33] See Gray, 1955.   [34] See Lewis, 1955, pp. 64–65.
[35] Nadel, op. cit., p. 241. See also more generally, Trimingham, 1959, pp. 76–7.   [36] Below, pp. 289–300.   [37] Above, p. 71.
[38] The institution of religious benefices or *waqfs* is particularly rare in West

notes a much wider range of meritorious gifts to all categories of the poor and includes formal sacrifice of meat and other offerings to God.

This should surprise no one: for in Islam all those who are weak in a secular sense are believed to enjoy the special care and protection of God. And those who give charity do so in the knowledge that in the process they stand to gain merit in the eyes of God. Such offerings, then, though associated with feasts (either at transition rites or in the great calendrical festivals) are essentially for the consumption of the poor, of children, and of the clergy—all those to whom the solicitous attentions of the pious bring their own reward.

Hence *sadaqa* becomes synonymous with sacrifice, and even in urban areas of the Sudan Republic is regularly used to mean a memorial service for the dead.[39] Its use is similarly widely extended to describe Muslim rain-making ceremonies, directed by the clergy, in West, East, and North-East Africa, when Quranic prayers are recited and offerings made to petition God to send rain. Indeed, the full range of ceremonies and ritual occasions involving prestation and containing the notion of sacrifice thus assimilated to the Muslim institution of *sadaqa* also includes such diverse activities as the free distribution of sacrifice at Hausa *iskoki* spirit ceremonies[40] and fund-raising parties held by rotating credit societies and mutual benefit clubs and associations among the Mossi and in West Africa generally. These diverse local interpretations and adaptations of one of the primary religious institutions of the faith illustrate something of the wide variety in forms of assimilation which can be achieved even within the minimal tenets of Islam.

Similarly, and lastly, accommodations of a different kind also occur with the cherished religious ideal of pilgrimage to Mecca, which, even with recent developments in air-communication, remains for most Africans perhaps the most difficult of the 'Five

---

Africa, though not quite so uncommon in East and North-East Africa. See Anderson, 1959.

[39] See Barclay, 1964, pp. 264–6. Elsewhere, as, e.g., among Swahili and Somali, the Arabic term *ziyara*, the 'visitation' of a saint's tomb, is generally used in this sense.   [40] Greenberg, 1946, p. 45.

Pillars' to accomplish. Nevertheless, the popularity of the *haj*, and, despite all the problems and expense it involves, especially in peripheral or isolated areas, is a remarkable testimony both to the strength of religious devotion shown by many of the most humble believers and to the prestige which its successful accomplishment brings. Here it is pertinent to ask to what extent pilgrimage to Mecca may be regarded as a form of sublimation of pre-Islamic ancestor veneration. This question, however, is easier to raise than to answer. For pilgrimage to Mecca is also widely observed in areas such as North-East Africa, where distance is not a great obstacle and where traditional ancestor cults are successfully assimilated to Muslim saint veneration.

Despite, or perhaps rather because of, its unique character, both in its geographical situation and in the emotional appeal which it exercises for the devout, local pilgrimage cults modelled on that at Mecca have arisen in some of the areas with which we are concerned. Thus, for example, in West Africa the shrines of the Murid leader Amadu Bamba at Touba,[41] and that at Tivaouane in the custody of the Hafid Tijaniyya,[42] attract crowds on a scale which is certainly comparable with the Meccan pilgrimage. The cult of Shaikh Hussayn Baliale at his shrine on the Upper Shebelle River in Ethiopia, which involves a unique blending of Muslim and animist Galla elements, provides a similar instance of these local attempts to emulate, if not eclipse, the orthodox cult at Mecca. The Somali veneration of Sharif Yusuf al-Kawneyn, at his shrine near Hargeisa,[43] is neither so elaborate nor ambitious in intention. It is, however, brought into equivalence with the holy pilgrimage to Mecca in the popular Somali view that to visit this local shrine three times is as meritorious and rewarding as to go once to the Ka'ba itself.

(e) ASSIMILATION OR ABERRATION

Some of the accommodations discussed in the foregoing, however much they testify to the vitality of traditional religious concepts and practice and to the generous catholicity of Islam, are

---

[41] See Bourlon, 1962, pp. 53 ff.
[42] Quesnot, 1962, pp. 133–55.   [43] Above, p. 63.

inevitably of questionable orthodoxy and frequently provoke long and bitter controversy. But, as those students of Islam whose conceptions derive from the study of documents rather than from the observation of actual behaviour must always be reminded, the gulf in Islam between ideals and practice, as with other religions with codified theologies, is generally wide, and the problem is to decide how far the boundary of apologetics can reasonably be strained. Variously extended by such cultural appendages as circumcision, the objective minimum criteria of Islam remain the 'Five Pillars', and while these are most realistically regarded as norms which all Muslims accept and, with varying degrees of success, seek to fulfil, the extent to which deviations from them may be tolerated and treated as the inevitable failure of practice to match ideals can only be decided by the Muslim community at large. In reality, of course, there is not one but many communities in Islam. And many who regard themselves as Muslims are scarcely accepted as such by those they take to be their co-religionists.

This is not the place to venture further into what is ultimately a metaphysical problem beyond the realms of sociological analysis. Here it is sufficient to recall that African Muslims, as other Muslims, tend to represent Islam to the non-Muslim as a totally religious creed and system of ritual observances and injunctions rather than as a way of life or complete cultural system. Yet, in truth, Islam is all these. Nor, and this is sometimes accounted Islam's distinguishing genius, do Muslims experience difficulty in dividing the imperatives which direct the conduct of their lives into those which are part of the Islamic heritage and those which belong to local tradition. This dichotomy which enables Muslims, if not Islam as such, to accommodate so much and so variously, not only of traditional but also of new influences, is not always adequately expressed in such terms as 'dualism' and 'parallelism', etc. For the strength of Muslim devotion, at least in many areas, is still such that in the last analysis these two distinct sources of legitimacy are seen as merging in a single Muslim way of life where all standards of thought and conduct are assumed to derive their final sanctity.

VI. ISLAM AND THE MODERN WORLD

(a) THE COLONIAL ERA

Our main purpose here will be to consider the effects of the colonial situation on the character of the relations between Muslim and non-Muslim peoples and, despite (or sometimes because of) the association of colonization with Christianity, the further consolidation and spread of Islam during this period. It need scarcely be added that this is an extremely broad question. In seeking to deal with it we shall find, as in other aspects of the development of Islam in tropical Africa, a similar range of apparently contradictory responses and reactions which reflect the diversity of circumstances and conditions in different regions and at different times during the colonial era. Notwithstanding this, however, certain broad generalizations will emerge.

The immediate effects of colonial rule naturally varied with the policies and attitudes of the colonizers, both official and unofficial, towards Islam. As well as by larger imperial concerns, these have inevitably been influenced by the degree and character of the attachment of the administering powers to Christianity, and even more significantly in practice, by the exigencies of local circumstances. Consequently, it is scarcely surprising that policy and practice should have varied considerably both among the colonial possessions of a single metropolitan power and within the same colonial territory at different periods and phases of its existence. These contrasts reflecting a necessarily pragmatic response to differing conditions are especially apparent in the early stages of colonization. Compare, for example, Leopold's initial alliance with the Arabs in the Congo with later events; or the use by Britain of Zanzibar's tenuous claims to the East African Coast, with British opposition to Islam in Buganda and Central Africa.

One of the clearest and least ambiguous instances of a colonial power's direct encouragement of Islam, and not merely as a religious force, is seen in the history of the Italian colonies of Eritrea and Somalia. In these territories once the work of pacification had been completed the local administrations sought to use Islam as a means of furthering the metropolitan government's aggressive ambitions against Christian Ethiopia. Here, in fact, to a large extent, and particularly in Somalia, which was in any case solidly Muslim, the colonial situation represented a continuation, and in some respects an intensification, of the precolonial political circumstances. In her North African colonies, and especially in Cyrenaica, where she had Senusi nationalism to contend with, Italy's enthusiasm for Islam was more restrained.[1] At the other extreme in the Belgian Congo, once the Arab flirtation had outgrown its utility, the administration's attitude was one of uncompromising hostility towards Islam. This, of course, was in part the result of Leopoldian clericalism, as well as the need to limit Arab trading competition, and the authorities' intolerance of Islam in this case virtually halted the spread of the new faith in an area where it had just begun to make a tangible impact.

In the British sphere, although the Kenya Coast and Zanzibar have some claim, Northern Nigeria and the Northern Sudan probably afford the best examples of territories where administrative sympathy and support for Islam was strongly expressed. Once the initial resistance to British control had been overcome in northern Nigeria, the agreements establishing the authority of the new rulers forbade all Christian proselytization in the Emirates, and left the field clear for further Muslim consolidation. Moreover, the incorporation of many elements of the traditional Muslim political organization in the new administrative system of indirect rule naturally enhanced the status of Islam and encouraged its wider dissemination. In the Anglo-Egyptian Sudan, after the storms and tribulations of the Mahdia were safely over, much the same position was reached.

On a much smaller scale a comparable degree of administrative partiality for the Muslim Somali of the Northern Province of Kenya (similar to that displayed in British Somaliland) led to the

[1] See Evans-Pritchard, 1949.

preferment of these nomads in their conflicts with non-Muslim Galla Boran, and helped to convince those Boran who were cut off from their traditional ritual centres that the best passport to success lay in their adopting Islam on the Somali pattern.[2] In quite other circumstances and with different effects, where administrative attitudes towards Muslim minorities were not so favourable, the Ndendeuli of Tanganyika provide an instance of a people to many of whom Islam seemed more attractive than Christianity, since they identified the latter religion with their traditional enemies the Ngoni.

In the French West African territories the establishment of colonial rule involved widespread conflict with Islam, for in the circumstances of the extensive influence of Haji 'Umar's Tijaniyya brotherhood it was as Richard-Molard has put it: 'the world of the *torobe* (clerics) that it was necessary to dominate entirely, or nothing at all'.[3] While this naturally fostered the continuance of the tradition of revivalist holy wars and their redirection against the Christian colonizers, a combination of strong measures with a later practical tolerance of Islam did not prevent the eventual attainment of harmonious relations between the two sides. Official French policy towards Islam vacillated considerably, but even at its most hostile made little difference to the situation on the ground. As Gouilly has aptly remarked: 'The same men, who at Bamako or Dakar elaborated directives destined to confound "The Peril of Islam", in practice took measures which were designed to strengthen it.'[4] And in any case, unlike the position in Leopold's Congo, many of the French officials held strongly secular and anti-clerical views which left little room for any religiously grounded intolerance of Islam. Others had come from Algeria.

If, then, official French policy was from time to time, and particularly in the first two decades of this century, deliberately concerned to restrain Muslim proselytization and ever watchful of foreign Muslim infiltration, this did not prevent the local

[2] See Baxter, in *Islam*, 1st ed., p. 242.   [3] 1949, p. 69.
[4] 1952, p. 254. For an excellent analysis of French policy see pp. 247 ff. of this work, and for an admirably concise statement Lord Hailey—in Anderson, 1954, pp. V-VI.

administrative officials from reaching something of the same sort of practical understanding with their Muslim subjects as was generally achieved under British rule. Thus, even such an initially intransigent movement as that of the Muridiyya in Senegal, formed at a time when orthodox Islam supported the colonial system, later lost its militancy and devoted its energies to the intensive cultivation of ground-nuts with the benevolent approval of the French authorities. Likewise, in Britain's small Somaliland Protectorate, where Shaikh Muhammad 'Abdille Hassan's twenty-years' *jihad* (1900–20) against the Christian Ethiopians and British affords one of the clearest instances of a Muslim protest movement which arose directly in circumstances of Christian colonization, the end of this turbulent period led eventually to a new understanding with the Administration in which Islamic institutions were respected and supported and all Christian proselytization was prohibited.

Thus, in general in those colonies where Islam was already strongly entrenched, whatever the character of the initial colonizing action, and whether or not traditional Muslim rulers were retained, as in most British possessions, or displaced, as was often the case with the more direct system of French administration,[5] the new authorities did not seek to disestablish Islam. Nor, indeed, except in the Congo, did the colonial administrations succeed in preventing proselytization or the further spread of Islam. On the contrary, the overall effect of colonization was rather generally conducive to a new expansion of the faith. And while the exclusion of Christian proselytization from the most ardently Muslim areas under British rule did not, of course, cordon these off completely from Christian influence, since, as in Northern Nigeria, Christians were frequently employed in the administrative services, almost universally the colonial administrations helped their Muslim subjects to build mosques and schools, and often directly subsidized pilgrimage to Mecca or facilitated its organization. Here administrative action was largely determined, irrespective of the official policy in vogue, by the inescapable fact

[5] The practical effects of French and British administrative policy must not, of course, be contrasted too strongly. See Deschamps, 1963, and Crowder, 1964.

that in Islam Muslims possessed a bridge mediating between the narrow particularism of traditional society and the wider impulses and requirements of modern life and economic interests.

Significantly, it was precisely in those regions where Islam was not already available to provide this vital service that the adherents of traditional African religions turned with enthusiasm to Christianity as the means to an effective participation in the wider world opened up by colonization. This was generally the situation in East Africa behind the Muslim coastal belt, and on the West African coast. In both these regions Africans achieved positions of prominence in the wider supra-ethnic society, not so much as in Muslim areas by success as traders and soldiers, as in the Christian Western occupations of teacher, clerk, and government official.

In areas in which both religions were represented the dichotomy between Muslim and Christian occupations was most marked where the British pattern of Indirect Rule had entrenched conservativist Islam and the young aspiring men of modernist outlook issued from the schools of the Christian missions. This division seems to have been less marked in the Sudan Republic, where British rule was more direct. The contrast was also much less striking in the French and Italian territories, where the system of administration and the 'civilizing mission' of the colonizers exerted a powerful levelling effect. These provisional generalizations, however, certainly require more detailed testing, and a comparative study of the cultural and religious backgrounds and school careers of officials and politicians in the different territories would be illuminating.

In British, French, and Italian territories a further important effect of administrative action directly favourable to Islam was the considerable, though varying, authority allowed to the Shari'a under colonial government and the widespread appointment of official *qadis* and Muslim courts whose jurisdiction was by no means restricted only to suits between professing Muslims.[6] Moreover, in many regions the use made of the Quran for swear-

---

[6] On the position in British territories, see Anderson, 1954, *passim*; and in French territories, Gouilly, 1952, pp. 236–7, 254 ff.

ing witnesses has exerted a notable influence. Where the un-
converted have been offered the choice of swearing on the Quran,
or on the Bible, or by some 'fetish', the general tendency has been
to adopt the Muslim practice.

More widely still, irrespective of particular colonial policies
and administrative procedures, the *pax colonica* itself created
conditions which greatly encouraged the dissemination of Islam.
Prior to colonization, as we have seen, Islam had spread most
successfully in circumstances of social change, of ethnic interaction and dislocation, and of the extension of economic and
political frontiers. With the new opportunities for trade and
commerce and the greatly improved and more secure communications, both within countries and between them, it is scarcely
to be wondered at that a new era of Islamic expansion should
have been ushered in. The trend now, moreover, was towards
individual conversion, the very personal character of which is
seen in the presence of Muslims, Christians, and the adherents of
traditional religions within the bosom of the same families and
kinship groups.

Increased travel and trading activities, migrant labour and
movement, the development of administrative and commercial
towns, all these played a vital part in throwing together Muslims
and non-Muslims of different origin and ethnic groups in circumstances in which co-religionists displayed an impressive solidarity despite their differences of origin. Nothing could more
persuasively demonstrate the supra-ethnic character of the community of Islam, and the many advantages open to its members.
Christianity of course, and Church and other Christian associations, offered similar benefits, but not, it would seem, on the
same scale or as readily.[7]

At the same time the local expansion of Islam received renewed
stimulus and encouragement with the arrival of new Muslim
immigrants from the Middle East and India and Pakistan, and the
introduction of dynamic modern missionary movements such as
the Ahmadiyya[8] sect in West Africa and the Isma'ili and other

[7] There would seem scope here for a comparative study of the functions and
success of Muslim (see Grindal, 1973) and Christian associations.
[8] See Fisher, 1963.

sectarian organizations in East Africa. Although these often gave rise to new lines of division and conflict, they also brought welcome new blood.

Finally, it is essential not to overlook the obvious consideration that, especially in areas subject to dual missionary activity, the association of the colonizers with Christianity usually tended to give Islam a special appeal as the religion of resistance and independence, and this effect was enhanced by the readiness with which Islam, unlike Christianity, adapted itself to local conditions and imposed few, if any, restrictions on the formation of a local indigenous clergy. Despite some tendencies towards unorthodox developments in Islam, it is perhaps this above all which accounts for the very small number of Muslim separatist movements in Africa, in contrast to the multitude of Christian separatist churches, and explains the remarkable unity of Islam throughout tropical Africa.

Thus, the total effect of the *pax colonica*, as much involuntary as intended, was to promote an unprecedented expansion of Islam. And, as Professor Froelich[9] justly observes for West Africa, and this also applies to a lesser extent in the other areas surveyed in this book, in half a century of European colonization Islam progressed more widely and more profoundly than in ten centuries of pre-colonial history. In this short space of time it seems probable that the number of Muslims in tropical Africa had at least doubled.

This rapid expansion has naturally not been completely uncontested, least of all by the Christian missions themselves. And, as we have seen, attachment to Christianity has furnished an important alternative avenue into the new world of larger allegiances and interests, and also another means for the expression of traditional hostilities and conflicts. This is especially evident in the contrasting cases of Ethiopia and the Sudan Republic. In the first, national integration has been pursued through the medium of the Christian culture of the dominant Amhara and the Amharic language, in opposition to the conflicting claims of scarcely less numerous but less powerful Muslim interests. In

[9] In *Islam*, 1st ed., p. 166.

the second, it is the Muslim culture of the dominant north which has become associated with national integration at the expense of the south, where a separatist tradition was fostered under British rule and found expression through Christianity.

Conflicting religious attachments, and not merely between Islam and Christianity but also within Islam itself, have thus sometimes served to entrench traditional differences, leaving many denominational conflicts to be resolved after independence. Yet they have, at the same time, also pointed to wider loyalties and interests, and have helped to override traditional ethnic particularism. From the point of view of the secular needs of the new states, this is certainly a most significant contribution; and what is perhaps most remarkable is the mutual tolerance and restraint which Muslim and Christian proselytizers have frequently displayed.[10]

(b) NATIONALISM AND INDEPENDENCE

The history of the role of Islam in the development of African nationalism has yet to be written. There are few studies, even in particular territories, of the political activities and alignments of Muslims, or of the influence of Pan-Islamic propaganda from Egyptian and other sources, far less any general examination of this important topic as a whole. Hence we can only conclude this brief survey by suggesting some points of comparative interest concerning the political positions associated with Islam in the growth of national movements, and the place of this religion and of its adherents in the newly independent states.

It will be apparent that the same factors which enabled Islam to act as a bridge between ethnicity and the wider system of relations established under colonial rule might also be expected to give African Muslims an initial advantage over their non-Muslim countrymen in the initiation and organization of nationalist movements directed towards sovereignty and independence. Thus, particularly in West Africa, as the heirs of a commercial and partly urban tradition concerned with long-distance trade

[10] For a sensitive appraisal of the situation in French West Africa prior to independence, see Gouilly, op. cit., pp. 267 ff.

and the pilgrimage, with at the same time a fund of Muslim knowledge and some command of a written language and administrative experience in both the pre-colonial and colonial régimes, as well as often of resistance to the colonizers, local Muslims clearly possessed a unique heritage which could be applied to the development of modern nationalism. Their special advantages, moreover, lay not only in the field of ideas, organization, and communication but also in the crucial realm of finance.

These resources, of course, could only be expected to be unreservedly harnessed to modern nationalist endeavour where this aimed at goals which were fully acceptable to the interests of the Muslims concerned. Where the attainment of independence was regarded as being likely to prejudice Muslim interests, the same organizational resources and skills could equally easily be applied in a manner which radical African nationalists would regard as conservative. The manner in which the Muslim factor has operated in the growth of African nationalism, therefore, has depended very largely upon the special circumstances of Muslim interests in different territories at different times.

The recent political histories of Mali,[11] Senegal,[12] and also Guinea[13] probably afford the best examples of the general coincidence of Muslim and popular nationalist aims in West Africa, while this is seen even more unequivocally in the rather different circumstances of Somaliland[14] and the Sudan Republic[15]. On the other hand, in territories where former ruling Muslim dynasties were preserved, or immigrant Muslim communities (such as the Arabs in East Africa) were assigned a specially privileged position by the colonial administrations, they naturally tended to adopt a more conservative ideology and position. Consequently, as in Zanzibar and northern Nigeria, such specially favoured Muslim

[11] See Hodgkin and Schachter Morgenthau, 1965. See also M. Chailley, 1962.
[12] See Bourlon, 1962; Quesnot, 1962; and Bourlon, 1964.
[13] See Gray Cowan, 1962. And for some indication of the political role of Islam generally in francophone West Africa, Thompson and Adloff, 1958; and more generally, Post, 1964. For the Muslim factor in Sierra Leone politics see Proudfoot, 1961.
[14] This term is used here to include all the Somali territories—those under Ethiopian and Kenyan jurisdiction, as well as those in French Somaliland and the Somali Republic. See Lewis, 1965(a).   [15] See Holt, 1961.

groups resisted the appeal to a wider nationalism, except when they were in a position to espouse a type of nationalism which seemed compatible with the advancement of their own particularist aims. The contrast here can perhaps be seen when the success of popular 'radical' nationalism in Mali is compared with its failure (at least up to the present) in northern Nigeria, following the French destruction of traditional Muslim power in Mali and its preservation by the British in northern Nigeria.

Nevertheless, although this distinction appears to have some value, and not least in suggesting lines along which further analysis might profitably be directed, it must not be maintained too rigidly. There is a sense, for example, in which it may be argued that nationalism in the Sudan Republic, despite its early Muslim Dinka direction,[16] may be regarded as concerned with the conservation of northern Muslim political control. And the case of Somalia is so unusual that it merits further brief mention.

The roots of modern popular Somali nationalism lie in the traditional cultural nationalism of this ethnic group, in which Islam has always been a vital component. From the beginning, Somali nationalism has aimed at the creation of a sovereign Somali state embracing the entire Somali population, and has consequently sought the re-unification of those parts of the nation dismembered by the colonial partition.[17] Hence although two parts of the nation (the former British and Italian Somalilands) are now joined in the Somali Republic, the struggle to unite with the remaining areas of Djibouti (French Somaliland), Ethiopia, and northern Kenya still continues. This, of course, is the reverse of the general trend elsewhere in Africa, where the movement is not from nation to state, but from state to nation; and parallel phenomena are only found in the particularistic ethnic divisions within states.

Given the particular advantages which the Somali enjoy, although they remain as yet not fully realized, it might be thought

[16] Holt, Ibid., pp. 127 ff. See also Beshir, 1974.
[17] Prior to colonization, however, despite their strong cultural nationalism, the Somalis did not form a single political group. See Lewis, 1965(a).

that in other new states, with their patchworks of peoples and language groups, Islam might be regarded as an aid to national integration. So far elsewhere, however, Islam seems rarely to have been viewed in this light, except in the Sudan Republic and, more questionably perhaps, to some extent in Mali and Senegal.

As far as actual Muslim participation in nationalist movements is concerned, in all areas where the Religious orders were strongly developed they played a significant role. In Senegal the Muridiyya movement's change of position from militant anti-French activity to quietist co-operation was followed subsequently by pressure-group activity in favour of the *Section Française de l'Internationale Ouvrière* and later by support for Senghor's *Bloc Démocratique Sénégalais*. Again in Senegal during the crucial period between 1958 and 1960 the Muridiyya and the Tijaniyya (almost three times as strong) both aligned themselves with those who favoured the retention of strong ties with France. But the Hamallist reformist branch of the Tijaniyya developed in the years between the two world wars in the Soudan (i.e. Mali) and neighbouring French territories as a proto-nationalist vehicle of popular protest against colonial administration and Muslim compliance. It appealed most to submerged social groups, and with such a following it helped to prepare the ground for the emergence of the *Rassemblement Démocratique Africain* after the Bamako conference in 1946.

In the Sudan Republic, as might be expected, recent political developments have been more strongly influenced by the activities of the Religious Orders. Here the critical factor is the association between the Khatmiyya *tariqa* and the Ashiqqa party, on the one hand, and that between their rivals the Ansar (led by the Mahdi's son) and the Umma party, on the other. The *tariqas* have also similarly played an important role in Somali politics, although in this case, with the overriding strength of clan ties, their political connexions are less clear-cut.

If the religious orders, by their very nature as organizations dedicated to promoting a wider sense of communal identity than that based on ethnicity, have facilitated the growth and achievement of modern nationalism (and, incidentally, pointed to wider territorial regroupings of African states), where they have come to be of importance in modern politics their inter-denominational rivalries have also necessarily exerted a significant force. This is evident, as we have seen in the competition between the Khatmiyya and Ansar in the Sudan Republic, and is also apparent in West Africa in the rival attractions of the Qadiriyya and Tijaniyya. Thus, in strongly Muslim countries the *tariqas* have not only contributed in various ways to the development of nationalism as such but have also markedly affected the character of internal politics in the pre- and post-independence phases. Detailed comparison of their political roles with those of Christian organizations in areas of mixed religious affiliation would be of considerable interest.

Passing now to Islamic education, we find that traditional forms of religious teaching and schooling, while showing remarkable resilience, have naturally tended to be weakened in competition with imported forms of Western secular education. Consequently, the products of the former system, malams, shaikhs, and *qadis*, etc., have generally only identified themselves strongly with the new nationalist movements in territories such as Mali, Senegal, the Sudan Republic, and the Somali Republic (and in different circumstances in northern Nigeria), where nationalist aims and aspirations have been couched, at least partly, in Muslim terms by parties under predominantly Muslim leadership or seeking Muslim support. And even then, although their co-operation has been important, they have seldom played a leading role. Their sustained allegiance has probably been most crucial in such countries as the Sudan and Somali Republics, where Islam is a fundamental part of local culture and where the rise of modern nationalist movements was at the beginning, at least, largely independent of any large-scale economic development and trade-union activity.

By contrast, those who have had experience of the modernist centres of Muslim higher education in Egypt and North Africa seem generally to have played a more active and critical role in the generation and diffusion of nationalist ideas and also in the organization of local independent Muslim schools as instruments of educational and social reform.[18] Equally, pilgrimage to Mecca, with greatly increased participation from such outlying areas as West Africa, and the growth of local interest and involvement in such organizations as the Islamic Congress[19] fostered the wider dissemination of reformist anti-colonial ideas from the Arab World, to say nothing of the extremely significant impact of the Arab Press and Radio, particularly from Cairo.

Faced with such a militant modernist interpretation of Islam, with its ready accommodation to the secular requirements of nationalism and the modern state, the old order of clergy has tended to become a conservative force wedded to traditional forms of religious education and opposed to the extension of modern secular schooling. Hence, even in predominantly Muslim countries, despite the deep commitment of the political *élite* to Islam, this old guard has naturally not been immune from criticism and attack. Friction similarly arises over the traditional activities of holymen and the custodians of saints' shrines where these are seen as profiting from the ignorance and unsophistication of the populace. This conflict between the guardians of traditional Islam and the new more secularly orientated political leaders is highlighted by such controversies as that over the status of Arabic and the Arabic script in countries such as the Somali Republic.

At the level of ideology itself the conceptual scheme of Islam (especially in its reformist modes), if secularized sufficiently, can readily be transposed into that type of modern nationalism which is the moving spirit of Pan-Africanism.[20] Thus, the leaders of Sekou Touré's *Parti Démocratique de Guinée*, much influenced by their experience of trade unionism and the theory of Marxism,

[18] For the effect of these in West Africa, see Cardaire, 1954. Cheikh Touré's *Li takune mu'minan. A fin que tu deviennes Croyant* (1957) provides an interesting statement of the reformist position in Senegal at this period. Here the faithful are exhorted to join the struggle against colonialism and capitalism and against the obscurantism and extortions of venal *marabouts*.

[19] The Sixth World Islamic Conference met at Mogadishu in the Somali Republic in December 1964. Egypt and Algeria did not attend.

[20] See Hodgkin, 1962.

could claim in 1954 that: '. . . we are in the pure line of Islam, conquering because humane and charitable'.[21]

In this accommodation to new circumstances and needs, in which, up to a point, the resilience of Islam is again demonstrated, the *jihad* becomes the struggle against colonialism (or neo-colonialism), the reformers become 'freedom fighters', as in Algeria, *dar al-Islam* becomes the body of sovereign African states, and *dar al-harb* those which have yet to shake off the colonialist yoke. And, stretching the analogy yet further, the unity of the community (*umma*) may be seen as the unity of the African or Afro-Asian peoples. The ideal universal state ruled according to the precepts of Islam in which justice, equality, and brotherhood shall prevail, is transposed into the model African union organized according to the principles of 'African socialism'.[22] These and other conceptual equivalences would seem to give the popularist ideology of Pan-Africanism (at least in the local context) a special appeal, actual or potential, among Muslim communities with a tradition of reformist or Mahdist ideas.

Once this has been said, however, it must immediately be added that these theoretical correspondences, however persuasive, have not so far been realized in any stable wider political association, despite several abortive attempts, between the Muslim and non-Muslim states of Africa and Asia. Pan-Africanism and Pan-Islamism remain two distinct, sometimes over-lapping, but never fully interlocked spheres of interest and attachment, and are both encompassed in that larger, vaguer, and even more fluid circle of alignments represented by the Third World block. And this seems likely to continue as long as a distinction is drawn within Islam between Arab and non-Arab. For those African Muslims who once vaunted their putative Arab connexions are now increasingly claiming that they are Africans.

[21] Quoted from *la Liberté*, 28 December 1954, by Ken Post, *The New States of West Africa*, Penguin Books, London, 1964. Sekou Touré is, of course, himself a Muslim. Similar claims are made to justify modern socialist trends in Somalia. See Lewis, 1979(*a*).

[22] For a valuable discussion of the nature of African socialism, see Friedland and Rosberg, 1964; and, particularly with reference to Islam, Monteil, 1964.

The difficulties involved in any wider political identification are perhaps most acutely revealed in the external policies of Egypt which sits uncomfortably athwart both worlds and aspires to a position of leadership in each. And here, of course, the traditional attachment of states such as Ethiopia, and of many of the new African leaders to Christianity, would seem destined to help to maintain these distinctions. In inter-African affairs the real importance of these cleavages is evident in the uneasy relationships between Egypt, the Sudan, and Ethiopia, to say nothing of the problem of Somali unification, on which the often vigorously voiced support of those Muslim states outside Africa has fallen upon deaf ears as far as those of their co-religionists who live in the continent itself are concerned.[23] The understandable interest of the latter in the preservation of their own sensitive frontiers and territorial prestige, and their natural fear of comparable particularist movements at home, have restrained such sympathy as they might perhaps otherwise have felt for a cause which to Somali nevertheless appears as a positive contribution both to African and Islamic unity.[24]

At the same time, it must also be remarked that those African countries which are officially constituted as Muslim states seem in African, as in wider extra-African, affairs to have shown little identity of interest or purpose. Often, indeed, they have adopted contrary positions on international issues (as, for example, in their attitudes towards Israel) and fallen into opposed camps in their larger allegiances, other principles of common interest exerting a greater attractive force than the bond of common adherence to Islam.[25] Nor could it be said that their various constitutions conform in any sense to a common 'Muslim' pattern. The extent to which Islam has in any constant fashion moulded the character of their political processes, save in superficial aspects,

[23] At the same time, however, it must be remarked that at the Sixth World Muslim Conference in Mogadishu in 1964 all the African Muslim countries and communities represented (including those from West Africa) pledged themselves to support the Somali struggle for unification. Although it would be premature to assess the significance of the Conference's resolutions on this or other wider issues (such as hostility towards Israel), it seems reasonable to suggest that the mounting of the meeting itself should be seen as a Muslim attempt to emulate the Addis Ababa Pan-African Summit conference of 1963. Somalia joined the Arab League in 1974.

[24] See Lewis, 1963 (*b*); 1979 (*b*)   [25] See Legum, 1962.

is equally open to question, although, admittedly, this is a topic which requires much more intensive research before a considered judgment can be given. Nevertheless, the presence of Islam as a unifying culturo-religious force might be supposed to endow these states with a sufficient sense of cohesion to permit the existence of democratically competing political parties without danger to their national solidarity. This potential, if it is such, has so far seldom been realized very effectively, except in the Somali Republic, where there is an unusually high degree of cultural homogeneity and national cohesion.

Finally, if everywhere in tropical Africa Islam is today on the march, the wider political consequences of any great new expansion of Muslim influence and Pan-Islamic solidarity seem likely to be tempered by the increasing secularism of modern Muslim states and the general recognition that secular aims and policies are more important in the modern world than common religious interest. Moreover, today in states of mixed denomination all religions are honoured, and at state ceremonies the Muslim, the Christian, and the traditionalist join together in offering prayers and libations, each according to his fashion. As with Christianity in the West, Islamic civilization is being gradually detached from its religious roots, and the gulf between the spiritual and the secular spheres of life is widening. While, as elsewhere in the Muslim world, continuing to influence deeply the private lives of individuals, it is thus at least questionable whether Islam can be expected in the future to exercise the profound political effect it has had in earlier periods of African history.

Thus, although Islam may be regarded as a distinctive mode of life and religion, as a historical heritage, or as a general ideology of universal applicability, or, indeed, as all of these, it is increasingly on the first two, rather than on the last of these that the emphasis falls today. Or so it seemed in 1966. Over a decade later, in the context of the world energy crisis, the concentration of oil resources in the Arabian peninsula gave Arab and Islamic identity an entirely new significance. However, if the Middle East and North Africa are reliable guides, there seems little doubt that as Islam becomes further entrenched within black Africa it will become equally riven by local divisions and disputes.

REFERENCES TO 1966

Abraham, D. P.
  (1961) 'Maramuca: an exercise in the combined use of Portuguese records and
     oral tradition', *Journal of African History*, vol. II, pp. 211–25.
Alexandre, P.
  (1963) 'Les Kotokoli et les Bassari', in *Les Populations du Nord-Togo*, by J. C.
     Froelich, P. Alexandre, and R. Cornevin. Paris.
Anderson, J. N. D.
  (1954) *Islamic Law in Africa*. London.
  (1959) 'Waqfs in East Africa', *Journal of African Law*, vol. III, pp. 152–64.
Banton, M. (ed.)
  (1965) *The Relevance of Models for Social Anthropology*, I. London.
Barclay, H. B.
  (1964) *Buuri al-Lamaab*. New York.
Barnes, J. A., Mitchell, J. C., and Gluckman, M.
  (1949) 'The Village Headman in British Central Africa', *Africa*, vol. XIX,
     pp. 89–106.
Bivar, A. D. H. and Hiskett, M.
  (1962) 'The Arabic literature of Nigeria to 1804: a provisional account',
     Bulletin of the School of Oriental and African Studies, vol. XXV, pp. 104–48.
Boullié, R.
  (1937) *Les Coutumes Familiales au Kanem*. Paris.
Bourlon A.
  (1962) 'Mourides et Mouridisme 1953', in *Notes et Etudes sur l'Islam en
     Afrique Noire*. pp. 53–74.
  (1964) 'L'evolution politique du Senegal 1962–1964', *L'Afrique et L'Asie*,
     no. 68, pp. 23–41.
Bovill, E. W.
  (1933) *Caravans of the Old Sahara*. London.
Bradbury, R. E.
  (1965) 'Father and senior son in Edo mortuary ritual', in *African Systems of
     Thought*, ed. M. Fortes and G. Dieterlen. London.
Cardaire, M.
  (1954) *L'Islam et le Terroir Africain*. IFAN.
Carter, Gwendolen (ed.)
  (1962) *African One-Party States*. New York.
Cerulli, E.
  (1936) *Studi Etiopici I. La Lingua e la storia di Harar*. Rome.
  (1941) 'Il Sultanato del Scioa nel secolo XII', *Rassegna di Studi Etiopici*, vol.
     I, pp. 5–42.
  (1957) *Somalia, Scritti vari editi ed inediti I*. Rome.
  (1959) *Somalia, Scritti vari editi ed inediti II*. Rome.
Chailley, M.
  (1962) 'Aspects de l'Islam au Mali', in *Notes et Etudes sur l'Islam en Afrique
     Noire*, pp. 9–52.
Chedeville, E.
  (1966) 'Quelques faits de l'organisation sociale des 'Afar', *Africa*, vol. XXXVI,
     pp. 173–195.
Chittick, N.
  (1963) 'Kilwa and the Arab settlement of the East African Coast', *Journal of
     African History*, vol. IV, pp. 179–90.

Cohen, Abner
  (1965) 'The Social Organization of Credit in a West African Cattle Market', *Africa*, vol. XXXV, pp. 8–20.
Cole, C. W.
  (1949) *Report on Land Tenure in Zaria Province*. Kaduna.
Coleman, J. S. and Rosberg, C. G.
  (1965) *Political Parties and National Integration in Tropical Africa*. Berkeley.
Colson, E.
  (1950) 'Possible repercussions of the right to make wills upon the Plateau Tonga of Northern Rhodesia', *Journal of African Administration*, vol. II, pp. 24–35.
Cory, H.
  (1947 (1951)) (1948 (1951)) 'Jando' (initiation and circumcision ceremonies in Tanganyika), *Journal of the Royal Anthropological Institute*, vol. LXVII, pp. 159–68; vol. LXXVIII, pp. 81–94.
Crawford, O. G. S.
  (1951) *The Fung Kingdom of Sennar*. Gloucester.
Crowder, M.
  (1964) 'Indirect Rule—French and British Style' *Africa*, vol. XXXIV, pp. 197–205.
Cunnison, I.
  (1963) 'Kazembe and the Arabs to 1870.' Paper presented to the History of Central African Peoples Conference, Rhodes-Livingstone Institute, Lusaka.
Delafosse, M.
  (1912) *Haut Senegal et Niger*. Paris.
Deschamps, H.
  (1963) 'Et maintenant, Lord Lugard?' *Africa*, vol. XXXIII, pp. 293–306.
Dupire, M.
  (1962) *Peuls Nomades*, Paris.
Encyclopaedia of Islam. London (1913).
Evans-Pritchard, E. E.
  (1949) *The Sanusi of Cyrenaica*. Oxford.
  (1956) *Nuer Religion*. Oxford.
  (1965) 'A final contribution to the study of Zande culture', *Africa*, vol. XXXV, pp. 1–7.
Fisher, H. J.
  (1963) *Ahmadiyyah: A study in Contemporary Islam on the West African Coast*. London.
Fortes, M.
  (1965) 'Some reflections on ancestor worship in Africa', in *African Systems of Thought*, ed. M. Fortes and G. Dieterlen. London.
Fortes, M. and Dieterlen, G. (eds.)
  (1965) *African Systems of Thought*. London.
Freeman-Grenville, G. S. P.
  (1962) *The Medieval History of the Tanganyika Coast*. Oxford.
Friedland, W. M. and Rosberg, C. G.
  (1964) *African Socialism*. Stanford.
Froelich, J. C., Alexandre, P., and Cornevin, R.
  (1963) *Les Populations du Nord-Togo*. Paris.
Gray, Sir John M.
  (1947) 'Ahmad bin Ibrahim', *Uganda Journal*, vol. XI.
  (1955) 'Nairuzi or Siku ya Mwaka', *Tanganyika Notes and Records*, vol. 38, pp. 1–22.

Gray Cowan, L.
(1962) 'Guinea', in *African One-Party States*, ed. Gwendolen Carter. New York. pp. 149–235.

Greenberg, J. H.
(1946) *The Influence of Islam on a Sudanese Religion*. New York.
(1947) 'Islam and clan organization among the Hausa', *Southwestern Journal of Anthropology*, vol. III, pp. 193–211.

Grottanelli, V. L.
(1955) *Pescatori dell'Oceano Indiano*. Rome.

Gouilly, A.
(1952) *L'Islam dans l'Afrique Occidentale Française*. Paris.

Gueye, Y.
(1957) 'Essai sur les causes et les consequences de la micropropriété au Fouta Toro', *Bull. IFAN*, vol. XIX (B), pp. 24–42.

Harries, Lyndon
(1964) 'The Arabs and Swahili culture', *Africa*, vol. XXXIV, pp. 224–9.

Hébert, J. C.
(1961) 'Analyse structurale des géomancies Comoriennes, Malgaches et Africaines', *Journal de la Société des Africanistes*, vol. XXXI, pp. 115–208.

Hodgkin, T.
(1962) 'Islam and Pan-Africanism.' Institute of Commonwealth Studies Pan-Africanism Seminar Paper, 10 January.

Hodgkin, T. and Schachter Morgenthau, R.
(1965) 'Mali', in *Political Parties and National Integration in Tropical Africa*, ed. J. S. Coleman and C. G. Rosberg, pp. 216–58.

Holt, P. M.
(1958) *The Mahdist State in the Sudan 1881–1898*. Oxford.
(1961) *A Modern History of the Sudan*. London.
(1963) 'Funj origins: a critique and new evidence', *Journal of African History*, vol. IV, pp. 39–55.

Hopen, C. E.
(1958) *The Pastoral Fulbe Family in Gwandu*, London.

Kirkman, J. S.
(1954) *The Arab City of Gedi*. Oxford.

Lebeuf, A. M. D.
(1959) *Les Populations du Tchad*. Paris.

Leiris, M.
(1958) *La Possession et ses Aspects Théâtraux chez les Ethiopiens de Gondar*. Paris.

Legum, Colin
(1962) *Pan-Africanism: A Short Political Guide*. London.

Lewis, I. M.
(1955) *Peoples of the Horn of Africa*. London.
(1959) 'The names of God in Northern Somali', *Bulletin of the School of Oriental and African Studies*, vol. XXII, pp. 134–40.
(1960) 'The Somali conquest of the Horn of Africa', *Journal of African History*, vol. I, pp. 213–30.
(1961) *A Pastoral Democracy*. London.
(1962) *Marriage and the Family in Northern Somaliland*. East African Studies, No. 15. Kampala.
(1963(a)) 'Dualism in Somali notions of power', *Journal of the Royal Anthropological Institute*, vol. XCIII, pp. 109–16.

(1963(*b*)) 'Pan-Africanism and Pan-Somalism', *Journal of Modern African Studies*, vol. I, pp. 147–61.

(1965(*a*)) *The Modern History of Somaliland*. London.

(1965(*b*)) 'Problems in the Comparative Study of Unilineal Descent', in M. Banton (ed.), *The Relevance of Models for Social Anthropology*, London.

Little, K. L.

(1947) 'A Moslem "Missionary" in Mendeland', *Man*, vol. XLVI, pp. 111–13.

(1951) *The Mende of Sierra Leone*. London.

MacMichael, H. A.

(1922) *A History of the Arabs in the Sudan*. Cambridge.

Mathew, Gervase

(1963) 'The East African Coast until the coming of the Portuguese', in *History of East Africa*, ed. G. Mathew and R. Oliver, pp. 94–129.

Mathew, G. and Oliver R. (eds.)

(1963) *History of East Africa*. Oxford.

Mauny, R.

(1961) *Tableau Géographique de l'Ouest Africain au Moyen Age*. Dakar.

Middleton, J. H. M.

(1961) *Land Tenure in Zanzibar*. London.

Mitchell, J. C.

(1956) *The Yao Village*. Manchester.

Monteil, V.

(1962) 'Une Confrérie Musulmane: Les Mourides du Senegal', *Archives de Sociologie des Religions*, vol. XIV, pp. 77–102.

(1964) *L'Islam Noir*. Paris.

Moreau, R. L.

(1964) 'Les marabouts de Dori', *Archives de Sociologie des Religions*, vol. XVII, pp. 113–34.

Nadel, S. F.

(1942) *A Black Byzantium*. London.

(1954) *Nupe Religion*. London.

Pageard, R.

(1962) 'Contribution critique à la chronologie historique de l'Ouest Africain', *Journal de la Société des Africanistes*, vol. XXXII, pp. 91–177.

Pankhurst, Richard

(1961) *An Introduction to the Economic History of Ethiopia from Early Times to 1800*. London.

Post, K.

(1964) *The New States of West Africa*. London.

Prins, A. H. J.

(1961) *The Swahili-speaking Peoples of Zanzibar and the East African Coast*. London.

Proudfoot, L.

(1961) 'Towards Muslim solidarity in Freetown', *Africa*, vol. XXXI, pp. 147–57.

Quesnot, F.

(1962) 'Les Cadres maraboutiques de l'Islam sénégalais' in *Notes et Etudes sur l'Islam en Afrique noire*, Paris, pp. 127–95.

Raulin, H.

(1962) 'Un Aspect historique des rapports de l'animisme et de l'Islam au Niger', *Journal de la Société des Africanistes*, vol. XXXII, pp. 249–74.

Richard-Molard, J.

(1949) *L'Afrique Occidentale Française*. Paris.

Rouch, J.
    (1954) *Les Songhay.* Paris.
    (1960) *La Religion et la Magie Songhay.* Paris.
Sauvaget, J.
    (1950) 'Les Epitaphes royales de Gao', *Bull. IFAN*, vol. XII, pp. 418–40.
Smith, M. G.
    (1953) 'Secondary marriage in Northern Nigeria', *Africa*, vol. XXIII, pp. 298–323.
    (1955) *The Economy of Hausa Communities of Zaria.* London.
    (1959) 'The Hausa system of social status', *Africa*, vol. XXIX, pp. 239–52.
    (1960) *Government in Zazzau.* London.
Smith, H. F. C.
    (1961) 'A neglected theme of West African history: the Islamic revolutions of the 19th century', *Journal of the Historical Society of Nigeria*, vol. II, no. 1.
Stenning, D. J.
    (1959) *Savannah Nomads.* London.
Tanner, R. E. S.
    (1964) 'Cousin marriage in the Afro-Arab community of Mombasa, Kenya', *Africa*, vol. XXXIV, pp. 127–38.
Thompson, V. and Adloff, R.
    (1958) *French West Africa.* London.
Thore, Luc
    (1964) 'Marriage et divorce dans la banlieue de Dakar', *Cahiers d'Etudes Africaines*, vol. IV, pp. 479–552.
Touré, Cheikh
    (1957) *Li takune mu'minan. A fin que tu deviennes Croyant.* Dakar.
Trimingham, J. S.
    (1949) *Islam in the Sudan.* London.
    (1952) *Islam in Ethiopia.* London.
    (1959) *Islam in West Africa.* London.
    (1962) *A History of Islam in West Africa.* London.
    (1964) *Islam in East Africa.* Oxford.
Tubiana, M. J.
    (1964) *Survivances Préislamiques en Pays Zaghawa.* Paris.
Vire, M. M.
    (1959) 'Stêles funeraires musulmanes soudano-sahariennes', *Bull. IFAN*, vol. XXI, pp. 459–500
Widstrand, C. G.
    (1964) 'Female infibulation', *Studia Ethnographica Upsaliensia*, vol. xx, pp. 95–124.

REFERENCES SINCE 1967

Arens, W.
    (1975) 'The Waswahili: the social history of an ethnic group', *Africa*, vol. 45, pp. 426–37.
Beshir, M. O.
    (1974) *Revolution and Nationalism in the Sudan.* London.
Caplan, A. P.
    (1976) 'Boys' circumcision and girls' puberty rites among the Swahili of Mafia Island, Tanzania', *Africa*, vol. 46, pp. 21–33.
Cohen, A.
    (1968) *Custom and Politics in Africa.* London.

Curtin, P.
  (1971) 'Jihad in West Africa', *Journal of African History*, vol. XII, pp. 11–24.
Donald, L. H.
  (1974) 'Arabic literacy among the Yalunka of Sierra Leone', *Africa*, vol. 44, pp. 71–81.
Fisher, H. J.
  (1973) 'Conversion reconsidered: some historical aspects of religious conversion in Black Africa', *Africa*, vol. 43, pp. 27–40.
Goddard, A. D.
  (1973) 'Changing family structures among the rural Hausa', *Africa*, vol. 43, pp. 207–18.
Grindal, B. T.
  (1973) 'Islamic affiliations and urban adaptation: the Sisala migrant in Accra, Ghana', *Africa*, vol. 43, pp. 333–46.
Hiskett, M.
  (1973) *The Sword of Truth*. New York.
Horowitz, M. M.
  (1974) 'Barbers and bearers: ecology and ethnicity in an Islamic society', *Africa*, vol. 44, pp. 371–82.
Horton, R.
  (1975) 'On the rationality of conversion', *Africa*, vol. 45, pp. 219–35, 373–99.
Last, M.
  (1967) *The Sokoto Caliphate*. London.
Levtzion, N.
  (1968) *Muslims and Chiefs in West Africa*. Oxford.
Lewis, I. M.
  (1971) *Ecstatic Religion*. Harmondsworth, UK.
  (1979(a)) 'Kim-il-Sung in Somalia', in *The Politics of Office*, ed. P. Cohen and W. Shack. Oxford.
  (1979(b)) *The Modern History of Somalia*. London.
Martin, B. G.
  (1976) *Muslim Brotherhoods in Nineteenth Century Africa*. Cambridge.
O'Brien, D. B. C.
  (1971) *The Mourides of Senegal*. Oxford.
Paden, J. N.
  (1973) *Religion and Political Culture in Kano*. London.
Parkin, D.
  (1972) *Palms, Wine and Witnesses*. London.
Person, Y.
  (1968) *Samouri: Une Révolution Dyula*, I. Dakar.
Salamone, F. A.
  (1975) 'Becoming Hausa: ethnic identity change and its implications for the study of ethnic pluralism and stratification', *Africa*, vol. 45, pp. 410–24.
Sanneh, L. O.
  (1976) 'Slavery, Islam and the Jakhanke people of West Africa', *Africa*, vol. 46, pp. 80–97.
Shepherd, G. M.
  (1977) 'Two marriage forms in the Comoro Islands', *Africa*, vol. 47, pp. 344–59.
Swantz, M. L.
  (1970) *Ritual and Symbol in Transitional Zaramo Society*. Uppsala.

Trimingham, J. S.
   (1968) *The Influence of Islam upon Africa*. London.
Willis, J. R. (ed.)
   (1979) *Studies in West African Islamic History*. London.
Yusuf, A. B.
   (1975) 'Capital formation and management among the Muslim Hausa traders
   of Kano, Nigeria', *Africa*, vol. 45, pp. 167–82.

II. SPECIAL STUDIES

I. THE PHASES OF ISLAMIC EXPANSION AND ISLAMIC CULTURE ZONES IN AFRICA

J. S. TRIMINGHAM

I. THE SPREAD OF ISLAM

The spread of Islam in Africa is marked by four phases, which also represent methods and depths and correspond to types of contemporary Islam.

1. *The Winning of North Africa* (A.D. 638–1050)

The first stage is the conquest by the early Muslim Arabs of all the Mediterranean littoral from Egypt to Morocco; then there followed a period of pacification, quickly succeeded by a break-up of the short-lived political unity into many Muslim states. Islam slowly won over the Berbers, but their Arabization took place during the next stage, following a new break-in of Arab nomads.

2. *The Spread of Islam into the Sudan Belt* (1050–1750)

This period witnessed the slow and largely peaceful spread of Islam southwards across the Sahara and up the valley of the Nile into the Hamitic and Black Africa of the Sudan belt. Across the Red Sea and by way of East Africa sea-routes it spread into the plains of the Eastern Horn, where it gained the 'Afar and Somali. Settlements were formed along the East African coast, where a new cultural group—the Swahili—was formed, but Islam had no effect upon the Bantu and other peoples of the region.

This phase began with the upsurge of the Berber Murabitun (from 1056) and the dispersion throughout North Africa of Arab nomads of the Bani Hilal (from 1045). These events principally affected the desert and North Africa, for though the Murabits conquered the Negro state of Gana on the edge of the southern desert, they were soon expelled. The Arab peoples did not spread Islam, but their conquest of the Berbers of Mauritania, south of Morocco, led to their Arabization. The Berbers of central Sahara, the Tuareg, were neither conquered nor Arabized.

The spread of Islam across the Sahara into the northern Sudan came through the work of Berber traders and clerics in the west and an influx of Arab peoples (A.D. 1300–1500) in the east, where the Christianity of the Nilotic Sudan disappeared.

The feature of this period is the adoption of Islam as a class religion—the imperial cult in the Sudan states like Mali and Kanem and as the cult of the trading and clerical classes. Just as various religious strata existed side by side in the mosaic of Sudanese religion, so when Islam came on the scene there was no feeling that it was incompatible with an African religious outlook, and, strange though it may seem, Islam was incorporated into the Sudanese religious scheme. Religious life was characterized by accommodation or, more correctly, by a dualism or a parallelism of the old and the new—the African idea of the harmony of society maintained itself over against any idea of Islamic exclusiveness. Consequently, Islam's elements of challenge to traditional life were largely neutralized.

The next period witnessed the triumph of Islam throughout the Sudan belt in a form which claimed its exclusiveness, while the modern period has seen the emergence among new converts of a secular Islam different from traditional African Islam.

3. *The Era of Theocracies and of states where Islam is the state religion* (1750–1901)

The nineteenth century was characterized by the appearance of a new, intolerant and militant Islam. Clerics made their appearance (the first in Futa Jalon in 1725) who waged the *jihad* or holy war and formed a number of theocratic states as they are usually called, though they should really be called divine nomocracies, since they all claimed to be ruled by divine law. These states appeared throughout the Sudan belt from Guinea (Futa Jallon

1776) and Senegal (Futa Toro, 1776), through Masina (1818) and Sokoto (1802) to the Mahdia of the Nilotic Sudan (1881). These states degenerated, and most of them were conquered or came under the rule of a new type of despot, for example, al-Hajj 'Umar (1854–64) in western Sudan and 'Abdallah al-Ta'aishi in Nilotic Sudan (1885–98).

The great change introduced by the nineteenth-century reformers lay in the stress placed on the uniqueness and exclusiveness of Islam and its incompatibility with worship within the old cults. These reformers brought an intensity into the former unchallenging Islam, so Africanized as to be at the point of losing its identity, which drove Islam into the centre of life as a transforming factor, whereby the very equilibrium of society was changed. Although under their successors this exclusive reference waned, yet sufficient had been done to bring Islam forward as the supreme arbiter of life and dominant in spite of all the accommodation with non-Muslim practices which was in fact allowed in life.

The conquests of the reformers resulted in a great expansion of nominal allegiance to Islam,[1] but their greatest contribution to the implanting of Islam came from the way they broke up social and ethnic groups (prisoners, slave-villages, forcible removals) and destroyed organized cults, leaving Islam as the sole cement for new or reconstituted organizations. This process was accelerated during the next phase, when all these territories came under European occupation.

4. *The Colonial Period to the Present Day*

The latter part of the last period coincided with the occupation of Africa by European powers with all its accompaniments: penetration of new forces, economic, ideological, and religious (Christianity). This period witnessed the continued expansion of Islam at an accelerated pace and over regions which had

[1] Many groups in the north with different types of organization remained uninfluenced until the period of European occupation loosened bonds. These included the centralized Mossi states, which were never conquered, Bambara (village state structures), and primitive palaeonegritics of the southern Sudan belt. Even in the northern Sudan belt there are few exclusively Muslim zones.

previously been closed to Islamic propaganda. It was only during this period (especially between 1890 and 1930) that Islam spread from the East African coast among the Bantu of the interior.

Although the nineteenth-century era of militant Islam was that of its greatest expansion in area, the subsequent period of European rule, while it stopped forcible conversions, facilitated its expansion in other ways. Peaceful conditions after years of warfare and slave-raiding, combined with new facilities for communication, enabled traders and clerics to circulate everywhere and spread the ways of their religion. In addition, the Muslim conquests of the previous century, followed by the impact of Western civilization, weakened the religious–social structures of many animist societies. Add to these, the migration of villagers to towns, plantations, and mines, the pressure of new ways of life, the weakening of respect for elders, traditional customs and social sanctions, all these opened the way for the penetration of a religious culture like that of Islam, which could provide a new centre for communal life and help to maintain social stability.

In parts where Muslim states had been established (even though overthrown as in French territory) Islam's spread and the nature of its adoption followed the old fashion. But other parts have witnessed the secular diffusion of Islam and the creation of neo-Islamic communities where Islam's position is much like that of Christianity in Western countries. This is due to the fact that the diffusion of Western influences accompanied the diffusion of Islam.

These four historical stages correspond to four different degrees or types of Islam found in Africa:

(a) The Islam of the first phase of expansion among Hamites. Two culture zones (Egypt and the Maghrib) where Islam is integrated into every aspect of life.

(b) Traditional African Islam, where Islam is fitted into the indigenous system and embraces many grades of allegiance. Religious dualism and tolerance are characteristic; chiefs recognizing all the religious usages of their peoples.

(c) The basic Sudan pattern, where Islamic law is incorporated into the pattern of social life. Intolerance and at the same time parallelism.

(*d*) The secularized Islam of neo-Islamic communities, where Western penetration accompanied the adoption of Islam.

II. THE RESULTANT ISLAMIC CULTURE ZONES

Islam spread through the accidents of historical necessity. We do not find the same pattern exactly reproduced throughout the Islamic world, for the formation of a new Muslim community like the Swahili or, and this is the more general and normal pattern of change, the transformation of an existing community through its adoption of Islam, comes about through the interplay of the aggressive culture, as expressed by Muslims from particular culture areas, upon people who have been moulded in very different ways.

In the meeting of Islamic and African cultures two currents of attraction and repulsion are set up; their interaction, the play of the various elements of the two cultures upon each other, eventually leads to a synthesis. One current is moving towards differentiation and the other towards homogeneity. From this interaction derives the actual state of Muslim peoples until the impact of Western secular culture.

Regional diversity derives from both internal and external factors of differentiation: (i) geographical and ethnic factors and the pre-Islamic religio-social substratum, and (ii) external influences, the nature, and differences in the historical penetration of Islam. Thus, East African Islam shows the strong influence of the Hadramaut, while West African Islam's characteristics link it with the Maghrib.

These factors operate to develop a culture along regional lines. On the other hand, Islam has acted towards unifying African culture. It is a strong cultural influence, and once it has been adopted by an African community it becomes eventually dominant. Certain Islamic institutions are universally adopted, and these elements not merely create a bond of understanding between peoples but develop common attitudes and patterns of behaviour. A distinctive outlook on life is created and a new religio-social pattern is woven.

Although the regional differences are clear, the dynamic tension between Islam and African culture finds expression in a remarkable unity of African Islamic culture. In spite of the fact that Islam normally penetrated integrated communities (exceptions are artificially formed groups such as the Swahili communities and slave villages), thereby transforming them, the Islamic aspects of the resultant culture are much the same everywhere. This is due to the fact that Islam brings the same institutions which modified African life, and it was around the Islamic institutions that the retained or kindred African institutions coagulated. The culture areas may therefore be regarded as having a common Islamic heritage.

However, since the integration of African and Islamic cultures is not complete (for Islam was only able to preserve its uniqueness by parallelism), African Islam may often have to be understood and studied in a double aspect as the local African manifestation of world Islam, and as Islamic variants of African culture.

In discussing the spread and historical role of Islam in Africa, as well as differences in the form that Islamic institutions eventually took, we need to divide Africa into various zones or Islamic culture areas. Such zones have no absolute values, the agreements are more important than the variants, but they are a useful method of treatment. There are three main Islamic culture zones: Egyptian, Maghribi, and Negro, each differentiated by the degree to which it has absorbed and been moulded by Islam and to the underlying cultural differences. The distinctions between the Negro African zones are due more to differences in the African cultural basis than to Islam. The culture zones are:

Egyptian: Basic Near Eastern Islamic culture, with Egyptian Nilotic culture showing itself in the village culture of the *fallahin*.

Maghrib: North African Mediterranean culture, though with Berber regional basis.

In the intermediary Saharan–Sahilian desert area the Moors and Tuareg belong to the Maghribi cycle and the Teda to the Central Sudan cycle.

Western Sudan: Negro Islam.
Central Sudan: Negro Islam.
Eastern or Nilotic Sudan: Hamitic-Negro.
North-eastern Hamitic (Eritrea, Ethiopia, and Somalia).
     The Islam of the nomads of the Eastern Horn.
Coastal East African: Swahili Islam.

Egypt and the Maghrib. The first two cultural regions, Egypt and the Maghrib, are those into which Islam spread from an early date and became so deeply implanted as to influence all subsequent history and every aspect of life. The two regions are, however, clearly differentiated. This derives from the fact that their basic (pre-Islamic) cultures were quite different, and each followed distinctive trends of historical development. Egypt formed a world in itself, and, though brought out of cultural isolation and subject to profound cultural change through adherence to monotheistic religions, it has always displayed distinctive political and social characteristics. Yet Egypt was, viewed in its Islamic orientation, almost entirely undifferentiated, belonging wholly to Arab Islam. Regional differences, however, show themselves especially in the folk (*fallah*) culture.

The other North African regions, the Maghrib to use the Arabic term, formed another historical and cultural entity, although politically distinguished for disunity. Berbers gave this region a definite individuality. Today the majority (more than two-thirds) are Arabized, while the rest have preserved their language, especially in Morocco. Maghribi Islam is Berber Islam —the result of the Berbers' assimilation of Islamic culture, and this type of Islam is present on the borderland with Negro West Africa. In this essay no attempt will be made to trace the relations of Egypt and the Maghrib with the rest of Africa, but simply to distinguish the two regions.

Three cycles of Islamic civilization can be distinguished in

West Africa. The first, the Saharan–Sahilian, characterizes more especially the Moorish tribes. The Tuareg belong to this cycle, but not the Teda, who belong to that of the Central Sudan. The Islam of this cycle is characterized by the North African form of the saint cult, a feature which was not transmitted to Negro Islam except to a limited degree (e.g. the Muridiyya). Similarly with the *tariqa-ta'ifas*, the religious brotherhoods with their multi-function *zawiyas* inseparable from the saint cult in North Africa, are different in psychological attitudes towards leaders from those of Negroes. Another characteristic, deriving from the religious apathy of nomads and particularly warrior clans, is the formation of clerical (maraboutic) clans to perform religious functions in their stead. This type of Islam has influenced the Sahilian zone, including towns like Timbuktu, and Negro slaves.

Though Islam came to West Africa through North Africans and Moors, Negro peoples have given it their own distinctive stamp. While the Saharan–Sahilian cycle belongs to the sphere of North African Islamic culture, the Islam of the Sudan displays distinctive African aspects.

Three main cycles of Sudan Islamic culture may be distinguished: West, Central, and East or Nilotic. The differences between the Western and Central cycles are so little perceptible that it is possible to speak of one West African Islamic culture, whereas the Eastern Sudan culture is distinctly different. That there is a difference between the first two is the sort of thing we acquire by direct contact, which we claim to know by intuitive insight, but which it is difficult to formulate or work out as a distinctive pattern by means of which we may explain what we feel.

Western Sudan. Tokolor and Soninke, the first Sudanese converted to Islam, have left their mark upon it. In certain ways West Sudan clergy have had a deeper influence than those of the central cycle in spite of the excessive worship of the Law in the latter. The difference can be seen if their effect upon newly Islamized areas is contrasted; for instance, the effect of Tokolor and Mande clergy upon animists in western Guinea and the effect of Hausa upon animists in the northern territories of Ghana, Togo,

Benin, and Nigeria. The primary influence upon Tokolor and Soninke was from North Africa, which established a distinctive type of Islamic consciousness and forms of observance. The agents of diffusion today are mainly Tokolor, Soninke, and other Mande teachers and traders.

Characteristics distinguishing it from the parent culture and the central cycle include a pattern of family festivals (e.g. at the eighth-day ceremony—the simultaneous pronouncing of the name, slaughtering of the victim, shaving, and, in Guinea, pounding of grain) at which the stress is on the *white* rice (or other staple food) 'sacrifice', rather than upon the offering of a victim. Spirit practices follow a distinctive Mande pattern. They believe in the 'crossing of the river' after death, and the place of waiting of departed spirits is called *arafo*. The cycle has its distinctive Islamic legends (e.g. the Prophet and the pig). The primary state structure is that of the village.

The Central Sudan Cycle, east of the Niger, has been subject to Islamic radiation from the Nile Valley (both Egypt and the Nilotic Sudan) as well as the middle Maghrib. The transition zone is roughly between the occupational caste system of the western cycle and the class system characteristic of the Kanuri–Hausa cycle, with its wide categories of grades and titles in the state system. Social mobility saved the peoples of the central cycle from developing any rigid caste system. Kanembu and Kanuri were the first people to be converted and gave a distinctive stamp to Chadian Islam, though they have never been active missionaries, regarding Islam as the cult of the city and aristocracy, and as a specialized occupation cult. The Songhay of the middle Niger, though so different from the Kanuri, belong to this cycle rather than midway, primarily because of the strength of the Paleo-Negritic foundation and the type of organized possessive-spirit cult which persists in flourishing, though no longer the folk cult, in spite of the disapproval of established Islamic authority. While dowry in the western cycle is given by the husband to the wife, in the central it is brought by the wife to the marriage. The city state, with its elaborate hierarchy of functionaries, contrasts with the village state organization of the Mande peoples before the formation of theocratic states. The failure of the attempt to found a theocracy in Hausaland was due to the power of this aristocratic state structure, which captured the clerical reformers, the Islamic religious hierarchy being incorporated into it. In the west, on the contrary, the reformers did not carry on the previous organization in any true sense, but formed a new type of state more clearly based upon the precepts of Islam.

Other West African Culture Areas (Western Guinea, Southern Sudan belt, Voltaic, and South Guinean) were not influenced by Islam until the nineteenth century. Islam spread rapidly in western Guinea, its type of Islam being derived primarily from Futa Jalon. The Voltaic peoples have remained relatively uninfluenced. In the southern Sudan belt many chiefs (e.g. Middle belt of Nigeria) have accepted it, but it has made relatively little impression upon their peoples. In the South Guinean region it has made significant gains only among the Yoruba. In many of these areas the penetration of Islamic and Western influences coincided, and this has affected their type of Islam. The interaction of the old heritage, Islamic and Western secular attitudes to life, is leading to a more secular religious attitude and outlook upon life.

The Eastern or Nilotic Sudan Cycle. The foundation so far as Islam is concerned was Eastern Hamitic, both riverain Nubians and rainland cultivators (Hamitic Negro) and nomads (Beja). Its geographical position in the Nile valley has made it a zone of interaction between Hamitic, Negro, and Arab Africa. Because Arabic spread along with Islam the Nilotic Sudan is, like the Maghrib, culturally part of the Near East as well as Africa, while the other regions of the Sudan belt (Mauritania being regarded as culturally belonging to the Maghrib) are not. This great cultural distinction is due to Arabic rather than to Islam. The penetration of Islam, late when compared with Egypt just to the north, came through the dispersion of nomadic Arab tribes in the early fourteenth century. The Arabs did not seek here, any more than in the early centuries of Islam, to consciously spread their religion, though, of course, surface Islamization went along with Arabization. Arabic became the lingua franca and then substituted itself for the languages of the sedentary cultivators (though not the northernmost Nubians and Beja nomads), but Islam claimed the souls of the people through the work of Arabized Nubians who formed an indigenous clerical class.

The conversion of the Nubians in great numbers took place especially between 1300 and 1320. Southwards Islamization went along with Arabization. The widespreading of Arab nomads from Upper Egypt was mainly responsible for the Arabization of Hamitic-speaking peoples (e.g. Sha'iqiyya and Ja'liyyin), but the whole-hearted adoption of Islam came after an indigenous clerical class grew up who 'lit the fire of 'Abd al-Qadir' in one riverain community after another, and in particular among Nubians such as the Mahas, who migrated southwards in large numbers and Arabized in the sixteenth century. These set the pattern of Nilotic Sudan Islam.

The most important aspect of this Islam was the harmonious blending of *fiqh* and *tasawwuf*, i.e. the tempering of legalism by mysticism. We do not find that rigidity (nor parallelism) which is characteristic of Muslim leaders in Northern Nigeria. The clerics were at one and the same time *fuqaha* and *fuqara*. The prevalent law school (*madhhab*) was that of Malik, though the Egyptian and Hijazi links—the principal external contacts—led to some teachers (e.g. Dushain of Arbaji) adopting the Shafi'i code. Popular religion was based on Sufism in the form mediated by personal and family *tariqa-ta'ifas* and inseparable from the cult of saints. We may note that the saint cult is characteristic of what, for want of a better term, I call Arabized Hamites, as in the Maghrib, Mauritania, and the Eastern Sudan, but not of the Negro Muslim world.[1]

---

[1] The weakness of the cult of saints and of belief in their *karamat* in Negro Africa is perhaps due to the fact that belief in miracles is linked with an historical and static view of the universe and does not accord with the Negro view of a dynamic universe. The cult of ancestors is not bound up with their graves. Similarly with the religious orders. Their reduced role in Negro Africa, where they are more in the nature of an Islamic label, seems to be connected with the fact that the saint cult did not accompany their diffusion, whereas in the Nilotic Sudan it was integral.

The North-eastern Ethiopic Zone, the Islam of the plains people of the Eastern Horn. This is a region which embraces the greatest contrasts, not only geographically but in human diversity, cultural levels, languages, and religions. The destinies of this region have been tied indissolubly with the Red Sea much more than with the Nile Valley, and it is from Arabia that it received the imprint of Semitic languages and culture and later of Islam.

The region, from the point of view of Islamic influence, divides into three zones. (*a*) The plains where the nomadic 'Afar (Danakil) and Somali live. These are wholly Muslim and historically connected with migratory and commercial currents across the Red Sea. (*b*) The northern and central plateau region, where the Christian Ethiopian state, with deep-rooted non-African traditions, which throughout history has arrested the expansion of Muslim peoples or states and maintained its religious integrity, provides the region's only unity. The northern Oromo of the plateau region (Yejju, Raya, and Wallo) are Muslim. (*c*) South-western Ethiopia, where Islam succeeded in super-imposing itself upon the animism of a group of Sidama and Macha Oromo peoples.

In accordance with the varied types of peoples there are considerable variations in their apprehension of, and the forms taken by, their Islam, as, for example, between Jabarti and Oromo of the highlands, the Oromo-Sidama of Jimma, the Oromo of the south-east, the townspeople of Harar, and the nomadic 'Afar and Somali of the plains.

The Swahili Cycle. Islam penetrated into East Africa from the Red Sea and the Indian Ocean. It gained all the Hamitic nomads of the Red Sea coast and the Eastern Horn of the last-mentioned cycle as communities, but inland south of the Somali it did not begin to penetrate until the nineteenth century and has spread largely by individual conversions. Whereas in the Sudan belt Islam claimed whole peoples and made its deepest impact upon Africans, it hardly affected the Bantu and other peoples of East Africa. Immigrants from overseas formed what were virtually closed-class communities based on settlements. These insular and coastal settlements led not to the spread of Islam among the Bantu or nomads but to the formation of a new population, the Swahili, characterized by a distinct Islamic–Bantu language and sub-culture, who stretch from Lamu to Mozambique. The Swahili so formed are not a homogeneous people. They consist of Shirazi (the inhabitants of Zanzibar and Pemba islands and a series of remnant families along the coast), Afro-Arabs who distinguish themselves on racial grounds from Africans, descendants of slaves, and settled detribalized labourers from the interior. They are a collection of different social classes, a stratified society, a cultural group, following an Islamic way of life.

The dominant Islamic influence in moulding Swahili culture came from Hadramaut (e.g. Shafi'ite in *madhhab*), an influence not only obvious in ritual and law but also in the details of *rites de passage* and superstitious usages.

Not until the end of the nineteenth century did Islam spread inland. It spread into Tanganyika in some strength, especially among the Yao and coastal peoples. A point to be stressed is that although all aspects of Islam which were adopted were those of coastal Swahili Islam, the characteristic medieval attitude to religion has not been able to establish itself. Islam in East Africa, contrary to what prevails elsewhere, still bears many of the characteristics of a foreign religion. Muslims form separate communities, and while Islam has its place in local issues, it has no wide influence upon affairs. The indigenous element which distinguishes the Islam of Tanzania is the *jando* circumcision-initiation, essentially a mainland Islamic initiation rite. The saint-cult and *tariqas* in their characteristic form are limited to the islands and coastal region.

Islam's penetration into central and south Africa is so slight that it may be ignored in this sketch. The proportion of Muslims in former French Equatorial Africa (except modern Chad and northern Cameroon which belong to the Sudan belt) and in Zaïre is insignificant; while in South Africa it is confined to special groups like the coloured people of Malay origin.

II. THE PENETRATION OF ISLAM
IN THE EASTERN SUDAN

YUSUF FADL HASAN

The term Eastern Sudan is used in this paper in the restricted sense of the Nile Valley and the region east of it, from the frontier with Egypt at Aswan to Sennar in the South. This area includes the three Christian Kingdoms of 'Alwa, whose capital was Soba on the Blue Nile, al-Muqarra, and al-Maris or Nobadia, which were united, possibly due to Muslim pressure, in the middle of the seventh century A.D. Henceforth this area was known as Nubia, with its capital at Dongola. Between these kingdoms and the Red Sea lies the Beja country, which extends from Aswan to Massawa and which was composed of a number of principalities. The original inhabitants of the Eastern Sudan, for the most part of Hamitic origin, akin to the pre-dynastic Egyptians, were diluted by successive waves of negroid people coming from the south. The indigenous inhabitants of the Gezira were probably more negroid than the Nubians farther to the north, while the Beja were of purer Hamitic stock than the rest. The northern part of the Eastern Sudan is mainly desert, while the southern part is rich grassland: the Nile Valley, with its rather limited amount of cultivable land, formed the heart of the country and the centre of its civilization. This civilization was basically Egyptian, with faint traces of Hellenic and Byzantine influences. The cultural heritage of the riverains, perhaps as far south as Soba, shows that they were not a backward people.

The introduction of Christianity in the second half of the sixth century marks the beginning of a new era in the history of the Sudan. Before this, the 'Sudanese' had worshipped Egyptian gods, stones, stars, animals, and trees. The Christian faith was adopted by the ruling class and nobility, who in the main adhered to the monophysite doctrine, and to a lesser extent by the rest of the population, who remained 'mainly animistic'. Some Beja on the Egyptian border and others living in the Red Sea ports also embraced Christianity, but it never took root to the same extent as it had done in the Nile Valley. There, it was adopted to such an extent that it became the state religion, and a symbol of Nubian 'nationality'. The new faith was closely identified with local ruling institutions, especially that of the kingly office. The monarch remained a focal point in religious and political matters, and the survival of the whole political fabric depended on him. Like the rest of his subjects, the king looked to the Patriarch of Alexandria for religious guidance and for a supply of bishops. As long as this bond was maintained, the Christian faith in Nubia was in no danger.

The appearance of Islam was an event of far-reaching consequence in Arab history. It gave the Arabs a bond which became the basis of their unity and achievements. Its emergence coincided with the recurrent over-population of Arabia which had repeatedly forced the Arabs across its borders. This time, under the aegis of Islam, Arab expansion was greater than ever before. Soon they overran Egypt as far as Aswan, which they used as a frontier town to ward off the raids of the Nubians and the Beja, who since the dawn of history had been accustomed to ravage Upper Egypt. The Nubians were particularly grieved by the disaster that had befallen their co-religionists—the Copts—in Egypt, and thus harassed the Egyptian border. It was this danger that prompted 'Amr b.al-'As, the Arab governor of Egypt, to order attacks to be made on Nubia. It is clear that this did not stem from a deliberate policy of spreading Islam farther south. Indeed, there is hardly any evidence to prove that the Muslim governors of Egypt, with the exception of a single incident in the Fatimid period, ever showed any missionary zeal towards the eastern Sudan. The spread of Islam was due mainly to the peaceful contacts of merchants and the penetration of Arabs who settled and mixed with Sudanese people.

Muslims were able to enter the Sudan by three major routes. The first was across the Red Sea, either via Abyssinia or directly to Sudanese ports such as Badi, Aydhab and Suakin. Although the Red Sea was generally difficult to navigate, it was at no time a formidable obstacle to movements. However, the number of those who migrated by this route could not have been as great as those who entered from Egypt. It was mainly by this latter route that the process of Arabization and Islamization of the eastern Sudan was accomplished. Immigrants avoided the Nile Valley, fearing the Nubians who forbade unauthorized entry, and the majority of Arabs infiltrated through the eastern desert, unnoticed by the Nubian authorities. The last, and probably the least important route was from North-West Africa, whose effect falls outside the scope of this paper. This route was, however, frequented by a number of men of religion who had great influence in the propagation of Islam after the sixteenth century.

The reports we possess of the first Muslim–Nubian clashes are somewhat confused, but it is evident that there were two main invasions: the first in 641 and the second in 651–2. The skilful Nubian archers bravely resisted the Muslim conquerors, and the Muslims were soon to discover that they were fighting against an extremely dangerous and disagreeable enemy. The Nubians were henceforth called the 'eye-smiters' or *rumat al-hadaq*. Muslims suggested to 'Amr b.al-'As that he make peace with those people 'whose booty is meagre and whose spite is great'. 'Amr refused and continued his attacks. In 651–2 the Muslims, led by 'Abdallah b.Sa'd b.Abi Sarh, penetrated as far as Dongola and destroyed its cathedral. As usual, the Nubians resisted gallantly, but were probably overcome by catapults and tried to seek peace. The Muslims, failing to defeat the Nubians decisively, accepted their offers. There was no victor or vanquished, and this fact is clearly demonstrated by the terms of the treaty that the Muslims granted to the Nubians. The treaty attempted to put an end to Nubian attacks and to regulate matters of common interest.

It is a unique treaty in the annals of Islam. In dealing with international relations Muslim jurists normally divide the world into two camps: *dar al-Islam* or the abode of Islam, which would ultimately dominate the second camp, *dar al-harb* or the abode of war. But Nubia had the unique position of *dar al-mu-'ahada* or *aman*, that is the abode of pact or guarantee. The treaty was a non-aggression pact in which neither side would defend the other against a third party. It conferred on the subjects of each side the right to travel and trade unhindered in the other's domains, but not to take up permanent residence. It is doubtful, however, whether the Nubians could have for long prevented the Muslims from settling in their lands. Muslim merchants soon penetrated Nubia and laid the foundations for the future supremacy of Islam. Judging by what happened later, it is reasonable to assume that they might have acted as missionaries among pagans and Christians alike at this early stage. The treaty also stipulated that the lives of Muslims and their allies were to be safeguarded and that runaway slaves were to be returned to their Muslim owners.

The most important part of the treaty is the transaction commonly known as the *Baqt*, which deals with the delivery of 360 (in practice, 400) slaves to the Muslims annually. This is not a tribute in the ordinary sense of the word, but an exchange of mutual advantages. The Muslims—though this was not specified in the text of the treaty—handed over provisions and textiles whose value was actually greater than that of the slaves they received. The practice arose from the fact that when the Nubians delivered the *Baqt* they included forty extra slaves as a present to 'Amr b.al-'As, who rejected them and told the superintendent of the *Baqt* to give their value in provisions to the Nubians. They also received cereals, textiles, and horses from 'Abdallah b.Sa'd b.Abi Sarh, to whom the Nubian king complained of a dearth of food. However, what began as a courtesy developed into an established practice.

The treaty shows that the Muslims had no intention of occupying Nubia, but were genuinely concerned in putting an end to Nubian raids. It is more likely that the Muslims wanted to keep it as a sphere of influence to give themselves greater opportunities for trade. However, the treaty remained the cornerstone of Muslim–Nubian relations and was kept in force with little change for six centuries. The first important amendment was during the caliphate of Al-Mu'tasim (833–42), when the Nubians complained of their inability to pay the annual tribute; henceforth it was delivered once every three years. At almost the same time the Nubian king protested to al-Ma'mun against Arabs who bought land from his subjects south of Aswan and north of Bajrash, which was guarded by a Nubian governor, the 'Lord of the Mountain.' The affair was decided in favour of the Muslims, and their ownership was established, but it is not clear whether they remained as absentee landlords or not. However, when Ibn Sulaym al-Aswani (*c.* 969) visited that region the Muslims were behaving as owners, and some of them did not speak Arabic.

Muslim contacts with the western coast of the Red Sea were established in the life-time of the Prophet, when Muslim refugees were offered protection by the Abyssinians. The caliph Abu Bakr (A.D. 632–4) is alleged to have banished a group of Arabs to the region of Aydhab in the Beja country, while the Umayyads and early Abbasids deported a number of Muslims, including poets, to the Archipelago of Dahlak opposite Massawa. Dahlak itself was occupied by Muslims in the year 702, putting an end to the Abyssinian pirates who endangered the safety of the Muslim ships. Meanwhile Muslim merchants were peacefully penetrating on the western coast and were developing trading centres. As early as the year 640, a Muslim migrated to Badi, one of the Sudanese ports.

On his way back from the Dongola campaign, 'Abdallah b.Sa'd encountered a Beja gathering, with whom, however, he neglected to conclude a treaty. Ibn Hawqal (*c.* 975) stated that 'Abdallah b.Sa'd subdued the Beja in the neighbourhood of Aswan, who then became Muslims in name. Meanwhile the Beja continued to harass Upper Egypt unhindered until 'Ubaydallah b.al-Habhab, the superintendent of Egyptian finance, defeated them and forced them to conclude a treaty. The Beja agreed to pay tribute of three hundred camels, to enter Egypt as travellers, and not to kill a Muslim or a *dhimmi* (a man of tolerated religion). This settlement however, did not put an end to the Beja attacks on Upper Egypt, and at the beginning of the ninth century the situation was made worse when they killed a group of Muslims on their way to Mecca. In reprisal the inhabitants of Qift killed some Beja who had come to trade. Relatives of the latter followed up by attacking Qift and capturing many Muslims. Hakam al-Nabighi of Qays

'Aylan volunteered, with a group of his people, to rescue the captives. After raiding in the Beja country for three years he was able to free them. Despite these efforts, the Beja continued their ravages in Upper Egypt, and in 831 'Abdallah b.al-Jahm was forced to fight them again. After defeating them in a number of engagements he concluded a treaty with their chief, Kannun b. 'Abd al-'Aziz. This treaty, though drawn up in the same spirit as previous agreements with the Nubians and Beja, shows a marked increase in Muslim influence in this region. This is clearly reflected in the terms of the settlement, which will be discussed at some length.

The Beja country from Aswan to the border between Badi and Massawa became the property of the Caliph, to be ruled by Kannun in his name. The treaty confirmed the payment of three hundred dinars or a hundred camels. Muslims were allowed to enter the Beja country as travellers, traders, or residents. The Beja agreed not to hurt Muslims or their allies, not to mention Islam disrespectfully, and not to destroy the mosques which the Muslims had built at Sinja (probably modern Sinkat) and Hajar. They were to allow a representative of the Caliph to collect alms from local Muslims. In return for these privileges, the Beja were allowed to enter Egypt unarmed as travellers or traders.

It is clear that the Muslims had before this penetrated into the Beja country in numbers large enough to warrant the construction of mosques and the appointment of a special official to collect alms. This conclusion is substantiated by the fact that two Arabs translated the treaty into Bujawi languages and that the Beja chief himself had an Arabic name.

These treaties therefore opened Eastern Sudan to the influence of Islam along this frontier from Massawa to Aswan. Small numbers of Arabs were able to infiltrate unnoticed, but as long as there was contentment in Egypt this infiltration was not enough to accelerate the spread of Islam farther south.

During the Patriarchal, Umayyad, and early Abbasid Caliphates the Arabs formed a privileged class of rulers and warriors. They received generous pay, and those who owned land did not pay the full tax. However, with the emergence of the Abbasid

Empire, which was launched by the discontented Arabs and *Mawali*, the situation began to change. Only warriors in active service received pensions, and these were gradually replaced by Turkish slaves or Mamluks. In 833 the Caliph Al-Muʿtasim struck the names of Arabs off the register of pensions and recruited large numbers of Mamluks, who in time became the dominant fighting class of the Muslim world.

The impact of this change was tremendous. A bitter struggle ensued, and an atmosphere of distrust embittered relations between the Arab nomads and the rulers of Egypt, who after a time became recruited predominantly from those of Turkish origin.

Failing to assert their pension-rights, some of the Arabs became farmers, others began to drift away. For the majority of nomads Egypt, with its limited cultivable land and scanty rainfall, was not ideal. Undoubtedly it was Al-Muʿtasim's policy of Turkification which induced the Arabs to migrate to the Eastern Sudan. The progress of this migration was closely connected with the degree of Turkification of both army and rulers in Egypt, which reached its climax during the Ayyubid and Mamluk régimes.

However, the growing Arab resentment of the first half of the ninth century coincided with the opening of gold-mines in the region between Qus, Abu Hamad, and the Red Sea, to which area many Muslims migrated. The Beja, resenting Arab interference, tried to stop them mining. In 855 Al-Qummi, after defeating the Beja chief, ʿAli Baba, confirmed the previous agreement and asserted Arab rights to work the mines. This Muslim influx led to closer contacts with the Beja. Male members of Arab peoples who married into the ruling Beja families benefited from the matrilineal succession—which was prevalent all over the Eastern Sudan—and their children became the chiefs of those Beja peoples. This process was repeated over a long period of time, and thus Muslims gained prominence. A group from Rabiʿa established the Kanz dynasty in the neighbourhood of Aswan. By means of the above-mentioned system of succession they extended their influence over the Nubians of al-Maris and the Beja in the region of Wadi al-ʿAllaqi, the famous mining centre.

Muslim penetration was stimulated further by the rise of the port of Aydhab, which by the twelfth century had attained importance as a great trading centre. Large caravans crossed the eastern desert between Aydhab and Qus, transporting merchandise and carrying provisions to the miners. It was not long before Suakin joined Aydhab as a trading port from which Muslims penetrated into the interior. Arabs used their camels in this traffic. Also for more than two hundred years, from 1058 to 1261, pilgrims from Egypt and North-West Africa on their way to Mecca used the same route. This intensive traffic exposed the Beja tribes to further Muslim influence.

After a time the mines fell into disuse, as they became no longer profitable to exploit, the pilgrims reverted to the Sinai route after the crusades, and trade caravans became less frequent. This general economic decline left many Arabs without work, and they therefore drifted towards the kingdom of 'Alwa.

Up to the time of Salah al-Din al-Ayyubi (1172) peaceful relations were maintained between Nubia and Egypt without difficulty. Muslim merchants were at home in the Eastern Sudan. Slaves were bought and sent to Egypt, where they became one of the chief supports of the Tulunid, Ikhshidid, and Fatimid régimes. They were brought in large numbers, male and female, and according to one source there were 50,000 Sudanese slaves at the time of the Fatimid Caliph, al-Mustansir (1035–94). Many of them had adopted Islam, and some of these may have found their way back to the Eastern Sudan after the fall of the Fatimid Empire. Ibn Sulaym al-Aswani, a Fatimid *da'i* or propagandist already mentioned above, invited the Nubian King, George, to pay the *Baqt* and embrace Islam. He records a discussion with a Sudanese about the latter's religion, in which Ibn Sulaym tried to influence him. This is perhaps the only recorded incident of straightforward missionary activity in the Eastern Sudan. He also stated that there were many Muslim merchants at 'Alwa and that they had a religious centre. It would appear that the two religions had learned to exist side by side.

In 1172 Turan Shah, Salah al-Din's brother, penetrated as far as Ibrim, where he stationed a Kurdish garrison. One of the reasons for this expedition was to use Nubia as a retreating ground in case the Ayyubids failed in their attempts to control Egypt. Nubia was soon found to be very poor and the Nubians themselves drove out the garrison.

The rise of the Turkish Mamluk régime in Egypt in the middle of the thirteenth century constituted a turning-point in Egyptian–Sudanese relations. The repeated revolts of the Arab peoples in Upper Egypt endangered the flow of trade, the backbone of the Mamluk economy, from Aydhab. The ruthless suppression of the revolts by Sultan Baybars (1260–77) angered these Arabs, many of whom began to drift southwards. Trade was also threatened by the Muslim rulers of Dahlak and Suakin, who from time to time appropriated the wealth of deceased merchants. The threats of Baybars were enough to frighten the Dahlak chief, but Suakin had to be put under Egyptian administration as Aydhab before it. The extension of Mamluk authority to the coast of the eastern Sudan meant that the Christian Kingdoms were almost cut off from the outside world. King Dawud of Nubia raided Upper Egypt, sacked Aydhab, and captured many Muslims in 1272.

Baybars was preparing an expedition against Dawud, when a Nubian prince, Shakanda, came to him to complain of his uncle who had usurped the throne from him. The Mamluk troops accompanied the Nubian prince, together with many Arab warriors from Upper Egypt, and marched against Nubia in 1275. Throughout their long journey the invaders were met with resistance. King Dawud, who engaged them near Dongola, was defeated and fled to the south. Some of his relatives were captured and taken to Egypt. Shakanda was installed as King of Nubia and representative of the Mamluk Sultan. He agreed to deliver half the revenue of the country and leave northern Nubia as a private property of the Sultan. Nubia had been for the first time conquered by force. Its inhabitants were offered the alternative of adopting Islam or paying tribute. They accepted the second alternative and agreed to pay a poll-tax of two dinars for each adult per annum. The puppet king was left in peace after he took a public oath to honour the treaty he signed with the Muslims.

A dispute among the members of the dynasty over the succession gave the Mamluks a chance to interfere in support of one party against another. After the murder of Shakanda in 1277 the issue was at last settled in favour of Shamamun, who soon, however, refused to pay the tribute. Sultan al-Mansur Qala'un sent a large expedition in 1287 in which many Arabs from Upper Egypt participated. It seems that the Mamluks wanted to get rid of these undesirable Arab nomads, who were a source of sedition, and so they encouraged them to join the expeditions. After his defeat Shamamun fled to the south and his nephew was appointed in his place. The new king agreed to obey his overlord, the Mamluk Sultan, and to pay the tribute. Sa'd al-Din, a nephew of King Dawud, was sent from Cairo to advise the Mamluk garrison in Dongola. However, no sooner had the Mamluk army returned than Shamamun reappeared and regained his throne. A large expedition was sent against him in 1289, and the same story of defeat, disappearance, and recapture of the throne was repeated once more. In 1296 Shamamun pledged to obey the Sultan, and was thus confirmed in office; but he did not honour his word. Another Nubian prince was sent from Cairo to take his place.

The effects of these repeated military Mamluk expeditions were of great significance. First, they weakened Nubia tremendously and strained its resources. Secondly, they were accompanied by large numbers of Arabs, some of whom remained in Nubia. Thirdly, they returned with large numbers of captives, including Nubian princes who had claims to the throne. After staying in Egypt for some time they embraced Islam. One of these was 'Abdallah Barshambu who accompanied an expedition in 1316 in order to become a king. When the Nubian King, Karanbas, heard that a Muslim was to take his place he suggested his nephew, Kanz al-Dawla of the Kanz dynasty, which had recently intermarried with the Nubian royal family. Sultan al-Nasir objected, however, and 'Abdallah Barshambu was crowned in 1317, but did not remain for long on the throne and was succeeded by a member of the Kanz dynasty. Henceforth Christian Nubia was ruled by Muslim Kings, who depended on Arab support and did not discourage the movements of Arabs towards Nubia.

The Islamization of the kingly office was probably the hardest blow that the Christian faith had suffered until then. It had for some time been cut off from any external stimulus or spiritual guidance, and thus it became intellectually moribund. The king was the only person capable of offering resistance to external influence and inspiring his subjects. But this institution, split by internal dissention and weakened by external attacks, was easily captured by the Muslims in the end through the matrilineal system of succession. This marked the end of the kingdom of Christian Nubia. The influence of the Christian faith remained active for some time, but then it was unable to withstand the impact of vigorous Islam. There is no record of any compulsory or mass conversion.

During the second half of the fourteenth century the unhappy relations between the Mamluk authorities and Arab peoples in Upper Egypt deteriorated further. The latter were subjected to heavy fiscal levies and were forced to follow the path of the previous emigrants. They found the Beja country already occupied by Arabs, who had succeeded, after marrying with the Beja, in spreading Islam. The new arrivals went farther into the interior. They wandered freely in the island of Meroe, the Gezira, and some even crossed the Nile in search of virgin pastures in Kordofan. The majority of these remained as nomads with their tribal system intact; and others, in smaller groups, settled with the riverain population and repeated the slow process of intermarriage and Islamization.

The end of the kingdom of 'Alwa was also inevitable. It was in no position to offer effective resistance to the marauding Arab nomads. The Christian faith had already declined for the same reasons as in Nubia. The kingdom of 'Alwa was followed in the early sixteenth century by an Islamized dynasty, the Fung kingdom of Sennar. This event marked the beginning of the supremacy of Islam over all the region under discussion.

The majority of the Muslims who entered the Sudan were nomads who were not well versed in the teachings of Islam. There were probably very few men of religion among them. It is not surprising to learn that when Ghulam Allah b. 'Ayd, the

Yemenite, migrated to the Dongola region in the latter part of the fourteenth century A.D. he found the Muslims in a state of ignorance due to lack of teachers. Wad Dayf Allah stated in his *Tabaqat* that when the Fung assumed power there were neither centres of learning nor schools for teaching the Quran. But the Fung Kings encouraged and welcomed the migration of men of religion who instructed both Muslims and pagans. After that time these men came in larger numbers from the Hijaz, Egypt, and North-West Africa and were successful in preaching Islam on a large scale. The process of Islamization was accompanied by a process of Arabization which left its mark on a large part of the country; for Arabic was not only the language of Islam but also of trade.

Thus, with the adoption of Islam in 'Alwa, the history of Christianity in the Eastern Sudan comes to an end, and a new chapter in 'Sudanese' history is opened: one to which the conclusion has not yet been written.

SELECTED BIBLIOGRAPHY

Al-Maqrizi
    (1922) *Al-Mawa'iz wa'l-i'tibar fi dhikr al-khitat wa'l-athar*, Cairo.
    (1961) *Al-Bayan wa'l i'rab 'amma bi-ard Misr min al-'arab*, Cairo.
Ibn Hawqal
    (1938) *Surat al-Ard*, Leiden.
Wad Dayf Allah
    (1930) *Tabaqat al-awliya wa'l-salihin fi'l-Sudan*, Cairo.
Mustafa M. Mus'ad
    (1960) *Al-Islam wa'l-Nuba fi'l-'usur al-wusta*, Cairo.
Trimingham, J. S.
    (1949) *Islam in the Sudan*, Oxford.

III. RELIGION AND STATE IN THE
SONGHAY EMPIRE, 1464–1591

J. O. HUNWICK

'Depuis le XIe siècle (l'Islam) a tenté de se répandre au Songhay avec une constance et une persévérance remarquables qui n'a d'ailleurs de comparable que la constance et la persévérance de ceux qui s'y sont opposés' (J. Rouch, *Religion.* p. 13).

I. INTRODUCTION

The Songhay people inhabit the banks of the River Niger and the bush country adjacent to them from the area of Jenne, round the northward sweep of the Niger into the southern extremity of the Sahara and downstream to near the borders of modern Nigeria. To the north they are bounded by the inhospitable country of the Sahara Desert, inhabited in the main by restless Tuareg nomads, and to the south by the almost equally inhospitable hilly country occupied by the Mossi people.

Our knowledge of Songhay history up to the beginning of Muslim penetration in the early eleventh century is sketchy. In prehistoric times the area was probably peopled by two main groups, 'the masters of the soil' and 'the masters of the water'. At some unknown date the Sorko fisherfolk entered the area from the south-east, travelling up the Niger, having come from perhaps as far away as Lake Chad via the Benue river. The Sorko settled in the region of the Lebbezenga rapids and supplanted the original 'masters of the water'. At roughly the same period, it is thought, the Gow hunters, who are probably related to the Sorko, moved in to occupy the bush land not cultivated by the 'masters of the soil'. The chief town of this Songhay nucleus was Koukya—probably situated on the island of Bentia in the Niger, about 100 kilometres south of present Gao and also, after its population had expanded, occupying an area on the left bank of the Niger.

According to Delafosse, it was around the seventh century A.D. that an organized kingdom began to take shape, centred on Koukya. The ruling house was the Za or Dia dynasty founded by Dia Aliaman, to whom Islamic tradition would ascribe a Yemenite origin. Delafosse is of the opinion that the Dia were Lemta Berbers from Libya who, at least on arrival at Gao, were Christians. As a result of the establishment of the Dia dynasty the Sorko fisherfolk were pushed out of the area and went farther upstream until their progress was finally halted by the Bozo fishers in the lacustrine region near Mopti.

The town of Gao, which was later to become the seat of the Songhay rulers, evidently existed as early as the ninth century A.D. Ibn Khaldun refers to it as the birthplace of the Kharijite Abu Yazid Makhlad b. Kaidad in A.D. 893 (*Ibn Khaldun*, iii, p. 201). Gao (*Kawkaw*) was evidently a trading centre at this time in which there were numbers of Muslim Arab and Berber merchants. It was not until after A.D. 1010, when the fifteenth Dia, Kossoi, was converted to Islam by Muslim traders, that the royal capital was transferred from Koukya to Gao. Al-Bakri, the Andalusian geographer, writing around A.D. 1068, tells us that when a new ruler was installed at Gao (Kawkaw) he was given a sword, a shield, and a copy of the Quran said to have been sent from the Caliph at Baghdad as insignia of office (Al-Bakri, p. 342). He adds that the king was called Kanda and professed Islam, never giving supreme power to other than a Muslim (p. 343). Court ceremonial was clearly pagan. When the ruler ate, a drum was beaten and women danced, shaking their heads. All work ceased during the sovereign's meal time, and when he had finished, the remains of the food were thrown into the Niger with loud cries and work was allowed to start again. This pattern of Islam as the official royal religion with the mass of the populace non-Muslim and with a largely traditional court ceremonial remained the general fashion up to the end of the period examined here and is an indication of the very delicate balance which always existed between Islam and the indigenous Songhay religious structure.

By the middle of the fourteenth century Ibn Battuta was able to describe Gao as 'one of the finest, largest and best provided towns of the Sudan'. He stayed there for nearly a month and met a number of the North African Muslims who were resident there, including Muhammad al-Filali, whom he describes as the 'imam of the mosque of the whites' (*Ibn Battuta*, iv, pp. 435 *et seq.*). This would seem to imply that there was also another mosque, used by the indigenous Songhay inhabitants. Islam was still at this time very much a foreign religion whose chief adherents were the Arab and Berber settlers or itinerant traders; in addition, it had become the official religion of the Court—at least in theory—and was gaining some ground among the local population. This again was to remain a general pattern for some centuries to come.

For a period in the late thirteenth and early fourteenth centuries Songhay appears to have been part of the domain of the emperor of Mali. The *Ta'rikh al-Sudan* states that a certain 'Ali Golom, son of the twelfth Dia, Assibai, and a former captain of the Mali army, freed Songhay from the Mali yoke and ruled Songhay under a new dynastic title of Shi or Sunni, but no date is given for this. The same work also states that Songhay passed under Mali control while Mansa Musa the Mali ruler was away on pilgrimage (1321–24) and that he visited Gao and Timbuktu on his return. However, a seventeenth-century fragment of a work which appears to be a résumé of the *Ta'rikh al-fattash* states that Mansa Musa went on pilgrimage in the reign of the Shi Makara, who was apparently the fourth Shi after 'Ali Golom. This would suggest that 'Ali Golom came to power some time in the second half of the thirteenth century. It may well be that Mali's hold over Songhay was ephemeral and that dominion was re-established a number of times, including once under Mansa Musa. The descendants of Shi 'Ali Golom all used the same title, but form part of the Dia patrilineage and are not to be considered a new dynasty. The eighteenth Shi was 'the oppressor, the libertine, the aggressor and tyrant' (*T/Sudan*, p. 64). 'Ali-Ber ('Ali the Great) known to history as Sunni 'Ali (reg. A.D. 1464–92.)

Rouch (*Contribution*, p. 185), basing himself on Dubois' paraphrase of Al-Maghili (*Tombouctou*, p. 122), speaks of 'l'évolution religieuse de Sonni 'Ali', and concludes that Sunni 'Ali began his reign as a Muslim and then reverted to idol worship and magic later on. This sounds like a plausible hypothesis on the surface, but it is unfortunately based on an inaccurate translation of Al-Maghili's Arabic. The key passage is translated by Dubois as follows: '*Les premiers temps*, il jeûna pendant le mois de Ramadan et fit des sacrifices et d'autres offrandes dans les mosquées. *Puis il revint* aux idols et aux devins. . . .' The correct translation should simply be: 'He fasted Ramadan and gave abundant alms of slaughtered beasts and other things in the mosques and like places. *In spite of that*, he used to worship idols and believe the words of the soothsayers and magicians. . . .'

When dealing with his successor, Askia Al-Hajj Muhammad Ture, Rouch sees the evolution the other way round and claims that Askia Muhammad began by resting his authority on the magic powers inherited from the Sunnis and that after the sons of Sunni 'Ali had removed the *Korte* (the seven drums which were the symbols of magic power) the Askia began to seek other bases for his authority and to lean on Islam for support (*Contribution*, p. 194). I believe both of Rouch's assumptions to be incorrect and that the truth of the matter may be almost the opposite of what he has suggested.

II. THE PROBLEM OF SUNNI 'ALI

The Muslim chroniclers all unanimously denounce Sunni 'Ali as a ruthless and bloodthirsty tyrant, given to fits of uncontrollable rage, who persecuted the Muslims, particularly the learned men, and wrought untold havoc in the Songhay lands. The *Ta'rikh al-fattash* compares him unfavourably with Al-Hajjaj, the notorious Umayyad governor of Iraq. Al-Maghili had no hesitation in adjudging him a pagan. Nevertheless, the same records also tell us that he prayed Muslim prayers, fasted Ramadan, gave alms, and showed great favour to some of the Muslim scholars. Both Muslim records (particularly Al-Maghili) and oral tradition show Sunni 'Ali as a magician who worked in close collaboration with the Songhay magicians, soothsayers, and priests. All are agreed that he was a man of immense energy and personal valour who, throughout the numerous campaigns of his thirty-year reign, was never once defeated.

Various solutions have been presented to the problem of Sunni 'Ali's ambiguous attitude towards Islam. Delafosse, evidently bewildered by the conflicting evidence, concludes 'il semble que ce conquérant avait peu de suite dans ses idées' (*H.-S.-N.* ii, pp. 82–83), which, when one considers the number of times he condemned even some of his favourites to death in a fit of rage, only to become bitterly remorseful in a mood of calm, may certainly have some truth in it. It seems unlikely, however, that he would constantly be in two minds about such a major issue in his empire as the influence of Islam. Sunni 'Ali was more than merely a powerful and ruthless ruler; he was evidently a subtle politician whose moves were carefully calculated and forcefully executed. Trimingham (*History*, p. 94) proposes the unrealistic view that he 'treated Islam as a joke'. Sunni 'Ali was not a monarch noted for his humour, nor can one imagine anything more unlikely than that such a mighty conqueror should amuse himself by poking fun at Islam. The matter was no joke to him; it was probably the most serious matter with which he had to deal during his reign.

Let us take the case of Sunni 'Ali first. Sunni 'Ali had been brought up as an adherent of traditional Songhay religion. 'His mother was from Fara (or Fari, which Rouch identifies with the area of Sokoto—but without making the case for this identification); they are a people who worship idols of trees and rocks and make sacrifices to them and ask help from them,' (*Al-Maghili*). They had certain shrines (Ar. *Buyut mu 'aẓẓama*) looked after by custodians (Ar. *Sadana*). These shrines, often near sacred rocks or trees, were the homes of gods who could be consulted through their custodians, who interpreted their utterances. (On the surface this sounds reminiscent of the Ifa oracle system of the Yoruba and appears to be not the only point of comparison between the two religious systems. Both have a very similar cult of the god of thunder—*Dango* in Songhay, *Shango* in Yoruba. Rouch suggests that this latter cult was spread by the Sorko along the waterways they travelled (*Religion*, p. 11).) Sunni

'Ali, throughout his youth, made constant recourse to them and became thoroughly imbued with the beliefs and practices of their adherents. From his father Sulaiman Dandi, he inherited the knowledge of the magic arts handed down through the line of magician-kings of Koukya. Tradition claims that his father initiated him and passed on to him the 'master-word' (*gyindize dyine*) by virtue of which all other divinities became subservient to him.

On the other hand, we may note that the kingdom of Gao had, for about five centuries, been exposed to an ever-increasing Islamic influence and that for about three and a half centuries the rulers of this empire had been at least nominal Muslims. Sunni 'Ali himself 'pronounced the two *shahadas* and spoke as a man well-versed in religion' (*Fattash*, p. 82). He showed favour to some of the '*ulama*, notably to Al-Ma'mun, cousin of the Qadi of Timbuktu, Habib (*T/Sudan*, p. 66) and 'Abdallah al-Bilbali, the first white imam of the Sankore mosque (*T/Sudan*, p. 57). On another occasion, after raiding a Fulani people he sent a number of female captives as a gift to some of the '*ulama* of Timbuktu (*T/Sudan*, p. 67).

What does this all amount to? It seems that Islam had probably become an important element in the royal religious cult, though not as yet the dominating element. Rouch believes that it was during Sunni 'Ali's rule that for the first time a coherent synthesis between Islam and the indigenous Songhay religion was evolved (*Religion*, p. 14), and he suggests that Islam may have supplied Songhay religion with certain elements which it lacked—particularly belief in a future life and an ordered cosmology. Certain facts might lead us to go further than this and to conclude that the magico-religious system of the Songhay had, by Sunni 'Ali's time, begun to decay and, further, had not within itself the necessary elements for providing a sufficient basis for authority and administration in the more sophisticated and far-reaching state which was beginning to evolve. Islam was capable of supplying these elements and was beginning to grow powerful in the kingdoms bordering on the Songhay territory, with the exception of the south. By the time of Sunni 'Ali there was the danger that

Islam might completely eclipse the Songhay religious system and hence destroy the basis upon which Sunni 'Ali built his authority as magician-king. It was an essential element of Sunni 'Ali's policy, therefore, to try and contain this force, exploit it where possible, and maintain a balance between it and the indigenous Songhay cult.

Firstly, Sunni 'Ali himself made some show of keeping up a Muslim appearance by saying prayers, fasting, and slaughtering sacrificial animals. His prayers would have been *batil* by the standard of any Muslim jurist—he often said all five daily prayers at one time in the early hours of the following morning, sitting in the *tashahhud* posture and inclining his body forward to indicate the *ruku'* and *sujud* and contenting himself merely with repeating the name of the prayer he was intending to pray instead of reciting the *Fatiha* and other suras. He no doubt had little or no idea of the import of his actions, but found it necessary to pay deference to the power of this mysterious oriental cult which had become woven into the prevailing Songhay religious system.

It seems further likely that he intended to keep this Islamic element as part of the royal prerogative, perhaps in order to prevent its magical properties from being acquired by the Songhay priests and magicians and the common people. According to Al-Maghili, he tried to prevent his court and his household from adopting Islamic practices, and none of them dared pray or fast a single day of Ramadan for fear that he would punish them. At the same time he persecuted the *'ulama* of Timbuktu and drove them out of the town in early 1469 on the suspicion that they were aiding the Tuareg. In 1486 he undertook a further purge of the Timbuktu scholars. He evidently respected their mysterious knowledge enough to fear it, and he therefore took pains to wipe out any one whose 'magical-religious' powers might prove equal or superior to his own, and thus endanger his life and sovereignty.

It would seem, then, that Islam, during the latter half of the fifteenth century, was rapidly gaining strength in the Songhay empire—particularly in the western half and, while it could not be ignored by the ruler and, indeed, had to be conceded a place in the state cult, it was in danger of becoming too powerful to the detriment of the indigenous religious system upon which the rulers of Gao had traditionally rested their authority. Sunni ʿAli, therefore, in his apparently ambivalent attitude, was but endeavouring to maintain the equilibrium and safeguard his own position.

This point of view seems further strengthened by the course which events took subsequent to the death of Sunni ʿAli, who perished in November 1492 under rather mysterious circumstances while returning from an expedition against Gourma. In January 1493 Sunni ʿAli's son, Abu Bakr Daʿu (Sunni Barou), was nominated ruler of Songhay. However, he had a contender in the person of Muhammad Ture, one of Sunni ʿAli's former commanders and favourites, who made an unsuccessful preliminary attempt to gain power in February 1493.

Sunni Barou had evidently decided to rest his authority solely on the Songhay magico-religious system and to reject the intrusive and increasingly powerful Islamic elements. He refused to declare himself a Muslim, and when Muhammad Ture sent messengers to him requiring him to declare his allegiance to Islam he expressly rejected the notion. The *Ta'rikh al-fattash* adds, rather significantly, 'He had fears for his sovereignty, as is natural on the part of a king.' However, it is evident that he and his followers had badly miscalculated the mood of the times. By now the Islamic impulse in the Songhay empire had become sufficiently strong to be able to provide a basis for authority which would find popular acceptance, whereas, while the Songhay magico-religious system might serve as the basis for a 'coalition' with Islam, as it had done under Sunni ʿAli, it no longer had the authoritarian force or the cosmopolitan appeal which was becoming necessary in the context of the late fifteenth-century Sudan, through which an Islamic wind of change was beginning to blow with increasing vigour.

Muhammad Ture came to power in April 1493, after defeating Sunni Barou in battle at Anfao—Muhammad's pretext being Sunni Barou's threefold public rejection of the demand to swear himself a Muslim. This was the critical moment for Islam in the Songhay empire. Sunni 'Ali had ruled by showing the Muslim religion some deference and skilfully using it as but one of the props of his power. Sunni Barou attempted to rule without it, but so far from being able to eliminate it from the structure of state power, had it turn upon him and defeat him, only to become the chief prop of power under the Askia dynasty. This did not, of course, mean that Islam immediately became all-powerful under the Askias; pagan practice and ritual still continued, even at the courts of the Askias, but the rule of Askia Muhammad Ture certainly accelerated a process of Islamization which had already begun gathering momentum.

III. ASKIA AL-HAJJ MUHAMMAD TURE 'COMMANDER OF THE FAITHFUL' (reg. 1493–1528)

During the latter half of the fifteenth century Islam was evidently on the offensive in the Western Sudan, and the mood of the times was apparently favourable to it. This was due in part to the awe which it inspired as an occult religion with its own powerful system of magic (charms, talismans, sand divining) and communicable spiritual power (*baraka*)[1] and its codified and unified system of ritual and belief. It introduced a common literacy in Arabic which made possible the stable government of large empires and facilitated contact—whether friendly or otherwise—between states partaking in the same system. Equally significant here was the combination present in Islam between religion and politics which gives to Muslim law, and even to its fiscal and territorial administration, much of the character of a divine dispensation.

By the end of the fifteenth century the Songhay empire was surrounded by areas of Islamic influence and was able to maintain its superiority—at least for the time being—by making use of Islam to the fullest extent. The rulers of Kano and Katsina had become Muslims during the fourteenth century, and in the mid-fifteenth century there was a further and more far-reaching wave of Islamization in these areas. During the reign of Yakubu,

[1] There are two very interesting chapters on *baraka* in E. Westermarck, *Pagan Survivals in Mohammedan Civilisation*, London, 1933. See pp. 87–144.

Sarkin Kano (1452–63), Fulani teachers came from Mali and
settled and taught in Hausaland. Muhammad Rimfa (1463–99)
appears to have been a strong supporter of Islam, and towards
the end of his reign took advice from the itinerant North African
theologian, Al-Maghili, on how to govern his state according to
the laws of Islam. In Kebbi the first Muslim Sultan was probably
Muhammad Kanta, who is estimated by Arnett to have reigned
c. 1454–*c.* 1492 (*Sokoto*, p. 89. To the north-east of the Songhay
empire the Sultanate of Agades is said to date from the early
fifteenth century (*Chroniques*, p. 151), and by the latter part of
the century interest in Islam was sufficiently keen for the Sultan,
Muhammad b. Sottofe (reg. 1486–93), to write to the Egyptian
scholar Al-Suyuti for advice (see 'Uthman b. Fudi, *Tanbih
al-ikhwan*).

On the western edge of the empire, Mali had a tradition of Islam
going back some four centuries (*Al-Bakri*, pp. 333–4), and Jenne
and Timbuktu had by the end of the fifteenth century become
important centres for the diffusion of Islam. The importance of
the latter in spreading and strengthening Islam in the Air region
and Hausaland is particularly significant. We know of a number
of scholars of Timbuktu who travelled in these regions in the
late fifteenth and early sixteenth centuries. For example, Ahmad
b. 'Umar b. Muhammad Aqit of Timbuktu is said to have visited
Kano on his return from the pilgrimage in or around the year
1487 (*T/Sudan*, p. 37). Aida Ahmad of Tazakht visited Takedda,
where he received instruction from Al-Maghili, and on his
return from the pilgrimage, some time after 1510, settled in Katsina, became *qadi* of the town, and died there in 1529. Even more
interesting as an example of a peripatetic scholar and teacher is
the case of Makhluf al-Bilbali. He studied first in Walata under
'Abdallah b. 'Umar b. Muhammad Aqit, travelled to the Maghrib,
and, on his return to the Sudan, went to Kanda (possibly a mis-
print for Kano) and Katsina, back to Timbuktu, on to Morocco
for the second time, and then back to the Sudan, where he died
some time after 1533 (*Nail*, p. 344; *T/Sudan*, p. 39). Finally,
there is Al-Maghili himself, who as a North African theologian
and author of many works was received in the Sudan as an

authority on Islam; indeed, he himself writes in an authoritative manner and rarely cites other jurists to back up his rulings. He was from Tlemçen originally, but had taken up residence in Tuwat, from which town he travelled to Takedda, thence to Katsina and Kano, and finally to Gao, where he wrote his famous 'Replies' for Askia Al-Hajj Muhammad. This must have been just at the turn of the sixteenth century, since he returned to Tuwat and died there in 1503/4 (*Nail*, p. 331).

The effect of this movement of Islamization, however, was still restricted mainly to the ruling dynasties and chief administrators of the various kingdoms and, as one would expect, it was only the capital cities and other large centres where Islam had much effect, and even in these places its influence was only partial. From al-Maghili's 'Replies' it is evident that the situation was much the same as the situation 'Uthman b. Fudi complained of in Hausaland four centuries later. Most so-called Muslims were half-hearted in their allegiance to Islam and, while making a lip-profession of the faith, still believed in other gods whom they called upon in their shrines and at their sacred rocks and trees. Free women walked about unveiled except in Timbuktu, (*Leo*, iii, p. 824), where the wives of the clerics had been secluded even in Sunni 'Ali's time (*T/Sudan*, p. 66), and in Jenne young girls customarily walked entirely naked until marriage. Leo Africanus complains that the village population of the 'kingdome of Gago' are 'ignorant and rude people, and you shall scarce find one learned man in the space of an hundred miles' (*Leo*, iii, p. 827). This appears to be the general situation during the early years of Askia Muhammad's reign and, though he is depicted in all the written sources as the man who supported and strengthened the faith, yet he was not able to Islamize the whole of his kingdom, and some of his successors were certainly lukewarm towards Islam, so that by the time of the Moroccan invasion in 1591 there seems to have been a marked relapse into paganism.

Askia Muhammad b. Abi Bakr Ture came to power in 1493 at the advanced age of 50 (*T/fattash*, p. 113) having narrowly escaped execution at the hands of Sunni 'Ali a number of times, though he was one of his favourites (*T/Sudan*, p. 68). This title Askia, which became the honorific of his successors, was not a new one and had been used as a military title under the Shi (Sunni) dynasty. (*T/fattash*, p. 88). His ancestors were probably Soninke of the Silla clan. Oral tradition claims that he was the offspring of a union between Sunni 'Ali's sister, Kossey, and a jinn. The *Ta'rikh al-fattash* also admits that Sunni 'Ali and Askia Muhammad share a common origin. They, and all people bearing the name Moi, are said to have come from the town of Yara, long ago destroyed, the inhabitants of which were originally from west of Wakore or Wangara (*T/fattash*, p. 94). This would most likely mean that they were Mandinka or Soninke.

Soon after assuming power he went to Mecca to perform the pilgrimage (1495), returning two years later in 1497. Tradition asserts that he went to Mecca virtually a pagan and had to prove himself a Muslim by magical acts. However, it seems unlikely that he would have been designated *Khalifa* if this were true, though the various accounts of his investiture as Caliph of Takrur do not speak with one voice. The most authentic account is probably that of *Ta'rikh al-fattash*, since the author was himself an eye-witness. According to this, the Sharif of Mecca gave him a green *qalansuwa*, a white turban, and a sword and made him his deputy (*Khalifa*) over Takrur (Western Sudan) (*T/fattash*, pp. 16 and 131). The incident is recounted in the words of Askia Al-Hajj Muhammad himself later on when, in 1537, he handed on these symbols of authority to his son, Isma'il saying, 'You are thus the *Khalifa* of the *Khalifa* of the *Sharif* who is himself, the *Khalifa* of the Grand Ottoman Sultan (*T/fattash*, pp. 161–2).

Strengthened by this authority and the 'magical' blessing (*baraka*) which was ascribed to pilgrims, the Askia could return to rule his kingdom without fear. Having abandoned the role of 'magician-king' which had been the prop of Sunni 'Ali's power, he had now taken on the Islamic guise of 'pilgrim-king' which would give him the necessary moral strength to rule his people. Islamic *baraka* had replaced Songhay magic as the chief ritual support of kingly authority.

Although, in theory, Islam does not have a priesthood, and

imams, qadis, and learned men have no sacerdotal functions or spiritual authority, nevertheless in practice they do tend to assume, or have thrust upon them, a marked measure of spiritual authority in certain times and places. In the context of sixteenth-century Songhay this was important. Officially traditional priests, magicians, and soothsayers were in disgrace; however, their very necessary functions of providing supernatural sanction for the authority of the ruler and for advising or ratifying his course of action could not be dispensed with. These functions now fell to the lot of the *qadis,* particularly the *qadi* of Timbuktu, and to the other Muslim clerics of the Songhay empire. By association with such men one could acquire some share of the *baraka* which they possessed; the *baraka* inherent in a pilgrim who had returned from Mecca after touching the Black Stone of the Ka'ba and visiting the tomb of the Prophet at Medina was considered particularly efficacious (see, for example, *T/fattash,* pp. 205–7). This may to some extent help to explain the great popularity of the pilgrimage throughout West Africa even in modern times.

Askia al-Hajj Muhammad, therefore, kept in constant touch with the *'ulama,* to obtain authority for his acts and to acquire a share of their *baraka;* he took good care to look after their interests and to ingratiate himself with them so as to keep a moderating hand on their influence. 'Askia Muhammad was full of respect for the *'ulama;* he lavished slaves and money upon them in order to assure the interests of the Muslims and to help them in their submission to God and in the practice of their religion' (*T/fattash.* p. 115). The relationship between the Askia and the *Qadi* is clearly brought out in the interview which Askia Muhammad had at the beginning of his reign with the *Qadi* of Timbuktu, Mahmud b. 'Umar. When the Askia asked the *Qadi* why he had expelled his messengers and beaten them, when in former times the ruler had always been free to do as he wished in Timbuktu, the *Qadi* simply recalled that Askia Muhammad had once visited him and placed his person under the *Qadi's* protection to be a barrier between him and Hell-fire (*T/fattash,* pp. 116–17). The Askia immediately recognized the legitimacy of this reply and asked for the *Qadi's* forgiveness.

Further, the *Qadi* was the only man in the kingdom who could enjoin a functionary of the Askia to undertake a task for him. The functionary did not have the right to refuse and had to serve him as he would serve the Askia. The *qadis* and other men of religion enjoyed certain other privileges. The *qadis* sat on a prayer mat when in audience with the Askia; only *Shurafa* (descendants of the Prophet) could sit with the Askia on his raised platform. The Askia only rose from his seat to greet the *'ulama*, the *shurafa*, the returning pilgrims, and the *san*, and they were the only groups of people allowed to eat with him. This was the situation during the early years of Askia al-Hajj Muhammad's reign, when he was anxious to conciliate these important groups. Later, when his power was greater and he was more sure of his position, these privileges fell into abeyance (*T/fattash*, p. 14).

The other Askia who followed the same policy and leaned heavily on the support of the *'ulama* was the only other who enjoyed a long reign, Askia Dawud (reg. 1549–83). Dawud even went a step further towards establishing the sacerdotal nature of the *'ulama* and used them as intercessors for himself with God! On one occasion he sent the *imam* of Gao twenty-seven slaves 'in order to obtain eternal safety' (from hell). His message was, 'I beg the *imam* to ask God on my behalf for His pardon and indulgence.' (*T/fattash*, p. 197). On another occasion he sent a hundred slaves to Al-'Aqib, the *Qadi* of Timbuktu, saying, 'Tell him to use them to buy my portion of Paradise from God; he will be my intermediary with God to obtain this' (*T/fattash*, p. 198). It was Dawud's habit when visiting Timbuktu to call on the *Qadi*. The *Qadi* would receive his guests at the door and entertain them. 'His guests, anxious to participate in the divine favour with which the *Qadi* was showered, would eat with him after addressing numerous prayers to God' (*T/fattash*, pp. 201–2). Evidently the almost ritual participation in a meal could be a means of imbibing the *baraka* of a holyman.

It has already been suggested that, even though the accession of Askia Muhammad, the pilgrim-king, might seem to have heralded a golden age of Islam in the Songhay empire, this was not entirely the case. Askia Muhammad himself knew how to use Islam as a political instrument—ingratiating himself with the *'ulama* to gain their support and blessing, at least in the early days of his reign. Only once, near the beginning of his reign, did he undertake a military campaign with their direct sanction and according to the Islamic rules—that was his *jihad* against the Mossi immediately after his return from Mecca in 1497–98. He made no attempt to re-form his administration according to Islamic theories (or even the actual practice of any Muslim country), but maintained and even enlarged the Songhay system of titles and offices which he inherited from Sunni 'Ali. We do not have much knowledge of court ceremonial except that it was the common practice for people entering the Askia's presence to prostrate themselves and cover their heads with dust (*T/fattash*, p. 13). The Askia evidently kept a large court with many slaves and concubines and dealt in patriarchal fashion with plaintiffs (*Leo*, iii, p. 827).

Askia Muhammad's son and successor, Musa, (reg. 1528–31) evidently had little time for Islam. He took over all his father's wives and concubines when he deposed him (*T/fattash*, p. 155). He refused to give ear to the intercession of the *qadi* Mahmud when he set out to fight his brother 'Uthman Yubabo and was not to be intimidated by the curse of a holy man (*T/Sudan*, pp. 84–5). Even in the reign of Askia Dawud (1549–83), who had the reputation of being a scholar himself and did much to aid the pursuit of Islamic learning, the court ceremonial was clearly non-Muslim in most respects. In spite of being a thoroughgoing Muslim in many ways, Dawud still felt himself obliged to pay deference to animist sentiment. Those who entered his presence prostrated and convered their heads with dust (*T/fattash*, pp. 184 and 193). At his Friday audience seven hundred eunuchs stood behind him dressed in silk. When he wanted to spit one of them ran forward and put out his sleeve for him to spit upon. Ahmad b. Muhammad b. Sa'id, a celebrated Timbuktu scholar witnessed this scene one day and afterwards said to Askia Dawud, 'When I entered I was constrained to think you must be mad, corrupt or possessed.' The Askia's reply was full of significance and shows how far the Askia still felt himself compelled to lean in both directions—towards tradition and Islam. 'I am not mad myself, but I rule over mad, impious and arrogant folk. It is for this reason that I play the madman myself and pretend to be possessed by a demon in order to frighten them and prevent them from harming the Muslims' (*T/fattash*, pp. 208-10).

During the last ten years of the independent Songhay empire, before the Moroccan invasion of 1591, it is clear that the empire was falling into rapid decay as a political entity. The vitality of the old animist empire under the 'magician-king' Sunni 'Ali and the well-organised and still expanding empire of his successor, the 'pilgrim-king', Askia Al-Hajj Muhammad, had crumbled away and succession quarrels had begun to eat away the fabric of the state. Askia Dawud leaned heavily on the *'ulama*, especially the *qadi* Al-'Aqib, for support, and was at least able to maintain the *status quo*. Although unsuccessful in his campaigns to the south-east, he was able to contain the restless peoples on his west and the Mossi to his south.

After Dawud's death three sons of his ruled in quick succession. During the reign of the first, Muhammad III (1582–86), came the first rumblings of trouble from Morocco. An embassy was sent to Gao by Mulay Ahmad Al-Mansur of Morocco in 1584, the object being to obtain an intelligence report on the strength of the Songhay empire. The report was evidently favourable, as the Sultan soon afterwards sent off a large expedition to the Sudan, though most of it perished in the deserts of Mauretania and the survivors returned to Morocco. Al-Mansur then occupied the Saharan salt-mines of Taghaza and for a time Askia Muhammad was obliged to abandon the mines. In 1586 the Askia was deposed by his brother, Muhammad Bani, who ruled for less than two years and died apparently during a fit.

It was during the reign of Muhammad Bani that a civil war, touched off by the murder of a state official, virtually split the empire in two. The Balama, Al-Sadiq, who had his residence at Timbuktu, killed the Kabara-farma, Alou, in a quarrel. Askia Muhammad Bani set out against the Balama, but died before defeating him. In April 1588 Ishaq II was proclaimed Askia in Gao, but when his messenger reached Timbuktu to announce his accession he was imprisoned, as the Balama Al-Sadiq had already been recognized as Askia by his own men and by the people of Timbuktu (*T/Sudan*, p. 200). The Balama was, however, eventually defeated by Askia Ishaq II and finally put to death.

It is evident that by this time the Songhay empire no longer had much cohesion, and as soon as the centre was attacked in 1591 by the Moroccan forces and the Askia's army sent fleeing in disorder, the western half of the empire was rapidly invaded by marauding peoples at Jenne, Bara, Dirma, and Ra's al-Ma' (*T/fattash*, p. 272). The Tuareg, too, seized the first opportunity to plunder when they descended upon Timbuktu in December 1591, while the main body of Moroccan forces were away in pursuit of Askia Ishaq II.

The *'ulama* were still a powerful force in politics even at this time. For example, the Askia's war council, which met to decide how best to face the Moroccan attack included among its members the *qadi* of Gao and one of the learned men of Timbuktu (*T/fattash*, pp. 268–9). It was in fact a 'man of religion', the Alfa Askia Bukar Lanbar, chief secretary and apparently chief adviser, of the Askia, who persuaded Ishaq II to abandon the field in the first encounter with the Moroccans at Tondibi in March 1591, and who later betrayed the Askia Muhammad Gao and his chiefs into the hands of the Pasha Mahmud.

In Timbuktu the *qadi*, and the learned men of Sankoré, particularly those of the Aqit family, were still an influential body of men (*Ahmad Baba*, p. 314 *et passim*). The house of the *qadi* had, throughout the Askia dynasty, been an inviolable place of refuge for deposed Askias, revolted governors, and disgraced officials. The clerics of Timbuktu were evidently no more favourable to rule by the Moroccans than they were to direct interference from the Askias, and they maintained a cold, though not openly hostile attitude towards them at first. This is the impression we get from the Arabic chronicles at any rate, though both Al-Sa'di and Kati would have been careful not to admit that the *'ulama* were actually rebellious. It is probable that the *'ulama* were, in fact, strongly hostile to the Moroccans and probably instigated the revolt of October–November 1591 in Timbuktu (*Ahmad Baba*, pp. 320–1). The course of action which the Pasha Mahmud subsequently took in arresting the Timbuktu *'ulama en masse* and later exiling a number of them to Morocco seems to indicate that he knew where the chief source of opposition to Moroccan rule lay. It was no doubt for similar reasons that Sunni 'Ali, over a century before, expelled and persecuted the learned members of this little state within a state. Furthermore, in the case of the Moroccan army, though it represented the authority of a Muslim state, its members were chiefly Spanish mercenaries who were either non-Muslims or Muslims only through force of circumstances and therefore had little time for the laws and precepts of the faith when they were so far away from their adopted country. Hence the *'ulama* would no doubt have felt amply justified in opposing their rule by all means at their disposal.

The coming of the Moroccans to the Sudan not only dealt the final blow to the already decaying Songhay empire but also largely sealed the fate of Timbuktu as a centre of trade and learning. After the final fall from grace under Pasha Mahmud and the exile of some of the leading *'ulama*, the city lost much of the intellectual and spiritual vitality which it had known throughout the sixteenth century. Furthermore, it became the capital of the state ruled over by the Moroccan Pashas and, being thus under very tight control from the new rulers, was never again able to enjoy the degree of autonomy it had had under the Askias.

Islam had, during the sixteenth century, gained ground in the urban centres of the Songhay empire no doubt; indeed, it had been a factor of urban life and an element of the royal religious cult for the preceding five centuries. The peasants and fisherfolk of the villages and hamlets seem to have remained little influenced; Islam could hardly have seemed relevant to such people of the soil and the water, whose cultural cycle inevitably revolves around seasonal change and natural fertility. If anything, by the end of the sixteenth century there appears to have been a hardening of lines between Islam and the Songhay indigenous religious system, exemplified in the isolation of the Dendi region which became the centre of political resistance to the Moroccans and which held most tenaciously to its own cults. All this, in spite of the encouragement given to Islam by some of the Askias, particularly the first, Al-Hajj Muhammad Ture, and the sixth, Dawud.

As I have tried to show, it was necessary for the Askias throughout the sixteenth century to maintain a delicate balance between Islam and Songhay religion in the structure of state power. It seems equally apparent that, on the whole, Islam had little popular support and remained largely an alien religion of foreign and élite groups, though this is not to ignore the Islamic elements, which may already by this time have become thoroughly integrated into Songhay religion itself. The coming of the Moroccans in 1591 broke down the already crumbling political structure of the Songhay empire and destroyed what religious equilibrium there was. Islam was then to become identified, at least in the early years of Moroccan rule, with a tyrannical alien ruling group. It had not penetrated deep enough into Songhay society to prove a rallying point in time of trouble or to hold together a tottering empire, and its chief protagonists, the *'ulama* of Timbuktu (a basically alien group), were among the first to suffer from the iron hand of a new Muslim rule.

REFERENCES

Ahmad Baba
  (1351 A. H.) *Nail al-ibtihaj bi tatriẓ al-Dibaj*. Cairo. (*Nail*)
Al-Bakri
  (1913) *Description de l'Afrique septentrionale* (*Kitab al-masalik wa'l-mamalik*).
    Trans. de M. de Slane, revised edn., Alger. (*Al-Bakri*)
Al-Maghili
  (MSS.) *Ajwiba 'ala as'ilat al-Amir al-Hajj Abi 'Abdullah Muhammad b. Abi Bakr*. (MSS. of Dakar, Paris, and Ibadan consulted.) (*Al-Maghili*)
Arnett, E. J.
  (1922) Introduction to the history of Sokoto (at end of *The Rise of the Sokoto Fulani*). Kano. (*Sokoto*)
Al-Sa'di
  (1898) *Ta'rikh al-Sudan*. Ed. and trans, by O. Houdas, Paris. (*T/Sudan:* page numbers refer to Arabic text.)
Béraud-Villars, J.
  (1942) *L'Empire de Gao*. Paris.
Boulnois, J. and Boubou Hama
  (1954) *L'Empire de Gao*. Paris.
Delafosse, M.
  (1912) *Haut-Sénégal-Niger*. Paris. 3 vols. (*H.-S.-N.*)

Dubois, F.
(1897) *Tombouctou la Mystérieuse*. Paris. (*Tombouctou*)
Hunwick, J.
'Ahmad Baba and the Moroccan invasion of the Sudan (1591)', *Journal of the Historical Society of Nigeria*, vol. II, no. 3, pp. 311–28. (*Ahmad Baba*)
Ibn Battuta
(1843–58) *Tuhfat al-nuẓẓar* (*Voyages*), ed. and trans. C. Defrémery and B. Sanguinetti, Paris, 4 vols. (*Ibn Battuta*)
Ibn Khaldun
(1925–56) *Histoire des Berbères*, trans, M.de Slane, Paris, 4 vols. Arabic text, 7 vols., Beirut, 1956–59. (*Ibn Khaldun*)
Leo Africanus
(1896) *The History and Description of Africa*. Pory's translation, ed. by R. Brown, London, 3 vols. (*Leo*)
Mahmud Kati
(1913) *Ta'rikh al-fattash*, trans. by O. Houdas amd M. Delafosse, Paris. (*T/fattash*)
Rouch, J.
(1953) *Contribution à l'histoire des Songhay*. (Mém. de l'IFAN, no. 29, pp. 137–259. (*Contribution*)
(1960) *La Religion et la magie Songhay*. Paris. (*Religion*)
Trimingham, J. S.
(1959) *Islam in West Africa*. London.
(1962) *History of Islam in West Africa*. London. (*History*)
Urvoy, Y.
(1934) 'Chroniques d'Agades', *Journal de la Société des Africanistes*, vol. 4, pp. 145–77. (*Chroniques*)
(1936) *Histoire des populations du Soudan central*. Paris.

IV. THE POSITION OF MUSLIMS IN METROPOLITAN ASHANTI IN THE EARLY NINETEENTH CENTURY

IVOR WILKS

I. THE KUMASI MUSLIMS: SHAIKH BABA

From the extant writings of the West African Muslim reformers, the *mujaddidin*, of the first half of the thirteenth century A.H., it is becoming possible to reconstruct the social and political conditions of the times in such central regions of the revolutionary movement as the Fulani emirates of Nigeria.[1] No similar body of evidence is available, however, for the study of those peripheral areas where influential Muslim communities continued to exist under the patronage of non-Muslim kings like Da Kaba of Segu (?1808–?1827) and Osei Tutu Kwame of Ashanti (?1801–24). Fortunately, in the case of Ashanti, there is evidence from a quite different source: between May 1816 and March 1820 Osei Tutu Kwame received as visitors to Kumasi no less than nine agents of the European merchant companies trading on the Gold Coast to the south, and of these, five left lengthy descriptions of his capital.[2] From them a detailed account of the Kumasi Muslim community can be pieced together, of its structure and functions, of the stresses to which it was subject, and of the influence which it exerted, during those four years.

The Kumasi Muslims lived in the centre of the town, their quarter lying along the avenue leading from the main market to the king's palace.[3] No definite information on the size of the community exists; like similar commercial groups elsewhere, its membership doubtless fluctuated with seasonal and other cycles of trade. Nevertheless, on two public occasions, his own

[1] See, e.g., M. Hiskett, 'Kitab al-farq: a work on the Habe kingdoms attributed to 'Uthman dan Fodio', *BSOAS*, vol. XXIII, no. 3, 1960.

[2] For the comparative value of these sources, see Bibliography at end.

[3] Bowdich, 1819, p. 129 and map facing p. 323; Dupuis, 1824, pp. 71–72.

reception and a subsequent Adae festival, Consul Dupuis estimated that three hundred Muslims made their appearance.[4]
The total adult male resident population was probably, then,
in excess of this, and with women and children there may perhaps
have been over a thousand Muslims more or less permanently
settled in Kumasi.

The head of the community was the elderly Muhammad al-
Ghamba', 'the Mamprussi', more commonly known as Baba,
who had first settled in Kumasi in 1807.[5] A man of piety and
learning, his obligations to the Kumasi faithful required the
exercise of both qualities. As *imam* he led them in prayer,[6]
and as *qadi* he administered justice in accordance with the Shari'a.[7]
Especially close to his heart was the school which he had founded
and over which he presided, where some seventy pupils were
taught the Quran, and thereby reading, writing, and elementary
Arabic.[8] Shaikh Baba's own educational attainments, however,
naturally extended farther.[9] Owner of a large library,[10] his studies
would seem to have included not only the conventional range of
Islamic sciences—*tafsir*, *fiqh*, and the like—presupposed by his
liturgical and legal functions, but also *ta'rikh*: he was, for example,
able to discourse interestingly on both Ashanti and Western
Sudanese history.[11]

As a young man, Shaikh Baba had travelled widely in the

[4] Dupuis, 1824, pp. 71–72 and 142.
[5] Apparently following a dispute with his relative, the King of Mamprussi
(capital Gambaga, Arabic Ghamba'), as described in Bowdich, 1819, p. 240. See
also Dupuis, 1824, p. cxxix n.
[6] Hutchison, in Bowdich, 1819, p. 405.
[7] Dupuis, 1824, p. 94. Cases between Muslims and non-Muslims, however,
would be adjudicated in Ashanti courts in accordance with Ashanti customary
law, though probably in the presence of a representative of the *qadi*, see Dupuis,
1824, pp. 117 and 124 n.
[8] Bowdich, 1819, p. 90; Dupuis, 1824, pp. 97 and 107; Hutton, 1821, p. 261.
[9] See Dupuis' general comments on the Kumasi Muslims, some 'men of
education and talent', pp. vi *et seq.*   [10] Bowdich, 1819, p. 144.
[11] See, e.g., Dupuis, 1824, pp. 250 n., xlix, xc. It is now known that a local
tradition of *ta'rikh* writing had already developed in the eighteenth century.
In the Arabic collection at the Institute of African Studies, University of Ghana,
for example, there are eight MSS of a chronicle of Gonja history completed in
1752; see I. Wilks, 'The Growth of Islamic learning in Ghana', in *Journal of
the Historical Society of Nigeria*, II, 4, 1963. An earlier but related work of c. 1711,
was extant in early 19th century Kumasi, and is preserved in *Cod. Arab. CCCII*,
III, ff. 236–7 Royal Library, Copenhagen.

regions between Ashanti and Hausaland,[12] but considered himself
at this period 'an indifferent Talb'.[13] However, he describes his
subsequent reception of 'the truth' from his *muqaddam*:

> God be praised, a certain Moraboth [*murabit*] from the north was sent
> to me by a special direction, and that learned saint taught me the truth; so
> that now my beard is white, and I cannot travel as before; I am content to
> seek the good of my soul in a state of future reward.[14]

Since this initiation occurred after Baba's arrival in Kumasi
in 1807, it would seem possible that, with the growth of the
Qadiriyya brotherhood in Hausaland (to which *tariqa* 'Uthman
dan Fodio himself belonged), Qadiri *shaikhs* also made their
influence felt along the great trade route that led through Bussa
and Nikki to Yendi, Salaga, and the Ashanti capital—a matter
for which there is some independent evidence.[15]

II. THE KUMASI MUSLIMS: RESIDENTS AND VISITORS

Of the resident members of the Kumasi Muslim community
who, in virtue of their social standing,[16] were especially prominent in civic affairs, most appear to have originated from the
immediate hinterland of Ashanti, so that Dupuis often refers to
them as 'the Moslems of Dagomba and Ghunja'.[17] Thus, Muhammad Kama'atay,[18] who had studied Arabic in Hausaland, has a
characteristic Dyula *nisba*, and probably came from one of the
ancient Wangara Kamaghate groups found throughout Gonja.
Abu Bakr Turay, Shaikh Baba's trading agent, also has a Dyula

[12] Dupuis, 1824, pp. 97, 109, and cxxix n.
[13] I.e. *talib*, student, disciple.
[14] Quoted by Dupuis, 1824, p. 97.
[15] In his *Tanbih al-ikhwan*, written in (?) 1811, 'Uthman dan Fodio lists
Dagomba among the 'lands of Unbelievers'. Since the rulers of Dagomba had
been at least nominally Muslim for almost a century, presumably the king *c.* 1811
was regarded as an apostate. An Arabic *ta'rikh* from Dagomba, however, that is
yet to be traced, is said to report the arrival in Yendi of emissaries from 'Uthman
dan Fodio. Bowdich, 1819, p. 178, refers to an increase in Hausa settlement in
Yendi at that time, and also speaks of the 'conversion' of the ruler. That this
might refer to his adoption of Qadiri *wird* is suggested by a later reference in
Bowdich, p. 453, to the Yendi king's 'proverbial repute for sanctity'.
[16] See, e.g., the reference to the 'seventeen superiors', in Bowdich, 1819, p. 37.
[17] Dupuis, 1824, p. 170; see also p. xiv.
[18] Dupuis, p. cxxviii, transcribes the name as Camati, but the Arabic reads
Kama'atay. See p. 163 below.

nisba—more familiar as Touré—and may have shared a similar background. From their *laqabs*, al-Hajj Mubarak al-Salghawi, Jalal ibn Qudsi al-Burumi, and Ibrahim al-Yandi were from Salaga in eastern Gonja, the Mbrom country to its south, and the Dagomba capital, respectively. From a more distant place, one Timbuktu man had been resident in Kumasi for a decade.[19] In general, however, most of the residents undoubtedly belonged to, or to the fringes of, Dyula or Wangara society—to those supra-ethnic trading associations, Kamaghate, Touré, Diabak-hate, Watara, and the rest, which, over the centuries, had extended their commercial activities across West Africa from the Senegal to Hausaland, and from the Sahil to the Guinea coast, trans-cending the borders of states, languages, and peoples.[20] It follows that the Kumasi Muslims of the 'deep south'—living in the high forest zone, little over a hundred miles from the surf-bound coast—were far from isolated from the greater Muslim centres of the Western Sudan. The rich natural resources of Ashanti, especially its gold and kola, attracted the interest of merchants from far away, whose representatives visited, and sometimes resided in, Kumasi. At each visit to Shaikh Baba's house, observed Bowdich,

> I found strange Moors just arrived from different parts of the interior, sojourning with him,[21]

and, doubtless with some exaggeration, he also described 'the hourly arrival in Coomassie of visitors, merchants, and slaves' from the hinterland, and of 'the daily departures of Ashantee caravans'.[22] The trade with Timbuktu through Jenne was of

[19] Bowdich, 1819, p. 194.
[20] For a glimpse from the northern end, see, e.g., the evidence of Muhammad Mustafa, emissary of the king of Segu: 'on the banks of the Niger . . . he met many "Jullas", trading natives, who mentioned to him that they had been to a far-distant country called Ashantee, the king of which was a pagan', *Royal Gazette and Sierra Leone Advertiser*, vol. IV, 219, 10 August 1822. For the early spread of the Dyula into Ghana, see I. Wilks, *The Northern Factor in Ashanti History*, 1961; 'The Growth of Islamic Learning in Ghana', paper cited; 'A Medieval Trade-Route from the Niger to the Gulf of Guinea,' in *Journal of African History*, vol. III, no. 2, 1962
[21] Bowdich, 1819, pp. 90–91.
[22] Bowdich, 1821 (*a*), p. 2.

considerable importance in this period,[23] and many Muslim merchants from these towns frequented the Ashanti capital;[24] such were the Timbuktu *'alim*, who arrived there in mid-1817 and who claimed to have witnessed the death of Mungo Park eleven years before,[25] and the elderly trader from Jenne, who arrived late in 1817, who had been in Cairo and Alexandria, and had apparently witnessed Nelson's victory at Abukir Bay in 1798.[26]

From even more distant parts came the occasional traveller, from Tripoli, Tunisia, Egypt, and even the Hijaz.[27] Among them were members of the *Shurafa'*, to whose presence the Ashanti government attached great importance:

> These descendants of the Prophet's family are received at Ashantee with hospitality unlimited in its scope; they became the honoured guests of kings and ministers, while the population in bulk venerate them as demi-gods, and look for an increase of wealth in proportion as they compete in tendering respect and offers of service to their visitors.[28]

An interesting representative of this group—the contribution of which to the economic organization of West Africa has yet to be adequately assessed—was the Sharif Ahmad al-Baghdadi, whose travels from Baghdad had taken him to Khorasan in the east, and Ashanti in the west.[29]

III. THE KUMASI MUSLIMS AND THE MUJADDIDIN

The constant and close contact of the Muslims in Kumasi with their co-religionists from all parts of the Western Sudan pre-supposes their awareness of, and acquaintance with, the doctrines of the *mujaddidin*, the 'Revivers of Islam', whose

[23] The evidence of a Malam Muhammad of Timbuktu on the gold trade between Ashanti and that town is on record, see Clapperton, 1829, p. 202. The trading accounts of al-Hajj Hamad al-Wangari give some idea of the volume of this trade at a slightly earlier period, see J. G. Jackson, *An Account of Timbuctoo and Housa*, 1820, pp. 347–8. Gunpowder also appears to have been traded in the same direction, see *Royal Gazette and Sierra Leone Advertiser*, vol. V, 251, 15 March 1823.

[24] Bowdich, 1819, p. 185.   [25] Ibid., pp. 90–91.
[26] Hutchison, in Bowdich, 1819, p. 407; Bowdich, 1819, p. 186 n.
[27] Dupuis, 1824, p. xiv.   [28] Ibid., p. xiv.
[29] H. Barth, *Travels and Discoveries in North and Central Africa*, 1857, II, pp. 283–5.

ascendancy had been established in Futa Toro and Futa Jallon by the later eighteenth century, and in Hausaland in the years following 'Uthman dan Fodio's call for *jihad* in 1804, and who were, around 1820 and under the leadership of Shehu Ahmadu, locked in struggle with the pagan Bambara for control of the Middle Niger delta.[30] There is, indeed, direct evidence of reformist influence in Kumasi. It has already been noted that, some time after 1807, Shaikh Baba of Kumasi received a *wird* from an itinerant *muqaddam*, 'sent by a special direction'. A comparable figure, perhaps, was the aged Katsina *shaikh*, who arrived in Kumasi early in 1820, and who

affected all the austerity of a Morabth (moraboo), among the Arabs, with whom he claimed consanguinity, by descent, from the conquerors of the Niger.[31]

Another interesting person, of whom more is known since he became the confidant of both Bowdich and Hutchison, was the Sharif Ibrahim, whose operational base seems to have been Bussa on the Niger[32] (then under Fulani control), but who arrived in Kumasi, in or about 1815, from Arabia, with two other sharifs.[33] His two companions left for Timbuktu and Tripoli in the following year, but Ibrahim remained until early 1818, when he departed for Mecca at the head of a large caravan of pilgrims.[34] His stay in Kumasi is notable for his uncompromising attitude of disapproval towards the Kumasi Muslims, with whom he would have no social intercourse[35] and with whom he quarrelled over matters of status:[36] he clearly regarded both their use of amulets

[30] For these movements of reform, see H. F. C. Smith, 'A Neglected Theme of West African History: the Islamic Revolutions of the 19th century', *Journal of the Historical Society of Nigeria*, vol. II, no. 2, December 1961. The two latter movements were closely related, in that Shehu Ahmadu, as Smith comments, 'regarded the Shehu dan Fodio as his example, and consulted him on the timing of the Macina *Jihad*'. The links between 'Uthman dan Fodio and the *mujahidin* of the Futas may turn out to have been closer than is usually allowed.

[31] Dupuis, 1824, pp. 137 and cxxxiii.

[32] Hutchison, in Bowdich, 1819, pp. 397 and 403.

[33] See P. Ainé, *Côte Occidentale D'Afrique, Côte-D'Or*, 1857, p. 27, paraphrasing from an unidentified work of Dupuis.

[34] Ibid., p. 27; Dupuis, 1824, pp. xiv–xv.

[35] Bowdich, 1819, p. 92.

[36] Hutchison, in Bowdich, 1819, p. 403.

and their general tolerance of non-Muslim Ashanti custom as indicative of apostasy.[37]

Awareness of the doctrines of the reformers generated, for the Kumasi Muslims, a moral dilemma, since the schoolmen of the reform movement laid great emphasis upon the simple stark dichotomy of *dar al-Islam* and *dar al-harb*:

> The government of a country is the government of its king without question. If the king is a Muslim, his land is Muslim; if he is an Unbeliever, his land is a land of Unbelievers.[38]

The Kumasi Muslims, therefore, were dwelling in *dar al-harb*, not *dar al-Islam*, a fact that committed them, it would be argued, to certain courses of conduct:

> . . . flight (*al-hijra*) from the land of the heathen is obligatory by assent. And the waging of Holy War (*jihad*) is obligatory by assent.
>
> And that to make war upon the heathen king who will not say 'There is no God but Allah' is obligatory by assent, and that to take the government from him is obligatory by assent.[39]

Failure to observe the twin obligations of *hijra* and *jihad*, of withdrawal and return, could, according to the reformers, itself constitute apostasy, since

> The approval of paganism is itself paganism . . . the *jihad* is incumbent on all who are able,[40]

and even trading with the Unbelievers is 'disgraceful'.[41] Those voluntarily remaining in heathen territories necessarily involved themselves in 'blameworthy customs', for example, in the payment of uncanonical taxes:

> One of the ways of their (i.e. the pagans') governments is their imposing on the people monies not laid down by the Shari'a,

[37] Hutchison, in Bowdich, 1819, pp. 397–8; Bowdich, 1819, p. 205. In view of Sharif Ibrahim's recent visit to the Hijaz, see also Bowdich, 1819, p. 92, one might suspect that his extreme puritanism reflected in part his acquaintance with Wahhabi doctrines.

[38] 'Uthman dan Fodio, *Tanbih al-ikhwan*. The doctrine is reiterated in Muhammed Bello, *Infaq al-maysur*.

[39] 'Uthman dan Fodio, *Wathiqat ahl al-Sudan*.

[40] Muhammad Bello, in *Infaq al-maysur*, charging Bornu—even Bornu—with being pagan.

[41] 'Uthman dan Fodio, *Tanbih al-ikhwan*.

and in compulsory military service:

> One of the ways of their governments is to compel the people to serve in their armies, even though they are Muslims[42].

That precisely such matters[43] were of grave concern to the Kumasi Muslims is evidenced in their complaints to Dupuis, that the believers in Ashanti were:

> compelled to pay tribute and fight the battles of heathen princes, whose religion and whose interests are necessarily the reverse of their own.[44]

The second consideration, that of military service, was especially unfortunate in two ways, so Dupuis was told:

> The first is religion, which forbids that the lives and liberties of true believers should be sacrificed to the caprice, or in the avaricious wars of heathen monarchs; the second is an innate repugnance to contribute to the aggrandizement of a power that is already dreaded by the Moslems in general.[45]

As *qadi* of the Kumasi Muslims, Shaikh Baba was necessarily highly exercised by the implications of his community's continued residence in *dar al-harb*. Although none of his writings survives intact, fragments quoted by Dupuis suggest that Baba and his associates made an intellectually skilful and vigorous defence of the position of the Muslims in Ashanti. Starting from the same—and therefore unassailable—premise as the reformers themselves, that the Muslims of the Western Sudan had failed to establish a true *caliphate*,[46] the Kumasi clerics argued for the (historical) inevitability of their peoples' position in Ashanti:

(i)

> the absence of that political co-operation in the north is mainly the cause why the southern believers are checked in their efforts to propagate God's

---

[42] 'Uthman dan Fodio, *Kitab al-farq.*

[43] Many of the works of the Fulani reformers quoted here are extant in Ghana, and copies are preserved in the Arabic collection at the Institute of African Studies, University of Ghana. It is not possible, however, to say at which date such works came into the hands of the Ghana *'ulama.*

[44] Dupuis, 1824, p. l.   [45] Dupuis, 1824, p. xxxiii n.

[46] See, e.g., M. Hiskett, 'An Islamic tradition of reform in the Western Sudan from the sixteenth to the eighteenth century,' *BSOAS*, vol. XXV, no. 3, 1962. This failure is what J. S. Trimingham has described as the 'Islamic stagnation and pagan reaction' of the seventeenth and eighteenth centuries, *A History of Islam in West Africa*, 1962, ch. 4.

worship by dint of arms; for the existing governments in the vicinity of the great inland waters [i.e. the Niger] are supine, and devoid of that energy which distinguished the career of the Arabs;

(ii) that, but for this,

every nation down to the sea coast itself, would have been converted to the service of Allah, long ere this, and the Koran would have been known throughout Africa; whereas now the idolators are strong in the south;[47]

(iii) and that consequently the Muslims of Ashanti have been obliged

to espouse the court politics in public life,

and even,

in wars religiously deplored, . . . compelled to fight in the ranks of the heathens, against their brethren in faith.[48]

Although, as we shall see, Shaikh Baba did effect a limited and revocable sort of *hijra* in 1818, in general the Kumasi Muslims would seem to have been too deeply involved in Ashanti affairs to be able to regard the pronouncements of the reformers as indicative of any practicable course of action.

IV. MUSLIM INVOLVEMENT IN ASHANTI AFFAIRS

The Kumasi Muslim community, numerically small, nevertheless wielded considerable economic power, having a complete monopoly in certain spheres, e.g. the cattle industry,[49] and controlling a large sector of the distributive trade. The Ashanti king, concerned to curb the growth of a native Ashanti merchant capitalist class—which he saw as a potential force of revolution[50] —did much to encourage foreign traders to Kumasi by his liberal economic policies:

If they come from another country to trade in Coomassy, they make friends, and give me a present; then to be sure, I cannot tell them to give me gold, when they buy and sell the goods. Besides, some traders are kings' sons and brothers, and great captains: I must not say to them, give me gold, but I must give them gold and provisions, and send them home happy and

[47] Dupuis, 1824, p. L.
[49] Hutton, 1821, p. 330.
[48] Ibid., pp. xxxiii n. and 241 n.
[50] See, e.g., Bowdich, 1819, pp. 335–6.

rich, that it may be known in other countries that I am a great king, and know what is right.[51]

In this way Muslim traders came to control the distribution, by the great trade routes leading north-west to Segu and Jenne and beyond, and north-east to Hausaland and beyond, of the primary products of Ashanti and its provinces, of its gold, kola, slaves, and salt. Where the Ashanti was unable to venture 'unless under the escort and protection of the Moslem',[52] the Muslim could travel with every facility:

> On the journey from Coomassy to Haoussa, he seldom disbursed a mitskal of gold or cowrees (the value of ten shillings) but, on the contrary, is frequently a gainer by the generosity of princes, and his daily wants are moreover liberally supplied at their expense, and oftentimes with unbounded hospitality.[53]

The participation of the Kumasi Muslims in the economic life of Ashanti led, since commerce was closely controlled by the State, to their participation in affairs of government. Thus Bowdich wrote of

> The Moorish chiefs and dignitaries by whom the King is surrounded, whose influence is powerful, not only from their rank but their repute.[54]

Dupuis similarly noted that

> The character of true believers ... stood very high with the king, for he consulted them upon many important occasions, where the interests of the nation were concerned,[55]

and Hutton observed that Muslims exercise 'the greatest influence at Ashantee'.[56]

[51] Osei Tutu Kwame, reported by Dupuis, 1824, p. 167.
[52] Dupuis, 1824, p. xc.
[53] Ibid., p. cx. Ashanti Muslim traders also spread their activities, on a more limited scale, southwards to the coast. See, e.g., PRO, CO 267/44, Report by Commodore Sir James Yeo of the Africa Squadron, dated 7 November 1816: 'Whilst we were at Cape Coast Castle I saw several of the Ashantees, they appeared shrewd, active and intelligent, not the least appearance of the common negro countenance but very much resembling the Moors and many of them wore turbans. Two of them said they had seen Whiteman in the back country, meaning no doubt the shores of the Mediterranean or Red Sea.' See also Dupuis, 1824, pp. 10–11.   [54] Bowdich, 1819, p. 53.   [55] Dupuis, 1824, p. 98.
[56] Hutton, 1821, p. 323. English awareness of the importance of Muslims in Ashanti appears to date from the time of the meeting at Anomabu on the coast in 1807 between Governor Torrane and Osei Tutu Kwame. 'The king,' noted

A number of the leading Muslims, including Shaikh Baba, Muhammad Kamaʿatay, and Abu Bakr Turay,

enjoyed rank at court, or were invested with administrative powers, entitling them even to a voice in the senate.[57]

Baba described himself as 'a favoured servant' of the king and as 'a member of the king's council in affairs relating to the believers of Sarem and Dagomba,'[58] and he and his associates certainly played an important role in the negotiating of the Anglo-Ashanti Treaty of 1820.[59] The vetting of visitors to the Court was another of their functions: Huydecoper, Bowdich, and Dupuis were all required to testify on the Quran to their goodwill towards the king.[60]

The king's desire to establish an Arabic chancery, remarked on by Bowdich,[61] also brought Muslims into his service and led him to send members of his household to Shaikh Baba's school.[62] The Gyaasewahene, head of the Ashanti bureaucracy, employed a Muslim secretary (formerly of Oyo) to keep records of political events,[63] and court proceedings were reported in Arabic.[64] Muslims were apparently responsible for keeping records of casualties in war,[65] and also served on the staffs of Ashanti commissioners in the outlying provinces of the empire.[66] Diplomatic relations between Ashanti and northern Muslim states were probably largely conducted by the Muslims. There

---

Torrane, 'is attended with many Moors . . . in fact the Moors seem to have spread over the whole interior of Africa' (*Report from the Committee on African Forts*, 1817, letter from Torrane to the Company of Merchants dated 9 October 1807).

[57] Dupuis, 1824, p. 95. See also Bowdich, 1819, pp. 49 and 146.

[58] Dupuis, 1824, p. 97. [59] Ibid., pp. 147, 152, and 158.

[60] Huydecoper's Diary, 22 April 1817; Bowdich, 1819, p. 56; Dupuis, 1824, pp. 72–3 and 179.

[61] Bowdich, 1819, p. 232; Lee, 1835, p. 174.

[62] Dupuis, 1824, p. 107. The king was also anxious to send pupils to the English school in Cape Coast, but was thwarted in this by his own chiefs, see Hutchison's dispatch from Kumasi dated 3 February 1818, in Bowdich, 1820. It is of interest that the English school in Cape Coast at this period had the same number of pupils as the Arabic school in Kumasi, see *Royal Gazette and Sierra Leone Advertiser*, IV, 209, 1 June 1822; Dupuis, 1824, p. 97.

[63] Bowdich, 1819, p. 296. [64] Lee, 1835, p. 164.

[65] G. A. Robertson, *Notes on Africa*, 1819, p. 151.

[66] Thus, the staff of Owusu Dome, Commissioner for Cape Coast in 1820, included two Muslims from Kumasi, see Hutton, 1821, p. 324.

was an ambassador from 'Malabar' in Kumasi in 1816[67] and evidence of communications around 1823 with 'a Mahommedan Priest of Tillibo'—probably the *almami* of Timbo in Futa Jallon—who,

> though not a Prince, has considerable influence over many strong and warlike tribes in the East, both Mahommedans and pagans; so that he is considered for his wisdom as a sort of oracle.[68]

Diplomatic correspondence may have been at times conducted in Arabic, as one leading member of the Kumasi community, 'Abdallah ibn 'Ata Suma, suggests:

> Praise be to God, who created the pen for use as speech, and who made paper that we may send it, in place of ambassadors, from country to country and place to place.[69]

Reindorf refers to Arabic treaties between Ashanti and both Dagomba and Gyaman.[70]

Military service was required of the Kumasi Muslims; indeed, it was observed that the king 'never engaged in any warlike enterprise without their society',[71] a matter creating, as we have noted, moral difficulties for them. In the capacity of *qa'id*, the head of the Kumasi Muslims had to lead the believers of metropolitan Ashanti to war. One of Shaikh Baba's predecessors in office 'excited some curiosity and attention' among the Christians who witnessed the arrival of the Ashanti armies on the Gold Coast in 1807:

> He was a tall, athletic, and rather corpulent man, of a complexion resembling an Arab, or an Egyptian. . . . He was a follower of the Mohammedan religion, possessed much gravity; but was communicative, condescending,

---

[67] Huydecoper's Diary, 16 June and 18 September, 1816. The exact sense of 'Malabar', or 'Mallowa' as Dupuis has it, is unclear. It is the same as the 'Murawa' of al-Hamadhani (A.D. 903), and, in an early-nineteenth-century context, seems to refer to the more westerly provinces of the caliphate of Sokoto.

[68] *Royal Gazette and Sierra Leone Advertiser*, VI, 319, 10 July 1824.

[69] Arabic text in Dupuis, 1824, p. vii. Translation revised. See also p. 163 below.

[70] C. C. Reindorf, *History of the Gold Coast and Asante*, 1895, pp. 140 and 174. Later in the century the British used Arabic for correspondence with Ashanti, but around 1820 they had few qualified Arabists; they contented themselves with sending Arabic translations of the Bible to Kumasi, see H. J. Ricketts, *Narrative of the Ashantee War*, 1831, p. 142.

[71] Dupuis, 1824, p. 98.

and agreeable. . . . He was native of Kassina, a country that appears to be situated to the South of East of Tombuctou. He said, he had been at Tunis, and at Mecca; had seen many white men and ships; and described the method of travelling over the great desert. This person commanded a body of men, who fought with arrows, as well as muskets; . . . He had many persons in his train, who were of the same colour, but varied a little as to dress.[72]

Shaikh Baba likewise, at the launching of the Ashanti invasion of Gyaman in 1818, found himself in command of seven thousand Muslim fighting men.[73] The king also kept a personal bodyguard which would seem to have been drawn from Muslim Malinke cavalry whose fighting qualities were highly respected by the Ashanti.[74]

V. THE MUSLIM IMPACT ON ASHANTI SOCIETY

In virtue of their important rôles in commerce and government—as 'traders and courtiers' as Dupuis has it[75]—the Kumasi Muslims also came to exercise considerable influence over the social and religious life of the capital. Bowdich, for example, was able to remark:

although the Moorish dignitaries are not yet so omnipotent as to abolish human sacrifices, yet they are certainly powerful enough, from the superstitious veneration they have excited, to prevent this becoming more frequent or more extensive. . . .[76]

The king extended his protection 'to Talbs or priests of all nations, but more especially those who came from Egypt, or any part of the Holy Land'; even prisoners taken in war,

if Moslems, were never put to death, like infidels; on the contrary, they were well used, and generally transferred to the eastern division of the Volta.[77]

Thus the king was, for the Muslims, 'a friend on whom they could always rely for protection'.[78] Proselytization was permitted, and

---

[72] H. Meredith, *An Account of the Gold Coast of Africa*, 1812, pp. 157–8.

[73] Dupuis, 1824, p. xxxviii. These were drawn, presumably, from Kumasi and the other large towns of central Ashanti. Muslim communities in the provinces were under their own *amirs*, for example those of the north-west, estimated at 80,000, who were governed, on behalf of the king, by the 'bashaw' of Kherabi, see Dupuis, 1824, p. cviii.

[74] For the basis of this view, see: Bowdich, 1821 (*b*), p. 52: Dupuis 1824, pp. 124 n. and xxxvii.   [75] Dupuis, 1824, p. cxxix n.

[76] Bowdich, 1821 (*c*), p. 19.   [77] Dupuis, 1824, p. 99 n.   [78] Ibid., p. 97.

every believer gained merit by adopting infidels into his house-hold—each according to his means—and bringing them up in the faith.[79]

While only a limited number of conversions were achieved through such orthodox educational processes, Islam nevertheless made an impact upon all levels of Ashanti society in its magical aspects, *ruqya*. The production of protective amulets[80] was a highly organized (and lucrative) affair:

> When a charm was applied for, one of the oldest [of the *talaba*] wrote the body of it, and gave it Baba, who added a sort of cabalistic mark, and gave it a mysterious fold; the credulous native snatched it eagerly as it was held out to him, paid the gold, and hurried away to enclose it in the richest case he could afford.[81]

Such amulets were especially valued for the protection they afforded the soldier, and Torrane noted of the forces on the coast in 1807, that

> every Ashantee man has a gregory, or fetish, which is a little square cloth, inclosing some sentences of the Alcoran: some have many.[82]

A six-line amulet might cost almost half an ounce of gold (some-what under £2), so that 'a sheet of paper would support an in-ferior Moor in Coomassie for a month'.[83] For a complete amulet-covered war coat the king was known to have paid the value of thirty slaves,[84] and

> a few lines written by Baba [commented Hutton] is believed to possess the power of turning aside the balls of the enemy in battle, and is purchased at an enormous price; writing paper is consequently very valuable at Ashantee.[85]

Arising from their confidence in the efficacy of Islamic magic, the Ashantis became 'by no means tenacious of their pagan doctrines.'[86] Thus, value came to be placed upon prayer:

[79] Dupuis, 1824, pp. 98, 107, and 163.
[80] The Twi terms for such amulets, *safe* or *sebe*, are both borrowings from the Mande, and perhaps ultimately from Arabic.
[81] Bowdich, 1819, p. 90. See also Dupuis, 1824, p. xi.
[82] Torrane, letter of 9 October 1807 cited above.
[83] Bowdich, 1819, p. 272.   [84] Ibid., p. 271.
[85] Hutton, 1821, p. 323.   [86] Bowdich, 1821 (*b*), p. 24.

The Ashantees believe that the constant prayers of the Moors . . . invigorate themselves, and gradually waste the spirit and strength of their enemies. Their faith is no less impulsive than that which achieved the Arabian conquest.[87]

And similarly on the Quran:

The Ashantees without knowing the content of the Koran, are equally persuaded that it is a volume of divine creation, and consequently that it contains ordinances and prohibitions, which are most congenial to the happiness of mankind in general.[88]

The matter was summed up, curiously yet revealingly, by Shaikh Baba: 'The king, and all his idolatrous subjects believed in it [the Quran] too.'[89]

In court circles Islamic influences were especially noticeable: side by side with the traditional state cults, that of Islam was being introduced. Thus, for example, the ritual preparations in late 1817 for the projected invasion of Gyaman included both pagan and Muslim observances:

2 November, 1817:

The king has been busy for the last twelve days making fetish, etc. for the success of the war; the Moors going every morning to the palace for prayer and sacrifice.

8 November 1817:

The king has been making human sacrifices for the success of the war, at Bantama, Assafoo, and Aduma, in the evenings and the Moors make their offerings of sheep in the palace according to the Moslem ritual.[90]

Muslim diviners were employed by the king, and it was thought possible to win the intercession of the Prophet Muhammad in the interests of Ashanti. The Sharif Ibrahim left Kumasi for Mecca in 1818,

entrusted with offering to the *manes* of the Prophet special gifts which the king and the chiefs had given him.[91]

---

[87] Bowdich, 1819, p. 272.   [88] Dupuis, 1824, p. 247 n.   [89] Ibid, p. 180.
[90] Hutchison, in Bowdich, 1819, pp. 393–4. 'The friends of humanity,' added Hutchison, 'will rejoice that the King favours the Moors, as many lives have been saved that would otherwise have been destroyed at the present crisis.'
[91] Ainé, op. cit., p. 27. R. S. Rattray, *Ashanti*, 1923, p. 227 n., also reports this.

In the overt behaviour of the king himself there were signs of his leanings towards Islam, in, for example, his use on some occasions of Muslim greetings,[92] in the Quranic charms hanging around his bed-chamber,[93] and in his public appearance from time to time in a cloth 'studded all over with Arabic writing in various coloured inks'.[94] Fortunately his own views in this matter are on record.

> I know [he is reported as saying] that book (the Koran) is strong, and I like it because it is the book of the great God; it does good for me, and therefore I love all the people that read it.[95]

Whereupon, Dupuis adds:

> The Moslems instantly prostrated themselves, and prayed aloud: the king too extended his arms, looking upwards as if to receive a blessing.

The king also developed his position in a reported exchange with his senior spokesman, Adusei.

> What have you to fear? [asked Adusei.] The great God of the Moslems, who is the same as the white men worship, is your guardian. He defends your dominions on the land side, where the believers live; and he protects you on the sea coast, for he gives you a great name in the land of white men, and turns their king's heart to do you good. 'Yes,' answered the sovereign, spreading out his hands and looking up towards heaven, as the Moslems do in prayer, 'I am a thankful slave of the God of all gods and men—I am not ungrateful, I am not proud and ignorant. . . .'[96]

and went on to agree in attributing the successes of his reign to God's espousal of the Ashanti cause. It was in his role of a humble servant of God that the king took possession of Sharif Ibrahim's Quran. Hutchison ruefully notes that Ibrahim:

> had a beautiful copy of the Koran which he intended to leave me, but the king had told him he must have it, that when any trouble came he might hold it up to God, and beg his mercy and pardon.[97]

The king's syncretizing tendencies—his readiness to recognize the God of Islam not as the only God but at least as the greatest of all gods—were well summarized by Dupuis:

[92] Dupuis, 1824, p, 109.
[93] Bowdich, 1819, p. 308.
[94] Dupuis, 1824, p. 142.
[95] Ibid., p. 161; see also p. 163.
[96] Ibid., p. 243.
[97] Hutchison, in Bowdich, 1819, p. 308.

That monarch is somewhat religiously inclined towards the followers of Mohammad, from a reverential awe of the universal God. . . . Notwithstanding this sovereign chooses to adhere faithfully to his Pagan rites in all their manifold horrors and enormities, he does not neglect to supplicate the Moslems for their prayers, particularly when oppressed with anxiety, when the state council is convened on business of emergency, or when the national priests or necromancers are unable to solve any problem to the satisfaction of majesty.[98]

The king's attitude was regarded by the Kumasi Muslims as conferring some merit upon him. Since he 'would sometimes give ear to the law (of Mohammed)', he was to be considered, although a 'misguided infidel', nevertheless,

superior by far, to many other sovereigns, and particularly to the king of Dahomey, his eastern neighbour, who was an infidel of infidels (Kaffar ben al Koufar).[99]

VI. THE KUMASI MUSLIMS: PROSPECTS

The great West African Muslim reformers of the early nineteenth century, preoccupied with their vision of establishing there a true *Caliphate* with a central imamate exercising authority based on the Quran, the Custom (*Sunna*), and the Law (*Shari'a*,) would no doubt have regarded the Kumasi Muslim community as in a state of virtual apostasy, and the Kumasi *'ulama* as *'ulama al-su'i*, venal malams.[100] To Shaikh Baba and his associates in Kumasi, on the other hand, the views of the *mujaddidin*, the reformers, must have appeared doctrinaire in the extreme, and of doubtful relevance to their position. For, as Baba saw it, 'the Prophet's cause was not neglected in these regions of ignorance',[101] and the possibility of the Ashanti king's conversion to Islam was ever present. Only twenty years earlier the king's kinsman and forerunner on the throne, Osei Kwame (1777–c.1801), had been 'a believer at heart', so Baba maintained, and because of his general 'attachment to the Moslems' had been dethroned by his chiefs on three specific grounds:

(a) 'the Moslem religion, which they well knew levels all ranks and orders of men, and places them at the arbitrary discretion of the sovereign, might be introduced';

[98] Dupuis, 1824, pp. x-xi.
[99] Ibid., pp. 97–98.
[100] For the 'venal malams', see Hiskett, op. cit.
[101] Dupuis, 1824, p. 97.

(*b*) the king's 'inclination to establish the Korannic law for the civil code of the empire',[102] and

(*c*) his prohibition of 'many festivals at which it was usual to spill the blood of victims devoted to the customs'.[103]

Furthermore, the dethronement provoked revolts in Osei Kwame's favour in the more Islamized parts of the Ashanti empire, which, although lacking the character of *jihad*, nevertheless took several years to put down.[104]

To the Kumasi Muslims around 1820, then, there appeared good reason to believe that internal forces within Ashanti were working in their favour. Externally, the *jihad* initiated by 'Uthman dan Fodio had extended the reformist power almost to the north-eastern limits of Ashanti dominion in Dagomba, while to the north-west Shehu Ahmadu of Massina was preparing the way for the overthrow of the pagan Bambara kingdom of Segu. And, underlying all, by their presence in Kumasi the Muslim traders were playing a vital role in the distribution of commodities to the northern Muslim powers essential for their continued expansion: gold, slaves, and gunpowder.[105] In such circumstances the insistence of the reformers upon withdrawal (*hijra*) from the land of the heathen, and upon even the cessation of trade, must have seemed quite unrealistic.

Nevertheless, the Kumasi Muslims were impelled to one act of protest, a limited sort of *hijra*, on the issue of being required to fight in the Ashanti armies. In 1818 Shaikh Baba, at the head of seven thousand Muslims, took his place with the king in the invasion of Gyaman to the north-west. Finding the Ashanti armies opposed by Muslim forces not only from Bonduku, the Gyaman capital, but also from Kong and western Gonja, Baba withdrew his troops and returned to Kumasi. The Ashanti king

[102] For the part that the introduction of Muslim law might play in the early stages of transition to Islam, see for comparison Mungo Park, *Travels in the Interior Districts of Africa*, 1799, pp. 15–21.

[103] See Dupuis, 1824, p. 245. For independent evidence of the king's conversion, see J. Gros, *Voyages, Aventures et Captivité de J. Bonnat chez les Achantis*, Paris, 1884, p. 169.

[104] For these revolts see I. Wilks, *The Northern Factor in Ashanti History* 1961, pp. 22–25.

[105] Note the problems presented to Muhammad 'Ali in Egypt by his shortages in gold and slaves.

subsequently 'swore that had he not been a holy man, he would have put him to death', but Baba, arguing that he could not have acted 'so contrary to the tenets of his religion,' asked:

> What would it have booted him in the world to come, had it pleased God to have him destroyed in the ranks of the infidels, when he was not fighting for the faith, but against it?[106]

Hutton (early in 1820) observed that 'it was a long time before the king would be friends with him', and maintained that as a result of Shaikh Baba's action,

> The Moors [who] have hitherto exercised the greatest influence at Ashantee . . . do not still possess this influence to so great an extent as they formerly did.[107]

Unfortunately, with the departure of Dupuis from Kumasi in March 1820, our sources come to an end, and not until half a century later does it become possible to form once more a clear picture of the position of the Muslims in Kumasi. By 1870 one significant development had occurred: an *imam al-bilad*, or personal *imam* to the king, had been appointed,[108] a position distinct from that of the *imam al-jum'a* who presided—as Shaikh Baba had done—over the Friday prayer and whose responsibility was to the Kumasi Muslim community as a whole. Otherwise little change in the relations of the Muslims to the court, on the one hand, or to the populace, on the other, seems to have occurred between 1820 and 1870. It is arguable that the failure of the Muslims to advance their cause was in part at least a consequence of the application of reformist doctrines to their position as residents in *dar al-harb*, the land of the enemy.[109]

POSTCRIPT

Since the above paper was written, Mr. N. Levtzion has been able to examine the *Cod. Arab. CCCII* manuscripts in the Royal

[106] For this episode, see Dupuis, p. 98.

[107] Hutton, 1821, pp. 323–4.

[108] The new imamate was vested in a Wangara group from Daboya in central Gonja, and has so far passed from father to son. By contrast, the older imamate is not vested in any particular group.

[109] I wish to acknowledge the assistance of my colleague, Mr. P. C. Gibbons, in the preparation of this paper.

Library, Copenhagen, and has found that these include early nineteenth-century correspondence between Kumasi and its northern provinces. There can be no doubt that the court of Kumasi maintained constant written communication with the northern chiefs and *imams*: the dozen or so letters that survive are concerned largely with the affairs of Osei Bonsu, 'the honest king, the saviour of the Muslims'. These letters also supply further biographical detail on the leading members of the Kumasi Muslim community: Baba himself, for example, was a son of the *Imam* of Gambaga, and Muhammad Kamaʿatay son or nephew of the *Imam* of Gonja. Mr. Levtzion's report on these MSS. appears in the *Transactions of the Historical Society of Ghana*, Vol. VIII, 1965.

REFERENCES

PRINCIPAL PRIMARY SOURCES QUOTED

I. Christian

(a) *W. Huydecoper*

Of Dutch-Fanti extraction, Huydecoper stayed in Kumasi from May 1816 to April, 1817 as representative of the Dutch governor, General Daendels. The nature of Dutch interest in the Muslims of the interior is revealed in Daendels' Instructions to Huydecoper, State Archives, The Hague: papers of the Dutch Possessions on the Coast of Guinea, 349—Instructions dated 25 April 1816:

> *Article 23.* That trade will not be confined to the Kingdom of Ashantee, but that the Ashantee caravans would carry European goods over the great Kong mountain-range, and replace the caravans of the Moors, who now take merchandise more than a thousand hours through sandy deserts on camels and horses.

> *Article 24.* The General has himself constructed in Asia a road 60 feet broad at least, which was 260 hours in length: thus with the help of the King of Ashanti he could very easily build good roads to Kachna, Tombuctou, and Houssa, and let the King ride in carriages as comfortable as the safest beds.

Huydecoper lacked the vision of his superior, and his *Journal of a Visit to Kumasi* is of limited interest. It is in the same series as the instructions cited above, and I have used a provisional translation prepared by Professor G. W. Irwin.

(b) *T. E. Bowdich*

Bowdich was in Kumasi from May to September 1817, where he superseded F. James as Conductor of the Mission sponsored by the African Company. By a commission of 19 April 1817 the mission was instructed, *inter alia*, to find out, of what nation are the Moors that frequent the Ashantee country, and for what purpose do they go there?

Bowdich, who considered the Muslims hostile to the objects of the mission, nevertheless established friendly relations with them, and his information is of great interest. The following works have been cited:

(1819) *Mission from Cape Coast Castle to Ashantee*, London.
(1820) *A Reply to the Quarterly Review*, Paris.
(1821(a)) *Essay on the Geography of North-western Africa*, Paris.
(1821(b)) *An Essay on the Superstitions, Customs and Arts common to the Ancient Egyptians, Abyssinians, and Ashantees*, Paris.
(1821(c)) *British and Foreign Expeditions to Teembo*, Paris.

In addition Bowdich's widow used his notes in:

R. Lee: *Stories of Strange Lands*, London, 1835.

(c) *W. Hutchison*

A member of the James–Bowdich mission, who remained in Kumasi as Resident untíl February 1818. He developed a close association with the Muslims, and was learning Arabic from them. His complete diary has not been located, but a section of it forms chapter XII of Bowdich's *Mission*, 1819.

(d) *J. Dupuis*

Dupuis was appointed British Consul for Ashanti in 1818, but was resident in Kumasi only in February and March 1820. In his Instructions it was observed:

. . . his royal highness the Prince Regent has been pleased to appoint you (your long residence at Mogadore, and acquaintance with the Moorish language peculiarly qualifying you for the situation), to be His Majesty's Consul at Coomassie.

Through his command of Arabic he established very close relations with the Kumasi Muslims, and his sympathy with Islam is apparent in his writings. Indeed, he was accepted in Kumasi as a believer, and 'for political reasons', he writes, he did not undeceive them, but 'thought it proper to return evasive answers'. His evidence is of the utmost value, and is cited from:

Journal of a Residence in Ashantee, London, 1824.

(e) *W. Hutton*

Hutton was a member of Dupuis' mission. In contrast with Dupuis, Hutton was strongly anti-Muslim:

I have always had a bad opinion of their character, which my late acquaintance with them at Ashantee has not at all tended to remove.

Because of its plagiarism his work is of little independent value:

Voyage to Africa, London, 1821.

II. Muslim

(a) *'Uthman dan Fodio*
1. *Wathiqat ahl al-sudan, wa man sha' Allah min al-ikhwan*, 'Dispatch to the folk of the Sudan and to whomso Allah wills among the brethren.' See

text, translation, and notes by A. D. H. Bivar in *Journal of African History*, vol. II, no. 2, 1961.

2. *Kitab al-farq bayn wilayat ahl al-Islam wa bayn wilayat ahl al-kufr*, 'The book of the difference between the Governments of the Muslims and the Governments of the Unbelievers.' See text, translations, and notes by M. Hiskett in *BSOAS*, vol. XXIII, no. 3, 1960.

3. *Tanbih al-ikhwan*, 'Advice to the Brethren', translated by H. R. Palmer in *Journal of the African Society*, vol. XIII, 1913–14, and vol. XIV, 1914–15.

(b) *Muhammad Bello*

Infaq al-maysur, part-translation in E. J. Arnett, *The Rise of the Sokoto Fulani* Kano, n.d.

V. LAT-DYOR, DAMEL OF KAYOR (1842–86) AND THE ISLAMIZATION OF THE WOLOF OF SENEGAL

VINCENT MONTEIL

The history of Lat-Dyor, *Damel* (King) of Kayor (1842–86), who was converted to Islam in 1864, demonstrates the factors which have determined the introduction and acceptance of Islam in Senegal, as well as the effects of Islamization on economic and political values and on the social structure. It throws light on the problem of contacts between Muslims and non-Muslims; it illustrates the confrontation between Islam and colonialism at the end of the nineteenth century; it shows the dialectical relationship between Islam and nationalism.

I. THE HISTORICAL BACKGROUND IN KAYOR

Kayor is a province of Senegal, 200 kilometres from south-west to north-east and 120 kilometres from north to south. Its inhabitants, almost all Wolof, are called *Aadyor* (the word *dyor* meaning the dry, red plain). Its history is known largely through oral tradition, which has remained remarkably unchanged over the last century: the chronology given by Yoro Dyao in the *Moniteur du Sénégal* in 1864 was recited to me, almost word for word, by the *griot* El-Hadj Assane Marokhaya 'Samb' at Dakar in 1963.

According to these traditions, Kayor was tributary to the Dyolof (Jolof) Empire from the thirteenth to the sixteenth centuries when it gained its independence. Some thirty rulers (*Damel*) reigned from then until the end of the nineteenth century. The *Damel* was selected by a college of 'grand electors', from within one chosen matrilineage (*kheet* or *meen*): there were thus seven royal families (*garmi*), of which the most important was that of the *Geedy*. The *Damel* used his mother's name after his own first name and then the 'honorific' (*sant*) of his father (thus:

Lat-Dyor Ngone-Latir Dyop). Since the sixteenth century traces of Muslim influence have intermingled with 'animist' beliefs and practices. A Moorish marabout introduced the 'ritual washing' which marks the enthronement of a *Damel*, alongside the 'fetishist' retreat to a sacred grove (sixteenth century). The site of the capital, Mbul, was chosen by reference to a talisman devised by a marabout. In the seventeenth century, the Aadyor went to greet their king (a non-Muslim), on the day of the Muslim feast of the Sacrifices (*Tabaski*). Increasing numbers of religious personages, more or less literate—marabouts or *sériny*—filtered in from Fouta and Mali. At the end of the seventeenth century, the Muslims of Kayor rebelled at the instigation of their *qadi*. They did so again a century later, and the *Damel* sold them as slaves and won a victory over the Almamy (*Imam*) of Fouta, who wanted to wage a holy war (*jihad*) in Kayor (1790). By the beginning of the nineteenth century, the *Damels* were consistently opposed to Islam. The explanation of these historical vicissitudes must be sought in the social structure of Kayor.

II. THE SOCIAL STRUCTURE OF KAYOR

The social classes were structured as a pyramid. At the top were the nobles (*garmi*), followed by the *dyaambur*: marabouts and ordinary villagers. All were free men (*geer*). After them came members of castes (*nyenyoo*) and, at the very bottom of the scale, slaves (*dyaam*).

The *Damel* was above all (like the *Mansa* of Mali) a formidable magician. His close matrilineal relatives bore (as among all Wolof) the title *linger* and it was through them that the royal blood was transmitted. Among the courtiers (*dag*) and dignitaries (*kangam*) the Chief of the Slaves of the Crown, the *Farba*, was pre-eminent.

The *Dyaambur* were free men, the majority of them villagers (*baadolo*) whose life, as proverbs show, revolved around the three agricultural activities: sowing, harvesting, eating. Their villages often had a marabout as chief, who was at the same time a 'settler' farmer. Like the monks of medieval Europe, the marabout of Senegal was a great clearer of new land. Since 1876 the so-called Dyambour Province has been composed exclusively of Muslim farmers. These marabouts entered the councils of the non-Muslim rulers, where they played a triple role as arbiter, healer and secretary: thanks to them Wolof was written down in Arabic script. As for the *Damels*, they were concerned to have on their side the marabouts' prestige and 'charisma' (*baraka*).

The *nyenoo* were members of castes (hereditary, endogamous professional hierarchies)—metalworkers, woodcarvers, leather-workers, tailors. One caste, the griots (*gêwel*)—undoubtedly from the Moorish *iggiò*—served as 'keepers of tradition' to the great and standard-bearers in combat. The base of the social pyramid in Kayor was, as elsewhere, made up of slaves (*dyaam*): captives bought in the market-place, slaves by birth or prisoners of war. In 1825 'household captives' accounted for 12,300 of the 16,000 inhabitants of Saint-Louis and Gorée. This category was in general well treated. In 1880 a horse was worth two captives; slaves 'took the place of money'. Slaves who belonged to the State were called the 'Slaves of the Crown' (*dyaam-u Buur-i*). Those belonging to the *Geedy* lineage were numerous enough to live in sixteen villages: these were the *Dyaam-Geedy-i*, who made and unmade *Damels*, won and lost battles, and controlled the exercise of power. They constituted the stable element in Kayor politics and did not, in the main, revolt.

It was from amongst the Slaves of the Crown that the warriors (*tyeddo*) were recruited: drunkards and pillagers whose exactions were undoubtedly a cause of the 'Marabout Wars' at the end of the seventeenth century. There were several thousand of them and they left behind them a great reputation for bravery. They were all-powerful because, although they belonged to the *Damel*, in reality the *Damel* belonged to them.

III. THE LIFE AND LEGEND OF LAT-DYOR

Lat-Dyor is a national hero in Senegal today, where the majority of the population is Muslim. The stages in his career are well known. He was a noble (*garmi*), of a *Geedy* mother and a *Dyop* father. As such, he was a claimant to the crown of Kayor. He was born, about 1842, in a non-Muslim environment (with historical 'traces' of Islamization) and the Slaves of the Crown attached to the *Geedy* branch (*Dyaam-Geedy-i*) chose him as their candidate for the throne. At the age of 19 he asked to be 'made adult' (*mag*), that is, to be circumcised—not in the Muslim fashion but according to the traditional 'fetishist' rite. He managed to supplant the reigning *Damel* (1862), but was forced to spend four years in exile in Saloum (1864–8). At this time he was converted to Islam by the Toucouleur marabout Ma-Ba Dyakhou, then ruler of Saloum, who made Lat-Dyor his main lieutenant. After the death of Ma-Ba, in the battle of Somb (1867), Lat-Dyor had no option but to make his 'submission' to the French—who sent an expeditionary column against him. As, in the end, his return to power appeared to be a guarantee of peace, Lat-Dyor once again became *Damel* of Kayor, from 1871 to 1882. In 1875, he allied himself with the French to defeat the marabout of Fouta, Amadou Sekou, and, in 1877, he extended his rule also over Baol whose king he had conquered. But, in 1882, he opposed the Dakar–Saint-Louis railway and had to flee. He was killed on 26 October 1886 at Dyaqlé by French troops.

An examination of the Senegalese archives shows that Lat-Dyor, *Damel* of Kayor, came into conflict with the social structure of his kingdom because of the contradictions raised, for his household slaves and the Slaves of the Crown, by his new behaviour as an 'oriental' Islamized monarch, that is, the representative of an egalitarian theocracy. His captives and concubines ran away. The Slaves of the Crown from 1879 onwards wanted to depose him and replace him with his nephew, Samba Laobé. The *Damel* ruined their chief, the powerful Demba-Waar—who was later to cause his own downfall. He was accused by his nobles of 'maltreating the chiefs, holding to ransom foreigners, the poor, herdsmen, farmers, bringing about the depopulation of the villages'. In fact, when he became a Muslim, he continued to let the *Tyeddo* pillage at will, even though his conversion ought to have guaranteed theirs. On the other hand, he considered himself to have the powers of an absolute despot and refused to make use of the traditional councils.

The railway affair, from 1877, is a good example of the conflict between, on the one side, Islam and nationalism, and, on the other, colonialism. The line from Dakar to Saint-Louis, crossing Kayor (which was to be opened in 1885) would allow the French to control the trade in groundnuts, to protect commerce, to establish their occupation of the territory, to intervene quickly everywhere. Lat-Dyor immediately understood that this was the end of his independence. His correspondence (in Arabic) with the Governor contains no arguments of a religious nature, but only: 'You are taking away my country and stripping me of all I possess.' He hesitated, considered the situation, but finally succumbed, because his fight was an anachronism: it was too late to maintain the old order (the 'established disorder'), but too early for the emancipation of Africa.

The legend of Lat-Dyor, his *'Chanson de geste'* epic poem, handed down by the griots, praises in the Damel the military qualities of a skilful tactician: his tenacity, pride and courage. His death, in oral tradition, is steeped in animist mystique: a talisman rendered him invulnerable (*tul*); it took a golden bullet to kill him. Islam is hardly mentioned in the griots' recitations about this Muslim ruler.

IV. THE ISLAMIZATION OF THE WOLOF

It is generally admitted, perhaps too readily, that Islam in Senegal began among the peoples of the Fleuve Province today called 'Toucouleurs'—a distortion of the ancient *Tekrour*—in the eleventh century. Then the first European travellers (Mosto, in the fifteenth century) testify to the beginning of Islamization in Walo and among the Manding in the south-east. The bulk of the Wolof seem to have remained animist until the middle of the ninteenth century, apart from numerous village marabouts, the Islamized province of Dyambour and the majority of Muslim inhabitants in Saint-Louis. It certainly seems as if the conversion of Lat-Dyor in 1864 triggered the conversion of his people.

In fact, as a dethroned refugee in Saloum, Lat-Dyor had no choice. If he wanted to retrieve his kingdom he had only Ma-Ba Dyakhou, the ruler of Saloum, to rely on. But Ma-Ba was a militant marabout who waged holy war on the infidel. He imposed conditions: Lat-Dyor and his warriors (*tyeddo*) would be converted to Islam. It was thus a conversion of convenience (at the same time, Al-Buri Ndyay, the king of Dyolof, did likewise). However, on his return to Kayor in 1869, the claimant to the throne presented himself as a good Muslim. Once reinstated as *Damel*, he called himself 'Commander of the Faithful'. As a sign of humility, he began to beg in order to feed his soldiers, which, according to custom, earned him the surname of *silmakha* beggar; blind man). If he had nineteen wives and thirty-nine children, this was just the custom then (and still today to some extent) for persons of rank. In his letters to the Governor, he seems preoccupied with respecting at least the letter and the code of Islam. He fought against other Muslims but such practice was then commonplace (El-Hadj Omar in the French Sudan [now Mali] is another example). He was illiterate but dictated in Wolof to his marabout secretaries who transcribed his words in Arabic script. A French and Arabic seal authenticated his letters. He had *qadis*. The first, in 1869, was Momar Anta-Sali, the father of the celebrated Amadou-Bamba Mbaké (1850–1927), founder of the Mouride Brotherhood (which today has nearly a million adepts of both sexes). Later, up until his death in 1886, Lat-Dyor had as *qadi* (*khaali*) Ma-Dyakhaté Kala, a famous man of letters. Lat-Dyor's grandson, whose first name was Amadou-Bamba, swears that on the eve of Dyaqlé (26 October 1886), the *Damel* announced his imminent death, predicting that he would go 'to say the evening prayer (*takkusaan*) with Ma-Ba' (his *sériny* who had been dead since 1867); he said his farewells to the marabout Amadou-Bamba Mbaké, who gave him a robe in which he died. Thus the family tradition has Islamized the griots' animist legend.

Whatever the truth, even if it is not certain that Lat-Dyor on his return to Kayor in 1869 suppressed pillage (*moyal*) and Islamized the villages by persuasion, and even if we cannot be sure that he envisaged a profound social reformation, based on Islam, it remains certain that he influenced part of the group of *tyeddo* by his example and that the villagers, in a natural reaction against the warriors—their oppressors—and the 'great men'— their exploiters—eagerly followed him. The villagers had for a long time had no recourse other than their marabouts. Now that their *Damel* had become Muslim, the development of class conflict accelerated and Islamization, in the social sense, became massive. Today the Wolof—who number more than a million—are almost all Muslim.

VI. ISLAM IN MOSSI SOCIETY

ELLIOTT P. SKINNER

The spread of Islam, like that of any cultural system, is influenced not only by its specific characteristics but also by the conditions it encounters. Islam first appeared in the western Sudan some time in the eighth century and reached its climax there in the fourteenth and fifteenth centuries.[1] During that period many of the rulers and peoples of Ghana, Mali, and Songhay became Muslims, and tried to spread their religion by peaceful means as well as by the sword. Nevertheless, a few Sudanese societies resisted the spread of Islam. Delafosse tells us that

certain populations seem particularly hostile to Islamization, which does not appear to have made any progress among them since the Hegira. It is the case, for example, of the very populous Voltaic family, and of the principal one among these peoples, the Mossi. These latter have been in contact with Muslims very close to ten centuries, they count among them an appreciable number of Mohammedan strangers (the Yarsés), and yet they have remained totally pagan.[2]

Unfortunately, Delafosse did not explain why the Mossi resisted Islam; nor did he report that the Mossi were subjected to *jihads*; that they were proselytized by traders; and subsequently propagandized by refugees. In 1912, when he wrote, the Mossi were still resisting Islam, but subsequently many of them did become Muslims. Today Islam is a growing religion among the Mossi.

Largely because of their strong political organization, the Mossi were able to preserve their ethnic identity and political autonomy throughout all the vicissitudes of Sudanic history.[3] Their society developed in the Upper Volta region as a result of the northward expansion of the Dagomba people of the Gold Coast (modern Ghana), who conquered and partially assimilated

[1] Bovill, 1958, p. 68; Oliver and Fage, 1963, pp. 80 ff.; Trimingham, 1959, pp. 45–6.

[2] Delafosse, 1912, Vol. III, p. 187.

[3] Cf. Marc, 1909, pp. 166–7.

the autochthonous peoples such as the Ninisi, Foulsé, and Habé. The resulting population, the Mossi, developed four important kingdoms and lesser principalities under rulers called *Naba* (pl. *Nanamsé*). All of these rulers, and most of their subordinates in the provinces, districts, and villages, were members of the royal lineage, and were linked by bonds of kinship, ritual, and military power. The important Mossi political units developed complex hierarchical administrative structures which extended the power of the Mogho Naba (king of the world) into the smallest villages and funnelled goods and services back to them.[4]

The village populations in Mossi country during pre-colonial times were divided into noble, commoner, serf, and slave, segmentary patrilineal groups who lived in polygynous, extended family households. The Mossi marriage system was based on the exchange of women between lineages linked by long-term reciprocal relations. However, since the older men were the ones who controlled most of their lineages' resources, they were the ones who obtained most of the wives. The young men either had to wait until their elders died to inherit wives or sought wives (*pughsiudse*) from chiefs against the promise of providing goods and services to their benefactors and giving them their first daughters to serve as future *pughsiudse*.[5] Lineage heads also supervised the economic activities of the people under their charge. These activities included the cultivation of several varieties of millet, sorghum, maize, rice, okra, sweet potatoes, cotton, and indigo; the herding of livestock; and trade, both local and to Timbuktu and the forest zones.[6]

The traditional religion of the Mossi people did not differ too greatly from that of other Sudanese groups. They acknowledged an otiose deity called Winnam, Winde, or Naba Zid'-Winde. Associated with Winnam was a deity called *Tenga*, whose local manifestations and propitiatory agencies were *Tengkouga* (sing. *Tengkougre*) which took the form of clumps of trees, mountains, rocks, or rivers and were served by sprites called *kinkirsé*. Earth priests or *Tengsobadamba* (sing. *Tengsoba*)

[4] Skinner, 1957.   [5] Skinner, 1960a.
[6] Skinner, 1962.

appealed to the *Tengkouga* on behalf of the local populations for help in sickness, for rain and good crops, and for children.

The Mossi had several concepts concerning the spiritual essences or animating principles of man: First of all they believed that there was the *seega* (*pl. seesé*), an entity which left the body during sleep and which if captured and destroyed by sorcerers during its nocturnal wanderings or in places where large crowds congregated, such as the markets, resulted in the death of its owner. Associated with the *seega* was the shadow (*sulensuka*). Persons about to die were believed not to have had shadows, since their *seesé* had either been stolen or had left of their own accord. The Mossi called a dead person *keema* (a person's breath, called *vousem*, was believed to leave the body through the nose when the body died). The connexion between *seega* and *keema* is not clear. Some people said that the *seega* remained about the haunts of human beings; others believed it went to a mountain called Plimpikou and disappeared for ever into a cavern. Still others believed that the *seega* became the *keema* and then went into Plimpikou. If this is the case, then Plimpikou and Keemsé-tenga (land of the ancestors) are the same place.

Mossi beliefs about the *keema* (*keemsé* or ancestors) were more specific, ancestor veneration being the core of their traditional religious system. The ubiquitous and omniscient *keemsé* took a vital interest in their descendants and were believed to punish the wicked with disease and death, and reward the righteous with health, wealth, happiness, and large families. These ancestors were often propitiated by means of the *seesé* of sacrificed animals (animals do not have *keemsé*). Annual sacrifices joined all the Mossi, rulers and subjects alike, in prayers of supplication to the royal ancestors, the sustainers of the group.

The Mossi people first came into contact with Islam when some time between A.D. 1328 and 1333 the Mossi of Yatenga attacked, sacked, and burned Timbuktu. The author of the *Ta'rikh al-Sudan* reported that:

Seized with fright the people of Mali fled and abandoned the city to its assailants. The Mossi ruler entered the city, and after killing all the people he found there and seizing all the goods he could, he burned the city and returned to his own country. Afterwards, the peoples of Mali returned to Timbuktu and remained there for the next hundred years.[7]

The Mossi continued to pursue a rather turbulent and aggressive policy in the region of the Niger bend, attacking Walata and Banku.[8] They were finally defeated and routed by Sunni 'Ali of Songhay in 1477. The tables being turned, the Mossi came under attack from subsequent Songhay rulers. In A.D. 1498 Askia the Great, filled with religious zeal derived from his pilgrimage to Mecca, launched a *jihad* on them because they had rejected his ultimatum to adopt Islam. The Mossi army was beaten and a number of the people were captured, but the rulers continued to resist Islam.[9] The Mossi rulers felt that they had to retain

[7] Sa'di, 1900, pp. 16–17.

[8] Ibid., pp. 45–46; cf. Delafosse, op. cit., vol. II. p. 141.

[9] Sa'di, op. cit., pp. 121–3. In the words of the *Ta'rikh*:

'During the year 903 (August 1497 to August 1498), he [Askia Muhammad] undertook an expedition against Na'asira the king of the Mossi. He took with him the holy *seyyid*, Mour Salih Djaaura, inviting him to give the necessary indications so that the expedition would truly be a holy war made in the name of God. Mour did not refuse this request, and explained to the prince all the rules relating to the holy war. The prince of the faithful, Askia Muhammad, then asked the *seyyid* to be his envoy to the Mossi king. The learned holyman accepted this mission; he went to the country of the Mossi and delivered the letter of his master which called upon the king to embrace Islam. The Mossi ruler declared that he wished first to consult his ancestors who were in the other world before replying. Accompanied by his ministers, he went to the temple of the idol of the country. The learned holyman accompanied them to ascertain how one went about consulting the dead. They began by making the customary offerings; then a very old man appeared. At his appearance everyone prostrated himself and then the king announced the object of his visit. Calling upon the names of the ancestors, the old man said: "I will never agree to this step for you. On the contrary, you must fight until you or they die to the last man."

'Then Na'asira gave his reply to the malam: "Return to your master and tell him that between him and us there will be only war and combat." Remaining alone in the temple with the personage who had shown himself in the form of an old man, the malam questioned him in these terms: "In the name of God Almighty I ask you to declare who you are." "I am Iblis (Satan)," replied the deceiving old man. "I have led them astray in order that they will all die in a state of disbelief."

'Mour returned to prince Askia al-Haj Muhammad and reported all which had transpired. "Now," he added, "your duty is to fight them." Straightaway he launched his war against them killing a number of their men, devastated their fields, plundered their habitations, and took their children into captivity. All of these, men and women, who were taken away as captives, were made the object of divine benediction [converted to Islam]. In all the country, no other expedition except this one had the character of a holy war made in the name of God.'

their ritual connexions with their royal ancestors, without whose help their people would be reduced to suffering and their polities destroyed. The Muslim Songhay did not respect the beliefs of the Mossi rulers and only ceased their *jihads* to convert them to Islam when they in turn were conquered by the Moroccans.

After 1591 Muslims made no further concerted attempt to convert the Mossi people by force. Islam now entered Mossi country by peaceful means, carried by merchants and emigrants from Mandingo cities, such as Timbuktu and Djenne, who sought refuge there. Beginning with Mogho Naba Ouaraga (*c.* 1684), many rulers granted Yarsé refugees permission to enter the country and allowed them to establish Muslim communities. Around 1780 Mogho Naba Kom, the son of Moro Naba Zombre and a Yarsé mother, permitted the Yarsé to live in villages throughout the country. About three subsequent Mogho Nanamsé ignored their ancestral beliefs and even became Muslims. Nevertheless, none of these rulers wished their heirs to adopt Islam.

It was during the reign of Mogho Naba Doulougou, grandson of Mogho Naba Sagha I, that Yarsé proselytizing increased throughout the kingdom of Ouagadougou. Mosques were built in the capital and in villages; many Quranic schools were founded; and Doulougou reportedly was the first Mogho Naba to appoint a Muslim *Imam* to his Court in imitation of his kingly relative, the Gambaga Naba, ruler of the Dagomba. Paradoxically enough, however, Doulougou objected to his eldest son, Sawadogo, being a devout Muslim. The young man persisted in his religion and was ultimately named Mogho Naba. He also encouraged the spread of Islam. Subsequently Mogho Nanamsé reverted to paganism until the reign of Koutou (*c.* 1850–71). This man is credited by Dim Delobson as being the 'only Mogho Naba who was truly a Muslim. . . . He was sent to the Koranic schools at Sagabtenga and is said to have made a creditable record there.'[10] Nevertheless, even Koutou tried to safeguard the royal relationship with the kingly ancestors. 'All [his children] except his eldest son, who succeeded him as Naba Sanum, were sent to

[10] Dim Delobson, 1959, p. 105.

Koranic schools, although none did any serious work there since they were more interested in becoming *naba*.'[11] With Koutou's death, Muslim influence declined and, while learned Muslims continued to serve at Court, they were circumscribed in their ability to propagate their religion. The first Europeans to reach Mossi country reported that the Muslims there were living under many restrictions. For example, they were enjoined by the Mogho Nanamsé not to recite their prayers in public places.[12]

[11] Loc. cit.

[12] Tauxier, 1912, pp. 585–6. On the other hand, we do have an excellent report of the celebration of Ramadan at Sagabtenga in Mossi country in 1888 by Binger. He found that, 'Moslem or not, all the blacks celebrate this feast.' His description of this festival and the role played in it by Boukary Koutou, the future Mogho Naba Wobogo of Ouagadougou, is significant for an understanding of Islam in pre-colonial Upper Volta:

'From the start Boukary sent to tell me that he would like me to accompany him to Sakhaboutenga where he is accustomed to go on the day of the festival. During the whole day the entourage of the chief occupy themselves with preparation: they distribute powder, clean guns, try on the harnesses, and polish the copper like they do in France on the eve of a great review. . . . It is an occason for them to revel, and they do not allow it to pass. They eat as much as they can, drink a great deal of beer, and shoot off many rounds of ammunition. . . .

'In the evening there is a moment of consternation: no one has seen the crescent; however, they console themselves in repeating that, if we do not sight it here, it has certainly shown itself elsewhere, and they sat down to drink beer all night long. . . .

'Monday, June 11: Early this morning Boukary sent a horseman to Saghaboutenga to consult the marabouts. The messenger soon returned and assured the chief that this evening he will see the moon. "All the marabouts have said so." The much desired crescent appeared for a few moments this evening; the powder speaks for half the night, and beer runs in floods. . . .

'Tuesday, June 12: From four o'clock in the morning the tam-tams resound everywhere, everyone is busy; one will really believe that this is the eve of an important event. . . . One half-hour after our departure we arrive at Sakhaboutenga. We dismount and camp under the trees at the entrance of the village. Some Muslims from the neighbourhood come and greet Boukary and offer him some kola nuts in lots varying from five to eight fruits. But they always presented them in the corner of their robes [it being forbidden for a commoner to hand a gift directly to a chief]. A village nearby sends twelve large jars of beer.

'From afar and from all directions long files of Moslems emerge from the village on their way to congregate together at the Imam for the prayers. Some curious people coming from the surrounding country are riding donkeys. The religious ceremony takes place on a plain to the east of the village. It is an imposing spectacle. There reigned a great silence in that assembly. The faithful, ranged in ranks about 20 feet deep, prostrate themselves and rise again with perfect harmony and with imposing langour. From time to time the voice of the Imam raised itself, and in the most profound reverence one heard an *amina* (amen) pronounced by that priest:

'There were about three thousand persons of both sexes there, almost all of

The Mossi Muslims were the persons who showed the greatest hostility to the first Europeans who arrived in the country. The *Imam* of Yako, influenced by his son (a member of the Tijaniyya Order and a former pilgrim to Mecca) refused to have any relations with the visiting Europeans. Furthermore, he is reported to have convinced the Mogho Naba Wobogo that death awaited any ruler who ever granted audience to a European.[13] When the French attacked the Mossi in 1896 an *Imam* from Béré, also a former pilgrim, told the ruler to flee and not depend on his ill-equipped soldiers to defeat the gun-bearing invaders. When the Mossi officials ignored this warning and were defeated in battle the Muslims reportedly went about telling the demoralized people that, 'As soon as all the blacks become Muslims, the whites will leave.'[14]

The French administrators would have liked to institute direct rule among the conquered Mossi people, but owing to the lack of sufficient administrators—they had one for every 60,000 inhabitants—they were forced to practise a form of indirect rule using the Mossi chiefs as instruments of their policy. The chiefs still retained enough power to slow down the spread of Islam, but as their power weakened, new communication networks were opened, and the rigours of colonialism grew among the Mossi, Islam started to spread.

There is no information as to the exact number of Muslims among the Mossi of Ouagadougou when the French arrived. Delafosse records that at the turn of the century there were approximately 42 Quranic schools with 230 students in and around Ouagadougou.[15] Tauxier, writing about the same period, states

---

whom were dressed in white. The *bournous*, the red tarboosh, and that assembly of black faces gave to that ceremony the grandiose character of an oriental fete. As soon as the prayers were finished, Boukary Naba, to the accompaniment of the sound of tam-tams, advanced to the Imam of Sakhaboutenga in order to receive his blessing, as well as the vows of the Muslims who wished on my illustrious host many horses and warriors. Boukary Naba ordered several sheep skins full of cowries. It is a present that he makes every year to the Imam and to Karamakho Isa, for whom he has a great veneration. These are old and reflective men who cannot help but give him excellent counsel.'

Binger, 1887–1889, vol. I, pp. 452 ff.

[13] Crozat, 1891, p. 4822.   [14] Tauxier, op. cit., p. 792.

[15] Delafosse, op. cit., vol. III, p. 193.

that there were 33 Quranic schools with about 358 students in the same area.[16] In 1926 there were 70 Quranic schools and 4,000 Muslims in Ouagadougou, with 7 per cent of the Muslims being non-Mossi. By 1944 there were about 240 schools and approximately 25,000 Muslims. The census of 1954 did not record the number of Quranic schools in Ouagadougou, but reported that there were 60,000 Muslims there. Today there are some 600,000 Muslims in all the *cercles* of the Republic of Upper Volta. Thus, over the past sixty years there appears to have been a substantial increase in the number of Muslims among the Mossi people. What follows is an attempt to analyse the diffusion of Islam and Islamic practices in the Kombissiri region of Ouagadougou, especially in Nobéré district, where I conducted field-work from November 1956 to January 1957.

The subdivision of Kombissiri, at the time of this study, was composed of about seventeen *cantons* grouping together some 177,661 people, of whom the majority were Mossi. There were small numbers of Silimi-Mossi, Fulani, Yarsé, Gurunsi, and Busansi in the region. Of this population, about 151,667 were pagans, 22,994 Muslims, and 3,000 Christians (most of whom were Catholics).[17]

The numbers and percentages of Muslims in the districts of Kombissiri varied quite widely (see table).[18] However, a comparison of the census of the Muslim population in 1954 with the rather sketchy figures for 1941 shows that while in some districts Islam gained a large number of converts, in other districts the percentage of Muslims remained static. For example, the number of Muslims in Manga had remained almost static over the preceding ten years, rising from 1,230 in 1941 to 1,557 in 1954, with the percentage remaining about the same. Similarly, the percentage of Muslims in Toudou remained the same, with a slight rise in number from 80 to 118. On the other hand, the number and percentage of Muslims in Koubry, the smallest *canton* of the subdivision, increased eight times over the same ten-year period, rising from 53 to 410. Of great interest, however, is the fact that in the two districts with the largest number of

[16] Tauxier, op. cit., p. 793.   [17] Skinner, 1958.   [18] See Table I.

Muslims, Kombissiri and Nobéré, about 65 per cent of the Muslims there were converted to Islam during the preceding five years.

Table I

Breakdown of the Number of Muslims in Some of the Cantons in the Subdivision as of the Census of 1954

Canton	Number	Muslim percentage
Kombissiri (*canton*)	5,718	37·2
Nobéré	3,387	42·0
Djiba	2,654	16·5
Doulougou	2,260	13·1
Manga	1,557	7·4
Barama	1,382	13·4
Bindé	1,064	13·0
Béré	943	11·0
Guirgo	851	9·3
Konsilga	627	6·3
Toece	626	6·9
Sapone	582	3·7
Mandie	465	15·0
Koubry	410	12·7
Kayao	233	2·9
Toudou	118	2·2
Tuili	117	2·8

The history of Islamic conversions in the subdivision reflects the history of the relationship between the Mossi and the Muslims. The first propagators of Islam in the area were those Yarsé who had been given permission by Mogho Naba Ouaraga to live in Guirgo, Rakay, and Sarabtenga. Yarsé Muslims also came into the area with Naba Tougma (a son of Mogho Naba Ouaraga) when he founded the Kombissiri district. Mogho Naba Kom I is remembered in the subdivision for having helped Islam by permitting Muslim Yarsé from Kombissiri to attend Quranic schools in Northern Gold Coast. Mogho Naba Sagha I, who succeeded Kom I, similarly permitted Muslim Yarsé to accompany those cadet sons of his, like Naba Ngado, chief of Nobéré district, who were sent out to replace district heads cashiered after a civil war.

It appears that the largest number of Mossi conversions to Islam occurred during the reigns of Kom I and Sagha I. The people of Nobéré, Manga, and Djiba date the first converts to

Islam from this period. When Doulougou followed Sagha I as Mogho Naba he permitted additional Muslims to settle in the districts of Kombissiri and Béré. Mogho Naba Sawadogo, the son of Doulougou, is credited with encouraging the Islamization of the village of Nyoida in Nobéré by a Muslim from Rakay.

Muslim Yarsé, under the patronage of Mossi rulers and their sons, were thus mainly responsible for propagating Islam in Kombissiri. Nevertheless, the spread of Islam in the region was controlled and even hampered by other Mossi rulers.[19] One of the reasons for the small percentage of Muslims in Toudou district was that its chiefs were usually hostile to Islam. Similarly, Islam did not gain many adherents in Manga because prior to the conquest the chiefs there were hostile to it, and after the conquest the chiefs favoured Catholicism. Thus, over time and until quite recently the Mossi chiefs largely determined whether Islam succeeded in their districts or not. Let us now look more closely at the status of Islam in the Nobéré district of Kombissiri, bearing in mind the importance of the Mossi chiefs in facilitating or hindering its spread.

The Nobéré chief, like many of the ruling heirs of Naba Ngado, was animist until he embraced Islam a short time ago in gratitude to a Hausa Muslim who had cured his illness. However, the descendants of the cadet sons of Ngado remained Muslims and lived as members of noble lineages in many of the villages of the district ruled by animist chiefs related to the man displaced by Ngado. The fact that the noble lineages of Nobéré were Muslims and the district chiefs, while not Muslim, were related to Muslim nobles, was a very important factor in the spread of Islam in the district. The reason for this was that the Nobéré chief, like most Mossi chiefs, was at the centre of the social, economic, political, and religious nexuses of his district. Muslim nobles shared his superior status and used their prestige to encourage the spread of Islam. For example, the animist chiefs of villages where many Muslim nobles lived invariably delineated

---

[19] It appears that many *nakomce* (nobles or children of chiefs) who became chiefs in their own right gave up Islam in order to follow the traditional religious prescriptions of the chieftaincy.

circles of stones (*missiri*) outside their compounds where visiting nobles could retire to pray when and if the time arrived. The animist chiefs and their followers remained quiet during the Muslim prayers, thus becoming symbolically part of the congregation. In time, many influential animists were persuaded to join in the prayers they had learned without realizing it.

Those animist village chiefs and family heads who engaged in marriage partnerships with Muslim nobles often contributed to the growth of the Muslim population by giving the prestigeful noblemen more wives than they received from them. The resulting children increased the Muslim community.[20] Another advantage that the Muslims, especially the nobles, had over non-Muslims as far as marriage and the family was concerned was that they did not have to surrender daughters of wives given them as *pughsiudse* by the chief. Both parties considered the *pughsiudse* as alms and the Muslims kept their daughters.

Ironically enough, the anxiety of all Mossi, whether nobles or commoners, Muslims or not, to have children, was often instrumental in leading many animists to Islam. When a Nobéré woman was feared barren, or her young children died, she consulted a diviner (*barga*) in the hope of discovering the reasons for her misfortunes. They sometimes told her that her *Tengkougre* benefactor was not amply rewarded and either had not given her children or had called them back, i.e., they died soon after birth. At other times she was told that she should consult a 'marabout' or that her 'Muslim' children (children who wished to become Muslims) had been angry and had died because they were given local names. In the latter case she was advised to give a gift to a Muslim, any Muslim, and to ask her husband to build a Muslim

---

[20] There was one interesting case in the district where a commoner who had become a Muslim tried to force his marriage partner, a chief, to become a Muslim in order to receive the hoped-for wife. The Muslim told his partner that he could not give his daughter to a non-Muslim, even a chief, since she might become a non-Muslim. The chief replied that his traditional obligations prevented him from adopting Islam and pointed out, with some justification, that since non-Muslim girls adopted the religion of their Muslim husbands, it would only be fair for Muslim girls to do the same. The Muslim community in Nobéré felt, however, that their religion was superior to that of the non-Muslims, and it was unthinkable that a Muslim girl should become one.

prayer circle outside his hut so that when her children 'returned' (were born again) they would see it. Furthermore, she was advised to give all her subsequent children Muslim names and rear them as Muslims, or they would die. I could discover no apparent reasons why animist diviners advised anxious parents to adopt Islam, except that they hoped that very difficult prescriptions would be more efficacious. Nevertheless, so effective was this technique for gaining converts to Islam that even the members of the family of the chief animist priest of Nobéré were not immune from it.[21] This old man viewed the birth of 'Muslim' grandchildren with resignation.

The French administrators and Christian missionaries around Nobéré believed that Mossi youths embraced Islam because they liked the beautiful robes and red fezes of the Muslims. This is indeed a naïve explanation for the conduct of a highly sophisticated people. Most of the young men in Nobéré wore Muslim-type clothes because such clothes were the mode. When sun helmets, dark glasses, and women's plastic raincoats *with hoods* came into vogue non-Muslims as well as the Muslims wore them. What is noteworthy is that when people became Muslims they became even more polite than the normally polite Mossi. They consciously tried to show by their behaviour that Islam had changed their lives. Undoubtedly they hoped that by so doing others might follow their way.

The belief among former colonial administrators and missionaries that a large number of those Mossi who had fled their homeland to escape forced labour (*travail obligatoire*), or military service, or who migrated seasonally to work in the mines and plantations of the Ivory Coast and the Gold Coast (Ghana) were converted to Islam while away from home was a simplistic view of a complex phenomenon.[22] Of course, some labour migrants did become Muslims while at work in foreign areas. For example, the first person in Koubry district to become a Muslim was converted

---

[21] Animist parents with all Muslim children were caught in a dilemma. Either they adopted Islam before they died, or they ran the risk of causing anguish to their Muslim children who would have had to participate in traditional funerals against their will or even refrain from participating in them.

[22] Skinner, 1960b.

when he worked as a migrant labourer in the Gold Coast some forty years ago. Similarly, out of the forty-two Muslims in Toece in 1954, three were converted to Islam while away in the Ivory Coast, and six while in the Gold Coast. Nevertheless, as far as I was able to discover, *most* migrants hesitated to alienate their relations by adopting Islam while away from home. They waited until they returned home before becoming Muslims. The reasons for this are interesting. Most migrants who left their villages for foreign lands had the opportunity to see the value in becoming a Muslim. The average Mossi who left on migration was surrounded by Muslims as soon as he started out. The chauffeurs and passengers on the trucks they rode were often Hausa, Songhay, or Mandingo Muslims. These Muslims all prayed together during the frequent stops on the roads, and shared food and water with each other, but not with the pagan 'kaffirs'. When the migrants arrived at their destination they often worked with or were supervised by Muslims who favoured their co-religionists. The Muslims often ate together with their supervisors and attended Friday prayer with them. Many animist migrants from Nobéré reported that they felt left out and discriminated against when this occurred. Other migrants reported that while Muslims and even Christians took care of their sick or dead fellows, sick animists were often ignored or unceremoniously dumped into a grave if they died. These experiences inclined men towards Islam, and after they informed their relatives of their reason for converting to Islam they felt free to do so. Many migrants not only became Muslims when they returned home but also encouraged their relatives to do the same.

There is no doubt that there were rewards for those Mossi in Nobéré and other districts who embraced Islam. Besides such tangible rewards as getting wives and children, there were such intangible ones as upward social mobility and the gain of greater prestige. It is important to note that almost all the liberated slaves and serfs in Nobéré had become Muslims. Those among them who made the pilgrimage bore the proud title of *Haji*, and even challenged the authority of district chiefs. In 1956, during a ceremony on the night before the *'id al-kabir* which marked the

end of Ramadan, a *haji* belonging to a former serf group chided
the Nobéré chief for his impiety, and voiced the hope that the
next chief would be a 'true Muslim'. He begged the chief to
accept the censure and regard it as coming not from a former
serf but from the heart of a servant of *Nabiyama* (the Prophet).
This same man had refused to pay homage to the chief at the
annual animist sacrifice to the ancestors held earlier that year.
When admonished by the chief at that time he returned the
daughter which the chief had given him as a wife. Of course,
no Mossi district chief would have accepted such behaviour from
any serf, whatever his religion, had the French not been there.

Islam was fairly well institutionalized in the subdivision,
especially in Kombissiri and Nobéré districts, in 1956. There were
various *tariqas*, mosques, and Quranic schools. The largest
religious order in the subdivision was the Tijaniyya, which regarded Al Haj 'Omar its patron. The second largest movement
in Kombissiri was the Qadiriyya, whose members revered Alma
Maliki (Al-Maghili). There were several hundred members of
the very orthodox 'eleven grains' Hamalliste (*Namisguesma*)
sect in the subdivision, especially in Béré district. There were
only two members of the Ahmadiyya (Hamadyya) in the subdivision, and they were non-Mossi who lived in Nobéré district.
With the exception of the Hamallistes, however, most Muslims
in the subdivision worshipped together irrespective of their
tariqa. They felt that the bonds of Islam over-rode all other
considerations.

The 250 or more Quranic schools in the subdivision were
affiliated with the various *tariqas*.[23] The Quranic students (*karem-
bissi* or *karem-camba* or *garibous*) were primarily boys ranging in
age from eight to fifteen, although several girls also attended
schools in Nobéré. Some of these schools drew boys from the
villages or districts where they were located; others were attended
by boys who came from other subdivisions and even from Bol-
gatanga in Northern Ghana. Foreign Quranic students often

---

[23] Kombissiri district had 28 schools, of which 15 were Tijaniyya, 11 Qadiriyya,
and two of unknown affiliation, and varied in size and quality. Only one of the
32 schools in Nobéré had more than 20 students, 10 schools had 8 students apiece,
and the others had even fewer.

worked for their teachers and supplemented their keep by begging for alms. Students learned to read and write Arabic with varying amounts of skill, but all of them learned to recite from the Quran. Clever graduates often visited the district chiefs to display their educational skills.

There were a number of eminent Muslim scholars in the sub-division. One of them, Souleymane Kafande of Bindé district and a member of the Qadariyya was considered a *wali* (Saint) of the prophet, and was credited with the miraculous feeding of several hundred persons for a whole day with a single calabash of milk. His Quranic schools included in their curricula higher studies in Islamic laws, and attracted Muslim scholars from as far away as Ouahigouya (north Upper Volta) and Bawku in Northern Ghana. Souleymane Diarra of the Tijaniyya sect was the other important scholar in the subdivision. This man attended a series of Quranic schools in Bawku around 1943 and was considered to be a brilliant Arabist. He left Bawku after a dispute with his teacher and tried to establish an Islamic centre in Manga district but was prohibited from doing so by the Catholic Manga Naba. The Doulougou Naba reluctantly gave him permission to establish a Quranic centre in his district. There were other 'marabouts' and *Imams* in the subdivision, but none of them approached the stature of these two men.

As far as the lay Muslims in Nobéré and in Kombissiri were concerned, they were recognizable as such, since they wore long robes and fezes, possessed phylacteries and used religious saluta-tions. They differed quite markedly in their knowledge of, and adherence to, the tenets of Islam, even though most of them knew the five articles of Islamic belief and tried to observe the *Amal* or five practical duties of Islam. The Muslims of Kombissiri, like Muslims everywhere, prayed five times a day and, as in Nobéré, most adult males were able to lead in prayer. The Mossi Muslims called their five prayer periods: '*fasiri*', '*zarafe*', '*lasa*', '*magrima*', and '*sanfo*', respectively. These Mossi Muslims prayed anywhere, but many tried to build prayer circles of stones (*missiri*) or miniature mosques near their compounds so that their families could pray together. The six large mosques in the subdivision were seldom used by people from outside the local areas. During important holy days prayers were held in the open, usually near the tomb of the founders of local Muslim communities.[24]

The *Carême*, or month-long fast, was attempted by most adult Muslims in the subdivision, with the exception of invalids and working men. However, while the 'Muslims of the Mouth' secretly broke the fast, the 'Muslims of the Heart' fasted throughout Ramadan. All Muslims, whether of the 'Mouth' or of the 'Heart', joined the joyous celebration at the end of Ramadan. The sighting of the crescent moon was greeted with shouts and gun-shots, and the district chief and even pagans took part in the festivities.

The Muslims in the subdivision seldom gave regular alms or *ʒakat* to their *Imams*. However, most of them attended ceremonies called *sadaqas* at the homes of other Muslims and placed articles, such as money, food, and goods, into a common pool from which all assembled persons received a share. Moreover, most Muslims fulfilled their obligations by giving presents to the young and often indigent students at the Quranic schools.

Few of the Muslims in the subdivision had any hope of going to Mecca on pilgrimage, even though many of them would have liked to do so. Most Muslims were too poor to pay for the trip and, although those who went were aided by their co-religionists, the initial outlay was just too much for the average Mossi. In the 1954 census seven men from the subdivision were listed as being on various stages of the pilgrimage—a not inconsiderable number when it is realized that even today not more than 100 Voltaics go to Mecca in the course of a year. My own field-work coincided with the pilgrimages of three Muslims from Nobéré. One of them died near the Red Sea, and most people believed that he would receive special dispensation from God for this effort. Another pilgrim was still away; and the third had completed the round trip

[24] For example, the Muslims of Nobéré held their prayers during Ramadan in a field near the tomb of Naba Ngado, the first Muslim district chief. However, in 1956 there arose some opposition among the Muslim *hajis* to the prayer site, because they claimed that for many superstitious Muslims Ngado's tomb had become a *Tengkougre*, or earth shrine.

to Mecca in an aeroplane, the mode of transport which most pilgrims now use. When this last pilgrim left, a great crowd gathered at his house to pray for his safe journey. Some of his friends even accompanied him to Ouagadougou and remained there until he left. While he was away the district chief encouraged the Muslims and even others to cultivate his fields. When the new *haji* finally returned a large crowd accompanied him to his house with cries of joy. There he killed a sheep in thanksgiving, sprinkled the crowd with holy water from Mecca, and recounted his experiences. His listeners were impressed by his aeroplane flight and by his description of Mecca, but they showed the greatest interest when he said that the Meccan women covered their faces and that most Meccan men were monogamous.

Despite the fact that the Muslims of Kombissiri were proud to be followers of Islam and tried to honour its tenets, they retained the major values of Mossi culture. They still valued children and, while they no longer believed in the cult of the ancestors and did not 'kill chickens' to the ancestors, they still felt that a man should have children to succeed him and that the best guarantee for this was polygyny. Mossi Muslims justified polygyny by saying that the Prophet Muhammad himself decreed that his followers might keep four wives, provided that they were all treated with the same degree of kindness and consideration. However, even those Muslims who, in contrast to the average Mossi who were monogamous, were able to obtain more than four wives did not appear overly concerned about transgressing the tenets of their faith. On the other hand, many Mossi Muslims had abandoned the practice of marrying their father's widows, holding that it was against Islamic rules to do so. They criticized this type of marriage among their animist brothers, and suggested that the levirate be used instead.

Mossi Muslims had not changed their attitudes about the position of women in Mossi society. Women were segregated behind the men at the open-air prayers during festivals and were not permitted within the mosques, in the *missiri*, or at *sadaqas*. The Muslims felt that the presence of women at prayers distracted the men from their devotion to God. Some Muslims in Nobéré, especially those who had been to Mecca, had started to place their wives in a kind of purdah. They refused to permit their wives to go to market for fear they would come into contact with 'ungodly' non-Muslim men. Some of the women who attended a reception for a returned *haji* were even seen to cover their faces with their headkerchiefs, but whether this represented an attempt at veiling or was a reaction to the presence of so many men was not quite clear.

The Muslims of Kombissiri did possess many other culture traits which, while shared by the non-Muslim populations, were of ultimate Islamic origin or syncretisms of Islamic and traditional culture. For example, the weekly calendar used among the Mossi is of Islamic origin; Mossi associated local spirits called *kinkirse* with *jinns*; and many persons believed in the efficacy of Quranic recitals as remedies for ill health. Some Mossi even considered an infusion prepared by soaking paper on which Quranic verses were written in water to be a cure for illness. However, one Muslim Mossi chief refused to accept the plea of a Christian litigant to permit the Christian and Muslim parties to a dispute to kiss and swear upon the Bible and Quran respectively. He refused to permit this blending of Christian, Islamic, and purely western legal traits in a Mossi court.

The drive for independence which had started in the Upper Volta during the period of my field work did lead to the emergence of latent conflict between the traditionalist, Muslim, and Catholic Mossi groups in the districts of the subdivision. The missionaries of the White Fathers had long conducted a school in one of the *cantons* and had used this institution as a means of recruiting converts. The Muslims had for some time refused to send their children to this school, and, in the absence of public schools, their children did not receive western education. The Muslims apparently voiced no complaints while there were no politicians, but as soon as elected representatives appeared they began to press them for a state-supported school. This demand caused some ill-feeling among the Catholics, who insisted that the mission school was large enough for all the district's children. But the Muslims were adamant in their demands that a secular school be built to open the road to social mobility, through education, for traditionalists, Muslims, and Christians alike. The Muslims and a few Christians also objected to the Government's paying substandard teachers to teach in the Catholic schools, while stating that even such teachers were unavailable for state schools.

A number of Mossi politicians also found that they had to appeal to Islam to gain the votes of Muslims. One such politician found himself caught between the Muslims and their chief, who, although a Muslim himself, was at odds with the Muslim community, which had decided to support a predominantly Muslim party. This politician was heard to tell a predominantly Muslim audience that he had even attended a Quranic school. This story was indeed true, because the man had gone to a Muslim *zongo*, or circumcision school, but it is not known how many Muslim votes he received for this admission. He did carry the district, because he was backed by the chief and the traditionalists.

Religion did not play a major role in the competition for political power which preceded Independence of the Upper Volta. There was a predominantly Muslim political party, but the real struggle for power was between the traditional Mossi chiefs and the young Catholic-trained Mossi politicians. The chiefs lost, and subsequently the Mogho Naba of Ouagadougou, the most important Mossi chief, became a Muslim. Whether this conversion was the result of internal conviction or a reaction to defeat by Christian commoners is still a moot question. However, for what it is worth, the Muslims had the satisfaction of seeing the conversion of the paramount Mossi chief coincide with the 'departure' of the Europeans (see above, p. 179).

The first government after Independence, presided over by a Mossi Christian, was composed of people of all religious persuasions. On Independence Day the President visited the major edifices of all the 'cults' in the capital of Ouagadougou, and asked all religious groups to pray for the success of the State. The desire that religious differences should not enter the political realm might be seen in the fact that there was no mention of any religious groups or religions in the handbook, published for Independence, describing the Upper Volta and its peoples. The Government was committed to the idea of a secular state, but there was some feeling that there was a pro-Catholic bias in official circles. Nevertheless, government officials still supported the Muslim community. For example, the President's brother, Denis Yameogo, Joseph Conombo, Mayor of Ouagadougou, and the Mogho Naba joined with El Haj Raghian in prayer during the celebration of '*id al-kabir* at the end of Ramadan in 1963. Madame Yameogo, the wife of the President, joined the folk-dancing Muslim women that afternoon.[25]

The problem for the Mossi Muslims, like that of Muslims throughout Africa, was that they had to modernize their practices, if not their tenets, to cope with a rapidly changing world. The Upper Volta appeared determined to modernize itself, and in so doing change the status of the Mossi woman by giving her more freedom than she then enjoyed in animist, Muslim, and even Christian homes. Whether or not the Muslims and the animists would agree to these changes remained to be seen. There was evidence, however, that the Mossi Muslims were prepared to co-operate with their government in developing their country. In response to complaints raised by the Ouagadougou community that Quranic students or 'garibous' were running wild in the town, the President of the Muslim community declared:

It is not necessary to point out that, especially during the rainy season, all worthy Voltaics should mobilize their energy for the economic development of our country.

Why then do the masters of Koranic schools remain indifferent to the vagabondage of their pupils instead of employing them in the noble task of cultivating the life-giving soil?

There is a possibility that all the vagabond children are not Koranic pupils, but we believe that a general measure should be taken to repress all of them in order to preserve our national prestige.[26]

The Muslims' President vowed to enlist the help of the local authorities to end what he called the 'vagabondage of the

[25] 'La Communauté Musulmane', *Carrefour Africaine*, 3 année, no. 46, 3 mars, 1963.
[26] 'Déclaration du Président de la Communauté Musulmane', *Carrefour Africaine*, 3 année, no. 12, 8 juillet 1962.

"garibous" in our Republic'. In so doing he hoped to take one step towards adjusting the Muslim community to the requirements of modern life.

REFERENCES

Binger, Capt. Louis G.
  (1887–89) *Du Niger au Golfe de Guinée par le pays Kong et le Mossi*. Paris.
Bovill, E.
  (1958) *The Golden Trade of the Moors*. Oxford: Clarendon Press.
Crozat, (Dr.)
  (1891) 'Rapport sur une mission au Mossi', *Journal Officiel de la République Française*, 5–9 octobre.
Delafosse, Maurice
  (1912) *Haut-Sénégal-Niger*. Paris: Larose.
Dim Delobson, A. A.
  (1959) *The Empire of the Mogho-Naba*, trans. Kathryn A. Looney. Human Relations Area Files, New Haven.
Lucien, Marc
  (1909) *Le Pays Mossi*. Paris: Larose.
Oliver, R. and Fage, J. D.
  (1963) *A Short History of Africa*. New York University Press.
Sa'di, 'Abd al-Rahman al-,
  (1900) *Ta'rikh al-Sudan*, trans. O. Houdas. Paris.
Skinner, Elliott P.
  (1957) 'An Analysis of the Political System of the Mossi', *Transactions of the New York Academy of Sciences*, ser. II, vol. 19, no. 8, June, pp. 740–50.
  (1958) 'Christianity and Islam among the Mossi', *American Anthropologist*, Menasha, Wisconsin, vol. LX, no. 6.
  (1960a) 'The Mossi "Pogsioure" ', *Man*, vol. LX, no. 28, February, pp. 20–22.
  (1960b) 'Labour Migration and its Relationship to Socio-Cultural Change in Mossi Society', *Africa*, vol. XXX, no. 4, October, pp. 375–401.
  (1962) 'Trade and Markets among the Mossi People', in *Markets in Africa*, ed. Paul Bohannan and George Dalton. Evanston: Northwestern University Press, pp. 237–78.
Tauxier, Louis
  (1912) *Le Noir du Soudan*. Paris: Larose.
Trimingham, J. Spencer
  (1959) *Islam in West Africa*. London: Oxford University Press.

VII. CATTLE VALUES AND ISLAMIC VALUES IN A PASTORAL POPULATION

D. J. STENNING

I. INTRODUCTION

This paper is about the place of Islamic observance in the ceremonial and ritual life of the Wodaabe pastoral Fulani of Bornu in Northern Nigeria. It attempts to arrange the cycles of ceremony and ritual so as to make clearer the Wodaabe view of their place in the world of Islam as they see it. This seems to me to be a necessary task in Africa today, where many of the populations are assimilating Islamic social ideas and religious practices.

II. DUALISM

The case of the Wodaabe is perhaps interesting, since there is a marked dualism in the social organization and value-system of this population, which I have tried to bring out in an earlier publication,[1] but which may be recapitulated here. This dualism arises directly from the economic structure of Wodaabe pastoral groupings, and from their historical role in the politics of northeastern Nigeria.

There is a structure of close-knit small groups, of which the simple or compound family and the limited agnatic descent group are the most important units. The subsistence and wealth of these groups derive solely from their herds of cattle. These are maintained by a system of transhumance in which agnatic descent groups congregate in northerly pastures which are free from tsetse fly in the wet season; these groups disperse southwards and split (often into their constituent families) as the dry season proceeds. The interests of the Wodaabe are narrowly circumscribed by the demands of this mode of pastoralism, which involves continual but conservative adjustment to subtle ecological changes. Their property, other than cattle, is exiguous. The system of

---

[1] D. J. Stenning, *Savannah Nomads*. London, 1959.

values associated with these circumstances, and its expression in ritual, is directed towards the ordering of relations between family and herd, and is concerned particularly with the fecundity of both animals and humans. Right conduct is the exercise of familial virtues, the fulfilment of duties towards elders, spouses, and coevals. In this way, good cattle husbandry is promoted, and the survival and wealth of future generations can be assured. The cattle themselves are in some ways seen as the arbiters in this situation. While they are manipulated, now 'rationally', now by magical means, they nevertheless possess sanctions on human conduct which a Bodaado cannot afford to ignore. Wodaabe, like pastoral Fulani in general, equate this distinctive way of life with their own ethnic origin and ideal physical characteristics, so that running through all the institutions implied in this sketch there is a strong attachment to the idea of ethnic exclusiveness and superior moral standing. The characteristics of this way of life may be summed up by the words familial, egalitarian, peaceful, conservative.

Pastoral life is familial. It depends on a family division of labour, on a family consumption of its products. Each herd is attached to, or rather one with, a family, and grows imperceptibly out of the dissolution of another family in the previous generation. In general, pastoral ritual has the function of marking the stages of family growth and dissolution. Pastoral life is egalitarian. A man who is wealthy in cattle is so because of his expertise, but expertise cannot be acquired, or brought into play, without reciprocity of many kinds with kinsfolk. He is wealthy because of his kin and not in spite of them, and his obligations are greater because of his wealth. Pastoral life is peaceful. While it would not be accurate to say that this kind of life does not permit conflict, it is revealing to observe that conflict of many kinds is minimized and often resolved by removal. A scolded child runs into the bush. The slighted wife takes herself off to her guardian. The deviant is banished. Herd-owners peacefully agree to separate, but only after interminable discussion, and when they go it is not known whether for a week, a season, or for ever. Pastoral life is conservative. Nomadism conveys a sense of *insouciance*, and the drawings of its migration arcs have an air of abandon. Nothing is further from the truth. Each step in the movement is planned with careful weighing of the evidence: there is cautious experimentation so that as far as possible the habitat is familiar and, as the Wodaabe say, 'like a house to us'.

This kind of configuration of values is common enough in anthropological literature. But its occurrence in Wodaabe society has added interest when we reflect that historically, and indeed today, they are maintained in circumstances which are patently hostile to them. The pastoral Wodaabe are an interstitial population. The formation of large groups with well-defined and specifically territorial rights to water and grazing has not occurred. Consequently, there is no past or present institution concerned with the acquisition or defence of territory for its own sake in perpetuity. At whatever period or time-span we care to choose we find Wodaabe negotiating, with aliens and in languages not their own, for temporary rights to pasture and water; usually doing so at the personal level. Again, we find that the domestic economy depends daily on small-scale market and barter relations, in which the Wodaabe exchange their milk for the cereal foods of the non-Fulani agriculturalists. Deeply committed to the world of the bush, with all it holds for the maintenance of their herds, the Wodaabe need, and move freely in, the networks of agricultural villages, market towns, and, occasionally, capital cities of north-eastern Nigeria. In Wodaabe thinking a continual distinction is made between these two worlds, but also a certain ambivalence of sentiment is expressed.

The interaction of the Wodaabe with what for the moment we may call—conveniently but somewhat inaccurately—'the outside world' takes place in a cultural and historical context which is plainly Islamic, and is phrased by Wodaabe in these terms. Their traditions tell us that the Wodaabe participated in the Holy War in north-eastern Nigeria from perhaps about 1820, and certainly from the 1850s, onwards. They did so opportunistically, now seizing the chance to aid an Emir's forces, now holding back. This kind of political calculation persisted in their dealings with the Islamic state down to the Mahdist incursion, and in a different form, into the Protectorate period. They gave tribute to Emirs, and they profited from the wars by acquiring slaves and horses. The growth of one or another Islamic state afforded them opportunities for acquiring general rights to pasture and water over wide tracts of country, which then had to be made good by more detailed arrangements. These relations with the Islamic state promoted a re-definition of the notion of leadership and a reorganization of the Wodaabe groups concerned. Wider groupings based on putative genealogical connexions began to assume a coherence *vis-à-vis* the State under the leadership of the *Laamibe*, whose political functions exceeded those of the *ardo'en* who led the small pastoral groupings. In these new circumstances the followings of the *Laamibe* became more heterogeneous, and this process was accelerated in the Protectorate period by the establishment of village headships, which put more precise duties towards the State on to the Wodaabe in general. Over the same period the politico-ritual relations which were a feature of the wider groupings diminished in importance and effectiveness, and the ritual office of *maudo laawol pulaaku* became more and more esoteric. This latter development was due mainly to changed political circumstances. It was partly due to the disruptive effects of the great rinderpest epidemic of the 1890s. But we cannot discount the effects of the dissemination of Islamic ideas and observances. The Wodaabe have no interest in describing a period when they did not 'know Islam'. They must have made at least a token gesture of support for the religious aims of the Holy War, although it may be that their ethnic solidarity was a stronger ideological force. But by the 1850s their leaders were 'praying the '*Id*' at Kukawa, the Bornu capital, and holymen were coming back to West Bornu with them. Today we can describe the Wodaabe as Muslims. They profess the Faith. They carry out daily prayers punctiliously, with one significant exception, which will be noted later. They observe the Fast, but in intention rather than fact, for many concessions are made to the rigours of their life in the bush. They are circumcised, where there seems to have been no 'traditional' institution involving circumcision. They give alms. They recognize a brotherhood with non-Fulani, although this is qualified by their sentiments of ethnic exclusiveness. They help the pilgrim on the way to Mecca, and a few Wodaabe are known to have started the pilgrimage. They trace tenuous descent from Shehu dan Fodio. It should be added that among the Wodaabe it is not possible to identify either segments or individuals who do not count themselves Muslims. Islamic observance is general, and varies only as between individuals who practise it.

This involvement of the Wodaabe with the State, and more generally with the Islamic culture of Northern Nigeria, gives rise to values which, as I have suggested, are antithetical to those of their pastoral life. These may be summed up by the words public, status conscious, martial, and opportunistic.

Wodaabe identify themselves with the world outside their camps by means of the legends of history. Their heroes in this context were men of war, but they were men who also sought their aims by duplicity and guile. These men, the first *Laamibe*, not only brought their people into the orbit of the state but divided them, since the perquisites of war were not only rights to pasture (which Wodaabe utilize in an egalitarian manner) but the status symbols of the society of which they now became a part. Titles, horses, slaves gave men status, and the force of the State was at times called in not to arbitrate conflicting claims, but to support one or another faction. These values are carried forward to the present day. Non-Fulani are arranged in a simplified form of the status-order evident, at least ten years ago, in Northern Nigerian society. While equals—that is to say their counterparts in the agricultural communities—are regarded as inferior on ethnic grounds, there is a continual aspiration to high status on the ladder afforded by the title system. At the same time the Wodaabe exact from their communities of ex-slaves the kind of servility they give their superiors, and the slaves themselves seek to emulate their Wodaabe lords.

Wodaabe know that these two sets of values are complementary and yet conflicting, and there are many examples of this in behaviour and linguistic usage, particularly of that well-known 'man of two worlds', the minor chief. Advantage in the outside world can be pursued, and success is acclaimed, since it may mean an advantage to the Wodaabe community. But it can be pursued only so far without detriment to family and kin—and herd.

III. CEREMONIES AND RITUALS

The antithesis I have tried to sketch here has its parallel in the formal structure of Wodaabe feasts. All Wodaabe ceremonies and rituals are marked by the slaughter and consumption of a feast-animal (usually a bull). The manner in which the beast's carcass is divided signifies which of two types of occasion is being celebrated.

The first known as *homtu* or *homturu* (the etymological root signifying 'appeasement', 'reconciliation') consists of the pastoral ceremonies of the Wodaabe—all those events having to do with the *internal* life of the clan, its constituent families, and its herds. In these feasts the whole carcass is divided for consumption according to principles of age and sex, and such strangers as have to be present are accorded a status of this kind for their part in the feast.

The second type of ceremony is known as *hirsu* (root signifying 'to slaughter' by cutting the throat in the Islamic manner). These ceremonies have to do with the *external* relations of the Wodaabe group. In these events the carcass is divided longitudinally, one half being retained by the Wodaabe donors, the other going to the non-Fulani guests.

There are additional distinctions between these categories of feast. In pastoral ceremonies the meat is distributed raw; in public ceremonies it is cooked, in two separate halves, before distribution. In public ceremonies it is a point of honour to select a good prime beast; in some, but not all, of the pastoral ceremonies, the beast is selected for convenience, and may turn out to be an ailing cow. In public ceremonies milk may be drunk by the hosts, and offered to guests, but is consumed casually by all participants; an integral part of pastoral ceremonies consists of ritual milk-drinking by the men. In public ceremonies there are usually many exchanges of kola-nuts between individuals, and these demonstrate the status or aspirations of participants. While kola-nuts are consumed at pastoral ceremonies, they are not a mandatory part of the feast, and no matter who supplies them, their distribution is in the hands of the donor or convenor of the feast. Public ceremonies are marked, wherever possible, by the horse-gallops (the Hausa *jafi*), and in this competition and reciprocity are in evidence in much the same way as in kola-nut exchange. Pastoral feasts do not, in principle, include this feature. Finally, the venues of the two categories of feast are somewhat different. A pastoral feast takes place with a single family homestead as its base, and indeed one part of the homestead is a focal point for the ritual. The disposition of the participants is made in accordance with the age and sex rules pertaining to family life. In a public ceremony the guests are given their own quasi-domestic area, including sleeping-shelters, which lies outside the Wodaabe camp. The action of the public ceremony takes place between this and the homestead of the donor, but never penetrates the domestic ground of the camp.

The public feasts are addressed to those whom Wodaabe regard as superiors, as equals, or as inferiors. The first of these may be called 'tribute' ceremonies, in which an important non-Fulani official of the State is present as a guest. The ceremony marks whatever business he has to transact (to check cattle-tax, promulgate a new regulation, install certain orders of chief); but also the social distance, competition, and status-reciprocity elements in evidence in public feasts are present here in full measure. The major characteristic of tribute ceremonies is that the visitors' retinue provides all the more obvious ceremonial elements—the drummers and praise singers; and, significantly, the *malam* who records the business of the day but may also act as the *imam* for public prayers. The Wodaabe contribution on this side is deliberately limited so as to be eclipsed by the visitors', but is correspondingly, and overtly, generous in provision of food for men and horses.

An important variant occurs when the tribute ceremony occurs between principals who are themselves Wodaabe. Examples of this are where a Wodaabe chief goes to collect cattle tax from his pastoral kinsmen; or where he installs a kinsman as chief. The feasts on these occasions take the public form, and status differentiation is marked in the appropriate way. But there is a point at which the kinship of the visitor with his hosts is demonstrated. He eats from their portion of the feast meat as well as from the guests', may be asked to distribute kola-nuts, and drinks milk at evening time with them in the pastoral fashion.

The feast for 'equals' is that which goes with the successful establishment of local pasture rights, particularly, in West Bornu, in the dry season. In the dry season I was there relations between the pastoralists and the District Heads of the dry-season areas were strained by the imposition of an illegal 'grass tax' and no tribute feasts of this kind took place. But the pastoral leaders made a point of giving sheep as *sadaqa* to the villagers in whose vicinity they camped, and because of milk shortages and considerable splitting of camps, the occasion for this was combined with (in one case) a name-giving feast, which falls into the 'pastoral' category. On this occasion representatives of the village were invited, given a separate feast area, consumed appropriate portions of the *homtu* beast, and a suitable share of the kola-nuts distributed by the donor, and joined in the prayers, for which they had provided the *malam*. There was no gallop, and the visitors did not get milk. They took their sheep away with them.

The feast for inferiors is the slave dance (*daddo*). This is a wet season feast in which the slave communities of the Wodaabe dance for their masters, who provide meat and kola-nuts for them. While unmistakably a public feast in all essentials, the *daddo* is not, as it were, the reverse of the chiefs' feast. The visiting party is itself a group of praise-singers, dancers, and drummers, and its activity is directed one way, towards the adulation of the Wodaabe; whereas in the chiefs' feasts the praise-singers, etc., draw attention to both parties with nice discrimination. Furthermore, this is not an occasion for prayers, and no *imam* is provided by either side. While the slaves profess Islam, and on other occasions pray together with Wodaabe, there is no atmosphere of brotherhood in the *daddo*. The prescribed Fulani behaviour on these occasions is ill-concealed derision of the slaves' antics, while the slaves' laudatory songs can turn into ribald lampoons.

The Wodaabe conduct of these feasts, which are their only formal contact with the outside world on their own ground, exhibits quite clearly a sense of social separation, of status-consciousness, of competition, and of tacit antagonism. The culture symbols of West African Islam are present, but are employed outside the domestic setting against which the ceremonies have to take place. Note that each event, except one, includes the necessity of prayers; and the exception itself arises from an historical (although at the present day unrealistic) view of the Wodaabe place in Islam in North-eastern Nigeria.

Let us turn now to the cycle of pastoral or 'internal' ceremonies. Each of these, as I have indicated, is familial, involving a *rite de passage* of an individual and the consequent adjustment of families and herds. But it is possible, without over-analysing, to see two types of event here. The first type is that in which the primary aim of the ritual is to deal with a person. The second is that in which the primary aim of the ritual is to deal with cattle. Into the first group fall, for purposes of this paper, naming, certain aspects of marriage, and mortuary ceremonies. The second group includes the establishment of the nucleus of a herd for a boy who has reached herding age; the establishment of a family herd; the cattle-increase ritual accompanying the slaughter of a lead-bull of a herd; and the administration of an estate.

The Wodaabe name-giving ceremony (*innde*) has been described elsewhere.[2] We need only note here that Wodaabe regard this important ceremony as an Islamic one and, apart from some elasticity in the time after the birth at which it is carried out, perform it in accordance with Islamic canons. The child is given an Islamic name; its head is shaved; an animal is sacrificed and the meat eaten within the family circle, alms are given;[3] the blood of the feast animal is not smeared on the head of the child, nor is circumcision carried out at this stage. There is no 'traditional' version of this ceremony: and, as far as can be gathered from Wodaabe names and other verbal evidence, all

---

[2] Stenning, op. cit., pp. 117–119.
[3] Note the concurrence of this with the establishment of pasture rights in one observed case.

Wodaabe children undergo it. In genealogies, evidence of non-Islamic naming begins to occur in the third ascending generation from present-day elders.

In marriage the use of Islamic ceremonies is somewhat more selective. There are five forms of marital union current in Wodaabe society: betrothal marriage; contract marriage; gift marriage; widow inheritance; and cicisbean unions. Apart from the last form, an Islamic wedding ceremony is part of the proceedings; and, where the bride has been married before, so is the observance of *'idda*.

Cicisbean unions are of short duration, and include none of the prestations or ceremonies associated with the other types of marriage. Where feast cattle have been transferred for a betrothed girl who engages in one of these liaisons, there is a claim on the male partner for the return of their equivalent; but this can rarely be made good, certainly not in an *alkaali's* court. Indeed, throughout Wodaabe society there have been strong moves to prevent cicisbean unions, which flout both the traditional expectations of betrothal marriage and the norms of contract implied in gift marriage, contract marriage, and widow inheritance. Nowadays they occur mainly as a result of breakdown in one of the early stages of betrothal marriage.

While in contract marriage, gift marriage and widow inheritance the Islamic ceremony is the only ritual to mark the occasion, including the transfer of other prestations, betrothal marriage is a series of rituals, of which the Islamic ceremony is not the most important. It starts, in fact, with the ceremony at which the herd boy is taken into his father's cattle-corral and is shown the beasts which will be the nucleus of his own herd. A *homtu* feast marks this occasion. But it should be noted that a boy 'qualifies' for this, as it were, by having been circumcised. Circumcision is carried out on groups of lads aged from seven to ten years of age by a junior elder, and no special rituals of a didactic or symbolic nature are attached to this. The 'first betrothal' or preliminary discussions between the intending parties to the match is the next stage; and this, again, is marked by a *homtu* ceremony. The next stage is the betrothal proper, which

occurs when the girl begins to menstruate. This ceremony includes a *homtu* feast, and also the Islamic wedding ceremony.
Then, after an interval, follow the ceremonies of bride-removal,
at which the couple are first expected to sleep together; this, again,
is marked by a *homtu* feast. The final stage is the home-making,
which occurs after the weaning of the couple's first-born. In this,
the homestead of the couple is constructed by the co-operative
effort of the parties to the marriage, and the herd of the husband
is ritually transferred to him by laying down his new calf rope
and attaching his calves to it, so that the dams and, perhaps, his
stock bull will return from pasture to their new corral.

In the course of a betrothal marriage, which sets up a new
family unit, all the stages are marked by *homtu* feasts. But an
Islamic ceremony is performed at what may well be regarded as
an unimportant stage, the ceremony at which intentions are
announced. The other stages all have to do with associating the
couple (or in the first instance, the future male herd owner) with
the family herd, or in ritually *disassociating* them from it in the
parts which involve procreation and child-bearing.

A similar form of selectivity is evident in mortuary ceremonies.
In Wodaabe society there is no ancestor cult, and no ritual
designed to install ancestors or re-align their descendants in
relation to them. Rights in the principal form of property—
cattle—are allocated progressively to heirs throughout the owner's
adult lifetime, so that on his death there is usually only a small
residuum. Today the dead are disposed of by burial, and great
importance is attached to the performance of the rite by a *malam*.
But, in the exigencies of the pastoral life, the ceremony is per-
functory and may include only the dead person's immediate
family. No cattle are killed, and there is no ceremonial accompaniment to the visits of condolence which take place, sometimes for
weeks after the funeral has taken place. When the whole round
of such visits has been performed, and nowadays when the
period of continence of widows has elapsed, the lineage group of
the dead man congregate to witness the distribution of his residual
estate. This is definitely not an occasion when any representative
of the State or any Islamic religious functionary should be

present, so as to avoid exaction of death-duties. The disposal of the dead, and of their cattle, are kept rigidly separate.

The pastoral ceremony which had to do primarily with the welfare of cattle was the increase-ceremony, at which the lead bulls which had served their time were killed and eaten by the herd owners of a clan. This ritual no longer takes place in Wodaabe society, but formerly it was part of the wet-season ceremonial cycles at which the politico-ritual relations of wider groupings in Wodaabe society were validated. The authority of the ritual leaders has now been superseded by that of the *Laamibe* in their relations with the Islamic state.

IV. CONCLUSION

This analysis suggests that while the values of their 'internal' and 'external' relations may be antithetical and yet complementary to the Wodaabe, they do not see 'external' relations as Islamic and 'internal' relations as non-Islamic solely. In the range of ceremonies which have to do primarily with the individual in his passage through life, there is a readiness and a desire to hallow the occasion with Islamic prayers and observances. Although they lie at the periphery of the Islamic world, this desire does not seem to the observer to be feigned or half-hearted. But where changes in the rights over cattle are concerned, no Islamic ceremony is countenanced, even in respect of the individual whose change of status is implicit in the event. Wodaabe explanations of this tend to turn on the interest which the State has in despoiling their herds by its exactions and penalties. But this is not the whole story, for Wodaabe herds are continuous objects of magico-religious observances in their own right, and no Islamic rite is allowed to impinge upon these. Some indication of this separation is given in the location and timing of *birsu* feasts. But it is better exemplified in the relation of cattle ritual to prayers. Evening prayers do not conflict with either the ritual lighting of the corral-fire or the ritual co-operation of man and wife at the calf-rope at milking time. But dawn prayers are invariably missed, because this is the time when the herd owner should be seated at his corral-fire in the closest contact with his beasts.

VIII. ISLAM AMONG THE FULBE OF ADAMAWA

P. F. LACROIX

I

The sedentary and semi-sedentary Fulbe living in Adamawa[1] are without exception Muslim; the same goes for the minority of semi-nomadic Fulbe (*bororo'en*) based there, although all the indications are that among them Islamization is more recent and, on the whole, more superficial than among their sedentary cousins. Among the latter religious faith runs deep and sincere, is accompanied by no more superstitious practices or beliefs than subsist among the majority of the Muslims of the Middle East or the Maghrib, and moreover harbours no typically 'African' traits. This faith—of a 'quality', dare one say it, which is rather rare in black West Africa—has never been ground down, among the majority of those concerned, by its contact with economic conditions or modern politics, and even seems to have been refined in certain respects in the last few decades (witness, for example, the abandonment of non-Muslim rites of circumcision). This faith may be considered a characteristic element of this society and has endowed it with a rich written literature (in Arabic and Fula) that still flourishes and reflects the society's preoccupations and conflicts.

II

The introduction of Islam among the Fulbe of Adamawa cannot be fixed at a precise historical time; but it is certain that at the beginning of the nineteenth century the majority of those called *Fulbe* established in what was to become Adamawa unleashed a *jihad* against the 'pagan' host populations. This suggests an already fairly extensive and, at least in some cases, deep-rooted Islamization, since the occasion threw up religious personalities like the *moodibbo 'aadama* and others whose memory is still green

[1] The territory of the precolonial lamidate of Adamawa comprises the modern Gongola State of Nigeria and the majority of the northern region of Cameroon.

among their descendants. This *jihad*, which was undertaken at the behest of Uthman dan Fodio, nevertheless took on a perceptibly different character here from that in the Hausa states. In Adamawa the war was against non-Muslims and not against Muslims accused, rightly or wrongly, of half-heartedness or 'apostasy'. It should therefore logically have led to the widespread Islamization of the conquered autochthonous peoples. Nothing of the sort happened, however, or very little: these peoples were subdued politically but no determined effort seems to have been made to convert them.

Fulbe motives for such an attitude may be reduced to two. The first is economic: the Islamization of the vanquished, which would have made them truly members of the community of the Faithful, was distinctly less advantageous for the conquerors than their subjection, in which case, since they were 'pagans', the Malikite Law left the conditions under which they were ruled to the discretion of their Muslim masters. A simple comparison of what a Fulbe ruler used to get, not so long ago, from his 'pagans' with the resources he could levy from his Muslim subjects proves the point eloquently. The second is psychological; for the Fulbe, especially those of Nigeria and Cameroon, who are descendants and heirs of the great tradition of Uthman dan Fodio, being Muslim is easily confused with being Fulbe. Islam justifies and explains in their eyes the social and political system which they have initiated (at least in Adamawa) and which they benefit from; it reinforces their sense of being 'different' from the peoples that surround them. In this context one might say they appropriate Islam to themselves, which partly explains their lack of inclination to proselytize. It is true that their domestic slaves have been Islamized, but this Islamization has remained very superficial and the efforts of those from this social category who have striven to deepen their religious knowledge have more often roused sarcasm than interest among their masters.

III

Viewed from within, the Islam of Adamawa prompts certain comments.

Just as the Fulbe people, as we have seen, have shown a distinct tendency to monopolize this religion to their own advantage, there has been a parallel attempt to monopolize Islam, at least as far as its spiritual leadership is concerned, by the Fulbe rulers (*laamiibe*, sing. *laamiido*) who wield political authority. A number of factors have aided and still continue to aid and abet this confusion of powers: on the theological level, the very teachings of the Muslim Law and Tradition; on the historical level, as well as the lessons of Islamic history, the example of the founders of the Fulbe hegemony in this region of Africa, for whom religious action was intimately connected with political action. Neither is there anything extraordinary in the fact that the *laamiido*, political head of a territorially defined state, should also be the head of the community of the Faithful living within the confines of that state, their religious as well as their political leader. It is striking, however, to find that, far from considering this spiritual leadership secondary, all *laamiibe* are, on the contrary, determined to exercise it unambiguously and to assert it to the maximum, relegating to the shadows or keeping in strict subjection their religious representative, the *limam*, and taking care that the men of letters (*moodibbe, mallum'en*) established on their land are not allowed to acquire too much independence or influence.

It is perhaps to this anxiety of the *laamiibe* to brook no other religious authority but their own that we should attribute the weakness of the 'brotherhoods' (*turuuq*) in this region, a surprising phenomenon in view of the role they play in other parts of West Africa. Although a certain number of men of letters have received the Tijaniyya or Qadiriyya *wird* (sometimes both), many others—apart from the Mahdists whom we shall mention below—are affiliated to no brotherhood. In addition and above all, their *moqqadems*, are few and, as such, enjoy neither great prestige nor great notoriety. Quite clearly, the authority of the *laamiibe* could hardly accommodate the proximity of strong religious personalities comparable, for example, to those found in Senegal. Perhaps historical differences may be able to give an explanation. In fact, the brotherhoods played no role at all in the *jihad* of Uthman dan Fodio (whose affiliation to the Qadiriyya is still doubtful and may have been concocted *a posteriori* by his direct successors for political ends), nor, with more reason, in its offshoots to the east. It should be remembered in this context that the brotherhoods have only attained a certain importance in northern Nigeria in the relatively recent past.

The merging of temporal and spiritual powers in the hands of the rulers in the southern lamidates, where the Fulbe element is, or was until recently, relatively small, also had the effect of making the *laamiido* appear, in the eyes of still non-Muslim or superficially Islamized tributary populations, a being quite out of the ordinary, an intercessor between God and his subjects. The extreme case of this identification of the Fulbe Muslim ruler with a divine, or at least essentially supra-human, ruler occurred in the lamidate of Rey-Buba (Bénoué Department, Cameroon). There, the *laamiido* is reputed to pray and fast 'for all his slaves', is thought not to die but to live after death on the summit of the Tcholliré mountain, from which he watches over his people and where up until recently two slaves were buried alive with him to accompany him on his last journey. Such beliefs and practices might suggest possible connections with those described for geographically close non-Muslim societies (notably the Mbum and Jukun).

IV

The evident lack of enthusiasm of the Fulbe for bringing Islam to the subjugated populations and their reluctance to convert their slave entourage except superficially have certainly been effective in restricting the number of conversions among the former and maintaining among the majority of the latter a mere façade of Islam, widely impregnated with heterodox practices. But this attitude has not been able to halt entirely the progress of the religion. Conversion appears to the more enterprising non-Fulbe an effective means of social mobility which allows them, if not to be fully accepted into, at least to enter the highest echelons of Fulbe society. Among the Fulbe's subject non-Muslim populations or neighbouring peoples, conversion is certainly attended by serious risk of conflict between the convert and his environment. Thus, in general, Islamized people remain few in number in northern Adamawa, where traditional cultural structures are solidly established. By contrast, conversion presents nothing but advantages for people belonging to groups where these structures have become enfeebled or for those who have become isolated from their original social context. Such tensions between the newly Islamized convert and his surroundings did not apply for former slaves whose diverse origins have clearly facilitated their adherence to the religion of their masters. However imperfect their knowledge of dogma is, as a general rule, and however heretical much of their behaviour may appear, these servile groups show a definite attachment to their religion, an attachment which is reinforced when they can vest in one man their spiritual aspirations and trust to him the burden of guiding them in the 'True Path'.

v

All the same, former slaves are not the only ones to feel this need for a religious guide and a number of pious Fulbe freemen, particularly those whose Islamization is not very far advanced, feel this too, which explains the ease with which the spiritual authority of the *laamiibe* has been accepted. But the frequently rather unedifying life of many of the rulers, the compliance and subservience towards them manifested by the 'doctors' of their entourage, not infrequently disappoint the ideal that the more demanding of the Faithful, and particularly the poorer among them, have of such a guide. Pious and willing to believe in the reign of a sort of 'Master of Justice', many of these common people suffer at least as much as many of the tributary populations from the exactions and abuses stemming from the social order, or at least from the influence on it of the greed of some of those at the top.

This sincere faith, in association with the resentment felt by the lower strata of society towards the politico-religious hierarchy, explains, in our view, the reception that has greeted the 'Mahdis' or 'Envoys of the Mahdi' who have appeared in Adamawa over the past three-quarters of a century. There have been, to our knowledge, six of them in the Yola Division of Nigeria or in Cameroon, the earliest being the *moodibbo* Abdullahi (near Yola, *c.* 1890) and the most recent, Ahmadu de Tourningal (near Ngaoundéré in 1952). Whether of high birth, like Prince Hayatu, a descendant of Uthman dan Fodio, or commoners, like Ahmadu, whether originating in Adamawa or foreigners (like 'Goni Waday' in 1910/11), all essentially found their Fulbe adepts among the common people and tributary populations. All, too, put in the first rank of the 'Enemies of God' the 'Bad Chiefs' and the 'doctors' devoted to them, and denounced not only the heresies of which they accused them, but also their rapacity and the abuses it led to, thus externalizing the conflicts latent in the society.

These attempts were always checked by the response of their adversaries and, in the event, first the *laamiibe* and then, after the colonial conquest, the European authorities, alerted by the traditional rulers (and worried by certain aspects of Mahdist preaching, notably the refusal to pay tax), rapidly broke the Mahdist movements with or without bloodshed.[2] Nevertheless, all over Adamawa, cells of faithful followers remain who reject any other 'Path' and proclaim themselves true to the Mahdiyya. Some of them believe that the Mahdi has already come and that the return of Isa and the end of the world, due 1,400 years after the death of Muhammad, are nigh. The majority, however, wait and hope for the coming of the 'true' Mahdi. They are not very active and have been made prudent by earlier events; their presence is hardly noticeable as far as overt acts are concerned but they nevertheless contribute towards strengthening belief in the reality of the 'Guided One'.

An expression of a faith which is not satisfied by the existing religious establishment, Mahdist movements have up to now always been suppressed by that establishment. Yet the hopes that they have raised remain, in a society where tensions, far from

---

[1] With the exception of the movement of Hayatu, whose followers were rendered impotent when Hayatu was put to death on the order of Rabah (1899). The bloodiest suppression of a Mahdist movement in Adamawa was conducted in 1911 by the German authorities against the supporters of Malam Jime ('Goni Waday').

diminishing, have rather been aggravated by recent changes and where those whom the tensions affect are always ready to pin their hopes with great confidence on the man who will, in his turn, assume the role of the Mahdi and show himself willing to accomplish the tasks expected of him.

IX. THE JIHAD OF SHEHU DAN FODIO: SOME PROBLEMS

M. G. SMITH

Among universalistic religions, Islam is distinguished by its emphasis on war as a means of spreading the Faith. Where likely to succeed, such war is a duty for the Faithful,[1] and it was largely due to the zealous prosecution of this profitable duty by its adherents that Islam spread as far and fast as it did. During the eighteenth and nineteenth centuries the Western Sudan experienced a succession of these *jihads*. Beginning in 1725 at Futa Toro, this wave of militant Islam was halted only by the French occupation. The leaders of all these recent West African *jihads* were Torodbe clerics from Futa Toro, who are usually classed as Fulani. Perhaps the most successful of these Torodbe *jihads* was that which Shehu Usumanu dan Fodio (also called Shaikh 'Uthman ibn Fodiye) launched against the Hausa chiefs of Gobir, Kano, Katsina, Zaria, Daura, their allies and congeners, in 1804. In six years of hard fighting the Shehu's followers overran these ancient states and passed beyond to carve out new chiefdoms in areas where no states had previously existed. Thereafter the north-western segment of what is now Nigeria has remained under the control of the Shehu's successors and their lieutenants. This *dar al-Islam* has been ruled mainly by Fulani Muslims. By 1840 it extended from Adamawa in the North Cameroons to Illo on the Niger, from Adar in the North to Ilorin on the borders of Yorubaland.

Assessments of this *jihad* have always varied. According to J. S. Trimingham, dan Fodio 'from 1786 preached the *jihad* in such a way that it became a racial as well as a religious war; (it) . . . differs from the other *jihads* on account of the number of nomads who joined in'.[2] For S. J. Hogben:

[1] Levy, 1957, p. 254.
[2] Trimingham, 1962, p. 162.

Religion was often made the pretext for the acquisition of worldly power. . . . [The *jihad*] had as its confessed object the purification of the Muslim religion, and it was directed against the corrupt rulers of Hausaland, who had been supposedly oppressing or ignoring the rights of their Muslim subjects. In reality, it was originally a national fight of the Fulani, both Muslim and pagan, against the forces of Yunfa, the king of Gobir, who had decreed their extermination. Only after the victory, when the pagan Fulani, who had borne more than their full share in order to achieve it, had retired to their flocks and herds, did the malams who had been the leaders, exploit the opportunity under the cloak of religion to oust the native rulers and put themselves into their places, with Usuman dan Fodio at their head. Henceforth the movement was no longer confined to a particular race; yet from its very nature it appealed more strongly to the fanatical and more highly-strung element in the Fulani clans.[3]

For W. F. Gowers, on the other hand:

The *jihad* was the raising of the standard of revolt by Othman dan Fodio against the tyranny of the non-Moslem rulers of Gobir, in defence of his co-religionists, whether Hausa or Fulani. It was not in any sense a conquest of the Hausa race by the Fulani; indeed, the Hausa adherents of Othman were probably as numerous as his Fulani followers. Even the leaders were not, strictly speaking, Fulanis. The Torabbe or Toronkawa (the tribe from which Shehu dan Fodio came) owe their origin to a mixture of the Jolof . . . element. They are blacker in colour than most Fulanis . . . they originally spoke the Wa-Kore language and are connected with the Suleibawa, who, like the Torabbe, are not Fulani—if there is any such thing as a pure Fulani race.[4]

Trimingham observes that Torodbe or Tokolor and Suleibawa are 'regarded as *rimbe*, assimilated free groups, but not as Fulbe proper'.[5]

Sir Ahmadu Bello, Sardauna of Sokoto, the late Premier of Northern Nigeria and a descendant of Shehu dan Fodio, has recently affirmed the 'official' Fulani view.

The Shehu Usumanu was a Fulani leader . . . a great preacher and man of the utmost piety . . . he was among a people who were nominally Muhammadan; . . . the religion had become very corrupt, and many pagan practices had crept in and had taken firm hold even in the highest quarters. The Shehu Usuman declared a Holy War against the polluters of the Faith. In 1804 he started by attacking the Chief of Gobir, one of the worst offenders, in whose

[3] Hogben, 1930, p, 73.   [4] Gowers, 1921, p. 10.
[5] Trimingham, op. cit., p. 195, note 2; see also Arnett, 1922, pp. 137–9.

territory he was living . . . Meanwhile, to cleanse the religion, the Shehu had organised revolts in all the great Hausa states; the Fulani living in them rose and overthrew the Hausa kings. The Shehu appointed new rulers, either from among the victorious generals, or from among other important Fulani.[6]

There are also other popular interpretations, radical and dissident. In one view the *jihad* was a political revolution against oppression and misrule; in another it was a cloak for racial conquest and imperialism.

These differing interpretations raise some important problems which can only be treated allusively here. As Trimingham observes, 'the history of the *jihad* of 'Uthman dan Fodio and of the Fulani states has yet to be written'.[7] Until this is done, and perhaps even afterwards, it may be wiser to suspend judgement between these conflicting views. They are in any case fully intelligible only in context. The late Sardauna saw himself as heir and custodian of a great and vital tradition derived from Shehu Usumanu. In 1959 those young Muslims who stressed the radical view of Shehu's *jihad* also advocated radical reforms in the Emirates of Northern Nigeria which were founded by this *jihad*. Others, with a dissident view of the *jihad*, preferred the wholesale elimination of the old régime and of the traditional Fulani ruling stratum. As we have seen, assessments of the Shehu's *jihad* made by British administrators who have worked in this area are very similar to these Nigerian views. Such divergent opinions might well reflect differing personal appraisals of the Fulani performance as a ruling stratum, *since* the *jihad*, and especially during this century.

Despite such contextualization, these differing viewpoints present important problems. Together, they obstruct and might well deny that an impartial historical account of these events is possible; yet the viewpoints are so opposed that instinctively one suspects the truth—that is, the historical reality of the *jihad*—to lie somewhere in between. What remains problematic is whether such 'historical truth' can be discovered at this stage, or would get a fair hearing if it were. Clearly, an individual's

---

[6] Ahmadu Bello, 1962, pp. 10–11.
[7] Trimingham, 1962, p. 195, note 1. [But now see, e.g., M. Last, *The Sokoto Caliphate*, 1967; M. Hiskett, *The Sword of Truth*, 1973—*ed.*]

view of this *jihad* is closely related to his ideological preference and his personal experience of recent Fulani administration. Traditionalists, Muslim or British, have tended to see the *jihad* as a genuine attempt to purify and spread Islam in this region. While admitting many subsequent lapses by its supporters and custodians, they argue that its historical effect was overwhelmingly beneficent in various ways; and that fairly moderate reforms, which will preserve and realize the spirit and aims of the *jihad* more effectively, are all that is necessary. Radicals and dissidents, who view the *jihad* as a revolutionary or imperialist war, derive quite different consequences which correspond with their ideology and personal experience. The British parallels to these Nigerian views strongly suggest that political involvement in North Nigerian affairs underlies all these conflicting interpretations. If so, this also seems to reduce the likelihood of an impartial historical account and assessment of the *jihad*, since this presupposes such knowledge and experience of the area that some sense of personal commitment is likely. Indeed, it may be unavoidable, since the *jihad*, whatever its merits or demerits, has had a decisive political impact on the region, and still exercises a predominant influence on current policy.

It is clearly unsound to seek an understanding of the course of this struggle, or the motives of its actors, in events which occurred long after the conflict had ended, but one suspects this retrospective interpretation to be rather common. Since the events of 1804–10 are fundamental to the present political order, there is scant hope that they will escape such ideological interpretation, or even that their presentation will proceed unaffected by political considerations, future and present as well as past. There is no doubt that the ruling Fulani, particularly in Sokoto Province, have actively nourished and reinterpreted the memory of this *jihad*, and especially the charisma of Shehu dan Fodio, in ways politically serviceable to their rule. The Shehu's books and writings, some of which might well be politically explosive, even today, have long been difficult for commoners and subjects, especially Habe, to come by. In their new independence and Federal political context the Northern rulers might now see fit to distribute these widely. Early British administrators, such as H. G. Harris, F. Edgar, Major Burdon, E. J. Arnett, and Sir H. R. Palmer, had access to various writings of primarily historical interest, such as *Tazyin al-waraqat*, by 'Abdullahi dan Fodio, the *Tanbih al-ikhwan*, by Shehu Usumanu, and the *Infaq al-maysur* by Sultan Mamman Bello. The great majority of free subjects in the Fulani empire were illiterate, and may hardly have known these titles, much less their contents. As late as 1959, Hausa Arabists in Northern Nigeria were surprised to learn of Shehu Usumanu's *Kitab al-farq* and *Bayan wujub al-hijra 'ala al-'ibad*. Yet it is clear from internal evidence that the Shehu intended these books for a wide public. No accurate assessment of Usumanu's *jihad* can ignore these critical documents. As political testaments, they rank with Lugard's Political Memoranda.

A further problem which these conflicting viewpoints raise concerns the nature of this *jihad* and of the *jihad* as a general form of Islamic expansion. *Jihads* fall into two main classes: revolts by Muslims against their non-Muslim rulers; and attacks by Muslims organized in autonomous political units against non-Muslims. The historically notable *jihads* are those which succeeded; but providing that other conditions are fulfilled, unsuccessful attacks might well be included.

The character of the Fulani *jihad* of Northern Nigeria is disputed mainly because it was launched against rulers who claimed to be Muslim, although undoubtedly lax in their observances. As the Sardauna put it, 'the Shehu Usumanu declared a Holy War against the polluters of the Faith'; that is, an armed rebellion aimed at enforcing correct observance of Islamic ritual and law. Much of the debate about the legitimacy of this *jihad* derives from the fact that it was a revolt against chiefs who were formally Muslim.

This problem receives extensive treatment in Shehu Usumanu's *Bayan wujub al-hijra*, especially section 1, 4–6, 12, 16, 31, 46–7. Citing a wide range of Muslim authorities, Koranic texts and traditions, the Shehu carefully distinguishes the various contexts in which *jihad* is obligatory or unlawful, and the rules which regulate it. He begins by discussing the obligation of *hijra*—

that is, for Muslims to withdraw from the lands of the heathen. Except for the physically disabled, this obligation is shown to be unconditional. Shehu argues that:

> Withdrawal from the towns of the heathen is an essential duty, both in the Koran and the Traditions, and in the consensus of the learned. . . . Now the capital cities of the Sudan are included in the towns of the heathen; . . . these cities fall into three classes . . . In one class of these towns, paganism predominates and Islam is very weak, for instance . . . Mossi, Gurma, Bussa, Borgu, Dagomba, Yoruba . . . and Gombe. . . . The rulers of these countries are all heathen, and so too . . . their subjects. . . . Another class of towns are those in which Islam is dominant and there is little paganism; but the countries of Bornu, Kano, Katsina, Songhai and Malle, as Ahmed Baba shows, . . . all these are heathen states without any doubt, since the chiefs . . . are heathens like the first group, although they practise religion of Islam, because they are polytheists also. They have obstructed the way of Islam, and have put worldly standards before the Faith. In the view of all the '*ulama*, all this is simply heathen.[8]

With these arguments, Shehu justifies his flight of 21 February 1804 from Degel in Gobir territory to Gudu near Kwonni just over the boundary, and also his summons to other Muslims to withdraw from the (heathen) Hausa states. In the *Infaq al-maysur*, Sultan Mamman Bello, the Shehu's son and successor, devotes more space to the documentation of heathen practices among the rulers of Hausaland and Bornu, and also reproduces the correspondence between the Shehu and himself, on the one hand, and the Shaikh Alhaji Aminu al-Kanemi, who defended Bornu, concerning this charge of heathenism and the counter-charge of an illegitimate '*jihad*' on the other.[9]

The charge of heathenism seems crucial to the legitimacy of this *jihad*, since the general weight of Muslim authorities prohibits rebellions against unjust or tyrannous chiefs, provided they observe Islam. The Shehu writes that:

> The Prophet said . . . 'he who obeys my Representative undoubtedly obeys me also; he who disobeys my Representative undoubtedly disobeys me also' . . . Subki says 'it is unlawful to withdraw allegiance from the ruler. All agree on this if the ruler is righteous, and even when he is not righteous this is the better opinion, that is, unless he becomes a heretic (*muntazil*).'

[8] Smith and Kumasi, 1959, Section 1.
[9] Arnett, op. cit., pp. 6-8, 21, 24–26, 47–48, and 99–120.

Ahmadu Zaruk says . . . 'It is forbidden to withdraw allegiance from a ruler, either in speech or in deed, and this consensus extends to praying under all rulers and their officials, good and bad alike.'[10]

For the classification of heathen, the Shehu relies on Muhammad al-Maghili's Epistle to the Askia:

> There are three classes of heathen; first those who are clearly heathen by descent; . . . second . . . the man who has been a Muslim, and then openly apostasized, returning to heathendom and abandoning Islam. His apostasy is quite open and he declares it with his own mouth; . . . third, there is the one who claims he is a Muslim while we for our part classify him as a heathen because that which does not occur apart from heathenism occurs with him openly.[11]

It was the substance of Shehu's and Bello's charges that the Hausa rulers of their day fell into this third category; that for this reason the withdrawal of Muslims from their kingdoms was obligatory, since 'the Prophet said . . . "he who associates with the heathen or lives with them is just like them" ';[12] and thus, that a Holy War against them was obligatory as well as legitimate.

Besides the evidence which Shehu and Mamman Bello cite themselves, observations by Landeroin in the Hausa successor-states of Tsibiri (Gobir), Maradi, and Tasawa (Katsina), and the recent account of Abuja, to which the Zaria Hausa retired, tend to support this charge of heathenism, while emphasizing that the Hausa rulers were formally Muslim.[13]

Shehu argues also that:

> Holy War becomes obligatory under three conditions. Firstly, on the orders of the (Muslim) ruler . . . Secondly, if the enemy launch a sudden attack on Muslim territory . . . Thirdly, to rescue captured Muslims from the hands of the heathen.[14]

The relevance of these doctrinal points is shown by the following outline of events which precipitated the *jihad* of 1804. For some years previously an uneasy situation had prevailed in the dominions of Gobir, where Shehu lived and taught, and where there were also many Fulani, some Muslim and sedentary, others

---

[10] Smith and Kumasi, op. cit., Section 6.   [11] Ibid., Section 46.
[12] Ibid., Section 1.   [13] Mission Tilho, 1906–9, vol. 2, pp. 528–37.
[14] Smith and Kumasi, op. cit., Section 13.

pagan and nomad. Some time around 1802 the Sarkin (Chief of) Gobir, Nafata, proclaimed that no one should be a Muslim unless his father had been one; and that without permission no man could wear a turban nor any woman a veil.[15] Bello says, 'Nothing . . . caused us so much fear as this proclamation.'[16] When Shehu 'saw the number of his assemblies and their desire to withdraw from the infidels and to begin the *jihad*, he began to urge them to prepare weapons for one year; and we set to to prepare it'.[17] Nafata died shortly after, and was succeeded by Yunfa, who pressed the anti-Muslim policy. In December 1803, at the request of his officials, Yunfa sent a force against a group of Arewa warriors who had accepted Shehu's teaching and leadership, under their head, 'Abdusallami. Following Nafata's proclamation and Gobir harassments, these non-Fulani converts had already *withdrawn* from Gobir territory to Gimbana, a site in the Kebbi chiefdom from which they originally came. They were ordered by Yunfa to return to Gobir, but refused unless the Shehu expressly required this. Gimbana was then overrun by Yunfa's troops during the Fast of Ramadan; its surviving occupants were captured and escorted towards Alkalawa, the capital of Gobir. 'Abdusallami, the Gimbana leader, escaped with some of his closest aides to a Fulani settlement near by.

The Sheikh ordered them (the Fulani) not to deliver him (Abdusallami) up to his enemy, and the enemy sent to them saying 'Hand over to us the remnant of the Muslim fugitives.' But the enemy was afraid to prove them and matters were adjusted for them, so they (the pursuers) returned, and as they returned they passed by the settlement of the Sheikh (at Degel); and they (the Gobirawa) began to mock at the Muslims and say 'You are the only ones left and you shall see us again soon.' And our foolish ones opposed them and took from them some of the treasures (booty from Gimbana) and let them (the Gimbana captives) go. The Gobir people fled. And when news of this reached their chief, he sent word to the Sheikh, 'Come out, thou and thy sons and thy brethren, from the village, for I propose to make an attack on the rest.' And the Sheikh made him refrain until he had emigrated with his company; and he fled from out of their country to a district called Gudu, and he bade the Muslims flee from the land of the infidels to the region to which he had removed. So the people emigrated to him steadily, until

[15] Arnett, op. cit., p. 105. [16] Ibid., p. 48. [17] Harris, n.d. (*a*); Hiskett, 1963, p. 105.

the infidels prevented the Muslims from further emigration, and his followers swore allegiance to the Sheikh on the Koran and the Law.[18]

The Sarkin Gobir then sent a messenger to recall Shehu. Even before the Shehu's messenger could set out with his reply to Alkalawa:

When the Sarkin Gobir blocked the roads to those who were fleeing to us, our people rose up on a Thursday and fell upon the Sudanese who were in the district and slew and captured and plundered and caught slaves. When God brought us to Friday, Shehu rose up and preached to his people. He commanded them to release those whom they had captured and to restore what they had taken away. Thereupon they released their captives and restored the property they had taken. It also happened before the journey of our messenger that the chiefs of Gobir were making war on us and harrying us. They were expelling our people and making captives of them. Shehu protested against this.[19]

While the Shehu's emissary to Yunfa was at Alkalawa, a force of Gobir horsemen attacked. The Shehu's followers defeated them at Matankare. The Shehu was also attacked three times by the chief of Kwonni near Gudu.[20] By then the situation was quite out of hand and war was inevitable. 'The prince of Gobir (with Tuareg allies) came out against us and met us in a place called (Tabkin) Kwotto, and God routed them.'[21] This was in June 1804. To celebrate the victory the Shehu's brother, 'Abdullahi, wrote a poem in which he says:

Now the different races among us Mohammedans were first the Toron-kawa (Torodbe): they are our kindred; then our Fulani and our Hausas. There were also some of other races who assembled and aided us in the service of God.[22]

In July 1804 the Shehu withdrew from Gudu to Nagabci and wrote circular letters to 'the chiefs of Sudan' relating the cause and course of his dispute with the chief of Gobir, enjoining their observance of Islam and its Law, and calling on them to assist him against Gobir, or at least to desist from assisting Gobir.[23] The Sarkin Gobir also

---

[18] Harris, n.d. (*b*).   [19] Arnett, op. cit., p. 52.
[20] Mission Tilho . . ., vol. 2, pp. 473-4, 485-6.
[21] Harris, n.d. (*b*).   [22] Arnett, op. cit., p. 58.   [23] Ibid., pp. 62-63.

sent messages to his brother chiefs, the Sarkin Katsina, the Sarkin Kano, Sarkin Zazzau, Sarkin Daura, and Sarkin Adar. He informed them that he had left a small fire in his country and it had grown until . . . now it had burnt him. He warned them to be careful lest a fire like this burnt them also. Thereupon each one of them rose up and attacked all those who allied themselves with Shehu; they slew them and captured them. They (Shehu's supporters) fled and took refuge in certain towns . . . till they became very numerous. Then they rose up, and in self-defence drove away the forces sent against them.[24]

This is Bello's version of the way the conflict spread; but when the chief of Gobir received help from other Hausa chiefs as well as the Tuareg, the Shehu also organized this general revolt. In this way the conflict spread from Gobir throughout and beyond Hausaland. This general spread was perhaps inevitable, but so were the alignments and composition of the opposing groups.

Some Fulani assisted the Hausa chiefs openly; others secretly; others remained neutral, and yet other Fulani groups sought to assist both parties in order to profit, whichever won.[25] But in most areas as well as Katsina 'some of their Fulani kindred (the non-Muslim nomads) joined our folk, the followers of the Faith'.[26] From Futa Toro, Sidi al-Mukhtar al-Kunti, the Qadiriyya *sufi*, sent others, Fulani and Torodbe, to swell the Shehu's *jihad*. Probably most Fulani who engaged in the struggle sided with dan Fodio's party irrespective of faith. For generations the nomads had suffered oppression and contumely from the Hausa rulers, and they had old scores to repay.[27] They were also tempted by the prospects of plunder and politically privileged positions, such as they received in eastern Katsina in return for their support. With only one known exception, the Chief of Zaria, the Hausa rulers uniformly declared against the Shehu and his followers and tried to help one another in certain campaigns, without much effect. In Bornu the Alhaji Shaikh Aminu, to whom this state owed its continued independence, like the nomad Fulani and Hausa warriors, took the side of the Kanuri ethnic group nearest his own Kanembu. The opposition between Muslims and non-Muslims was thus confused from the very start of

[24] Arnett, op. cit., p. 105.
[26] Arnett, op. cit., p. 77.
[25] Smith, 1958–59.
[27] Smith, op. cit.

the conflict by other ties and alignments, such as kinship, ethnic identity, secular political resentments and loyalties, calculations of advantage, communal solidarities and antagonisms, etc. Given this coalescence of very diverse interests among their followers, the control exercised by leaders on either side was uncertain and incomplete. As can be seen from the events just related, the initial conflicts developed inevitably, but were not under the direction of Yunfa or Shehu. Party followers took matters into their own hands. The Shehu's chief lieutenants, his brother 'Abdullahi and his son Bello, exercised a tenuous control over their undisciplined warriors.[28] In Kano, Katsina, and Zazzau the Shehu's supporters disputed precedence and political claims with one another, even before the struggle was over, and often to their adversaries' advantage.

Especially in Western Hausaland, there was a large and widely dispersed Fulani population, pastoral nomads being non-Muslim, the sedentary Fulani mainly Muslim. Both divisions were for different reasons dissatisfied with their lot under the Hausa chiefs; before the Shehu's *jihad* there had been a number of clashes between Fulani and Hausa throughout this area from Zaria to Zamfara. The processes of polarization brought to a head by the Shehu's declaration of *jihad* would probably have generated conflicts, even without this; but when Shehu and Yunfa came to blows these latent hostilities and cleavages between Muslim and heathen, pastoralist and farmer, immigrant and native people, Fulani and Hausa, all poured themselves into this conflict, with the result that the critical principles for which the Shehu stood were often obscured. Perhaps it was his recognition of the need to clarify this situation, and to regulate conduct according to Islam, that led the Shehu to devote himself to writing political and religious tracts such as the *Kitab al-farq* and the *Bayan wujub al-hijra*, for the guidance and enlightenment of his followers. Moreover, once this conflict had come to a head at Tabkin Kwotto, it could not be localized within a single Hausa state; inevitably it spread to the limits of the social field in which this combination of forces and cleavages was general. For the

[28] Arnett, op. cit., pp. 53, 77–8, 82, 107; see also Whitting, n.d., p. 4.

Muslim leaders, this multiplied the problems of directing and regulating their *jihad* in accord with the rules of religion and of good policy. But perhaps this need to pursue political advantage while observing the Law and religion is a general feature of all those *jihads* which originate as revolts against 'heathen' rulers. The results are always liable to differing interpretations. Where religious scruples obstruct effective political action, the *jihad* will normally fail; where political action of a secular, instrumental type disguises its nature under religious banners, its religious claims are easily discredited; but no one who has studied the Shehu's writings or life can doubt his primary religious commitment. His *jihad* was successful through a skilful combination of religious and political factors; yet it is precisely this combination which lends it an ambiguous character. As I have tried to show, the Shehu and his closest supporters, having identified themselves as the focus of opposition to Gobir government, were very largely governed by the circumstances of their situation and had to adjust, within the limits their religion permitted, to its requirements. This pattern is a general characteristic of Islam, enshrined in the doctrine of *ijma'*, by which consensus legitimates necessary changes. As Weber pointed out, Islam is one of the very few major religions which has a practical orientation to the affairs of this world, 'an essentially political character',[29] as seen in the injunction of *jihad*. The ambiguous character of Shehu dan Fodio's *jihad* derives from the ambiguous character of *jihad* itself.

REFERENCES

Ahmadu Bello, Alhaji Sir,
  (1962) *My Life*. Cambridge.
Arnett, E. J.
  (1922) *The Rise of the Sokoto Fulani, being a paraphrase and in some parts a translation of the Infaku'l Maisuri of Sultan Mohammed Bello*. Kano.
Gowers, W. F.
  (1921) *Gazetteer of Kano Province*. London: Waterlow.
Harris, H. G.
  (n.d.(a)) A Précis and Translation of the *Tazyin al-warakat*, by 'Abdullahi dan Fodio, first Sarkin Gwandu. (Unpublished.)

[29] Weber, 1963, p. 263.

(n.d.(*b*)) A History of the Rebellion of Abdusallami, being a translation of the *Sardu'l Kalami* by Sultan Muhammad Bello. (Unpublished.)

Heath, F.
(1952) *A Chronicle of Abuja*, being a translation of Hassan and Shu'aibu: *Makau, Sarkin Zazzau na Habe*, and *Tarihi de Al'adun Habe na Abuja*. Ibadan University Press.

Hiskett, M. (1963) *Tazyin al-waraqat by Abdullah Ibn Muhammad*. Ibadan University Press.

Hogben S. F.
(1930) *The Muhammadan Emirates of Nigeria*. Oxford.

Levy, Reuben
(1957) *The Social Structure of Islam*. Cambridge.

Mission Tilho . . .
(1906–9) *Documents Scientifiques de la Mission Tilho, 1906–1909*. Paris. (Ministère des Colonies, République Française, 1911.)

Smith, M. G.
(1958–59) Field Notes.

Smith, M. G. and Kumasi, M. Muntaka
(1959) An Account of the Obligations of Withdrawal, being a translation of the *Bayan Wujub al-Hijra alal Ibad* of Shehu Usumanu dan Fodio. (Unpublished.)

Trimingham, J. Spencer
(1962) *A History of Islam in West Africa*. London.

Weber, Max
(1963) *The Sociology of Religion*, transl. Ephraim Fischoff. Boston: Beacon Press.

Whitting, E. J.
(n.d.) *History of Sokoto, being a translation of the Tadhkiratu 'Inisian by Hajji Sa'id*. Kano: Ife-Olu Printing Works.

X. THE SUDANESE MAHDIYYA
AND THE NIGER–CHAD REGION

SABURI BIOBAKU and MUHAMMAD AL-HAJJ

The idea of the 'expected Mahdi' or the 'awaited deliverer', who will appear at the end of time and 'fill the earth with equity and justice after it has been filled with tyranny and oppression', is well known in the history of Islam. Nevertheless, it may be worthwhile to begin this paper with a brief account on the origins and historical development of Mahdism.

The term Mahdi (the guided one) occurs neither in the Quran nor in the Prophetic traditions of Muslim and Al-Bukhari which had been acclaimed as authoritative by the consensus of the Muslim community. It does occur, however, in other traditions of doubtful authenticity, i.e. Ibn Maja, Al-Tirmidhi, Abu Da'ud, and others. In these traditions the Mahdi is described as a descendant of the Prophet who will appear at the end of time and rule the world with equity and justice, i.e. 'The world shall not pass away until my nation be governed by one of my house whose name agrees with mine.'[1] A number of early Muslim scholars have questioned the authenticity of such traditions and rejected the idea of a Mahdi as false and unsupported by either the Quran or the *Sunna*.[2] Nevertheless, the idea developed into a popular belief which has been held with great tenacity up to the present day. During times of religious degeneration or political upheaval, a devout person may assume the office of the 'expected Mahdi' and take upon himself the duty of rectifying the Faith and re-organizing the State by force of arms if necessary. Instances of such manifestations are numerous in the history of Islam.

The historical origins of Mahdism could be sought in the civil wars which followed the death of 'Uthman, the third Caliph

[1] *Encyclopaedia of Religion and Ethics*, vol. VIII, p. 336.
[2] Ibn Khaldun, 1958, vol. II, p. 725.

(644–55). It appears that the perturbed condition of Islam at the time led the Muslim Community to look forward to a saviour similar to the 'expected Messiah' of the Jews and the Christians. The idea was first adopted by the Shi'a when their hopes for succession to the Caliphate were shattered by the Umayyad supremacy. It was soon, however, absorbed by the Sunnites as well. The main point of difference between the Shi'as and the Sunnis as to the idea of the Mahdi is that among the former it is an article of faith, while among the latter it is little more than a popular notion. Again, to the Shi'as, the Mahdi is equated with the 'hidden *imam*' who is absolute and infallible and whose return (*raj'a*) is awaited to restore the leadership of the Muslim Community to the '*Ahl al-Bayt*' (the Prophet's house). To the Sunnis, on the other hand, the Mahdi is simply a reformer who will restore the Faith to its original purity of the early days as it had been during the times of '*al-Khulafa' al-Rashidun*' (the 'Four Rightly Guided Caliphs').

For the purposes of this paper, we need not be detained by the Shi'a concept of the Mahdi, since there is no evidence of any connexion between Shi'ism and Islam in the Sudan or the Niger–Chad region.[3] The purpose of this paper is to discuss the interrelation between the reformist movements in the Niger–Chad region in the early years of the nineteenth century and the Sudanese Mahdia at the close of the century. We will attempt to show that the Fulani *jihads*[4] gave rise to the Sudanese Mahdia[5] and that the latter sought support and expansion (outside the Sudan) mainly in the Niger–Chad region.

[3] The term 'the Sudan' refers to the 'Nile-Sudan' or the present 'Republic of the Sudan' as distinct from the larger *Sudan* of the Medieval Arab geographers. 'The Niger–Chad region' refers to the Savannah Land of West Africa extending from Darfur westwards through the old kingdoms of Wadai, Bagirmi, Bornu (Kanem), the Hausa states, Melle, and so on up to the Atlantic.

[4] The Fulani *jihads* of the nineteenth century are connected with the names of Shehu Usuman dan Fodio (d. 1817) in the Hausa states; Seku Ahmadu (d. 1843) in Masina; and al-Hajj 'Umar (d. 1864) in the Bambara states of Nioro and Segu. For a brief account, see Smith, 1961, pp. 169f.

[5] Muhammad Ahmad al-Mahdi rose against the Turko-Egyptian régime in the Sudan in 1881. He achieved enormous victories, and by 1885 the Egyptian régime virtually ended after the death of General Gordon. The Mahdi himself soon died and was succeeded by the *Khalifa* 'Abdullahi who ruled the Sudan until he was defeated and killed by Lord Kitchener in 1898. See Holt, 1958a.

The major movement among the Fulani *jihads* was that under the leadership of Shehu Usuman dan Fodio. In 1804 the Shehu called for a *jihad* against the Hausa state of Gobir. This was soon followed by local Fulani risings throughout Hausaland and Bornu. By 1831 the Fulani succeeded in establishing an Empire comprising: 'Some fifteen Muslim emirates controlling a total area of some 180,000 square miles, and owing allegiance to an "*amir al-mu'minin*" in the newly founded town of Sokoto.'[6] The most effective resistance against the Fulani came from Bornu under the leadership of Shaikh Muhammad al-Amin al-Kanemi, who was himself a learned Muslim reformer, but he could not see any justification for the Fulani *jihad* besides political ambition. The Sokoto Empire, however, included parts of Bornu and managed to survive until the British occupation in 1902–3.

The influence of the Sokoto Empire on the rise of the Sudanese Mahdia was mainly intellectual. The leaders of the Fulani *jihad*, Shehu Usuman, his brother 'Abdullahi, and his son Muhammad Bello, were well read in Arabic literature, and they all possessed a vast knowledge of the classical Islamic sciences. This learning showed itself in their writings, which reached the total of '258 books and pamphlets'.[7] Among this literary output we find extensive material dealing with the subject of the 'expected Mahdi'.[8]

In his book *Tahdhir al-ikhwan*, the Shehu says:

know, O my Brethren, that I am not the *imam al-Mahdi*, and that I never claimed the *Mahdiyya*—even though that is heard from the tongues of other people. Indeed, I have striven beyond measure in warning them to desist from that, and declared its refutation in some of my writings, both in Arabic and '*Ajami*.[9]

The Shehu, then, declined the office of Mahdi in the most emphatic terms, though it was widely believed that he was the

---

[6] Smith, op. cit., p. 175.　　　　　　　　[7] Ibid., p. 176.

[8] For example: Shehu Usuman, *al-Mahdi fil-muntaẓar; Tahdhir al-ikhwan min 'iddi'a' al-mahdiyya al-mau'uda akhir al-ẓaman* (Arabic MSS., Ibadan University Library); Muhammad Bello, *al-qawl al-mukhtasar fi amr al-imam al-muntaẓar* (Sokoto Native Authority Collection—Divisional Library).

[9] *Tahdhir al-ikhwan*, op. cit., fol. 2. '*Ajami* is the vernacular language: in this case, Fulani and probably Hausa.

'awaited deliverer'. He argued that he did not fulfil the requirements of the office as described in the classical Islamic traditions.
First, the Mahdi should be a descendant of Fatima, the Prophet's
daughter, and the Shehu had no claim to such pedigree. Secondly,
the Mahdi should be born at Medina while the Shehu was born
at Marata in '*Bilad al-Sudan*'.[10]

But while the Shehu refused to assume the office himself, he
contributed to the current prophecies regarding the appearance
of the expected Mahdi. Muhammad Bello relates the following:

> The Shehu sent me to all his followers in the east among the people of
> Zanfara, Katsina, Kano and Daura. . . . I conveyed to them his good
> tidings about the approaching appearance of the Mahdi, that the Shehu's
> followers are his vanguard and that this *Jihad* will not end, by God's permis-
> sion, until it gets to the Mahdi. They listened and welcomed the good
> news.[11]

It is clear, then, that as early as the Shehu's life-time (d. 1817)
there was a strong tradition about the approaching end of time
preceded by the Mahdi's appearance. Manifestations of Mahdism
appeared here and there in the Niger–Chad region, but it seems
that none of the claimants succeeded. We are told of a certain
Hamma who proclaimed himself Mahdi among the Taureg in
1813 and gained some success before he was defeated and cruci-
fied by the Shehu's orders.[12] The fact remains, however, that the
Shehu's statement linking the Fulani *jihad* with the Mahdi's
appearance had inspired prophecies, written and oral, about the
appointed day. Classical books of Islamic eschatology were
extensively read and copiously quoted by the Shehu's companions,
and their successors, in their literary output about Mahdism.[13]
The central point in these prophecies is that the Mahdi will
appear in the East, and that his advent will be preceded by a
period of drought, civil strife, and general turmoil in the Maghrib

[10] *Tahdhir al-ikhwan*, op. cit., fol. 2.
[11] *Infaq al-maysur* (Arabic MS., Ibadan University Library, uncatalogued),
fol. 129; Whitting's edition, pp. 104–5.
[12] *Tahdhir al-ikhwan*, op. cit., fol. 3; see also, 'Abd al-Qadir b. Mustafa,
Akhbar al-bilad al-Hausiyya (Ibadan Arabic MS. 82/18), fol. 10.
[13] Muhammad Bello, *Tanbih al-'Afham 'ala anna 'l-mahdi huwa l-khitam*
(mentioned by Gidado in *al-Kashf wa'l bayan*). Khidir b. Jibril al-Fallati,
Muntakhab al-kalam fi 'amr al-mahdi al-imam (Kano N. A. Collection).

and the Niger–Chad region. The outcome would be the migration of hordes of people from the Maghrib and the Niger–Chad region to the 'Nile and Makka'. As early as the time of *amir al-muʿminin*' Abu Bakar Atiku (1837–42)—probably owing to the perturbed conditions within the Sokoto Empire—a number of people started to migrate from Hausaland to the Nile valley in anticipation of meeting the 'expected Mahdi'. This created so much unrest and agitation that the Sultan had to issue proclamations declaring that the time of the exodus had not yet come, 'since there is still some good remaining among us'.[14] It appears, however, that the unrest continued throughout the second half of the nineteenth century, causing the migration of many people from the Sokoto Empire to the Sudan and Hijaz.

At this juncture we may turn to discuss the early contacts between the Niger–Chad region and the Sudan. The distinction between the two regions is, of course, modern, because to the early Arab geographers, *'Bilad al-Sudan'* extended from the Red Sea and the Horn of Africa in the East to the shore of the Atlantic in the West.[15] Divisions within this extensive territory were genealogical and geographical rather than political. We are concerned here with the Zaghawa group, who seem to have controlled communications between the Niger–Chad region and the Sudan. Al-Yaʿqubi says about them:

As for the 'Sudanese' who sought the west, they traversed the land and established many kingdoms. The first of their kingdoms is that of the Zaghawa who settled at a place which is called Kanem.[16]

Yaqut's account runs as follows:

The Kingdom of the Zaghawa is said to be a great kingdom among the kingdoms of the 'Sudan'. On their eastern boundary is the kingdom of the Nubians who are above upper Egypt. Between them there is a distance of ten days journey. They are many tribes and the length of their land is a fifteen days journey through habitations and cultivations all the way. . . .[17]

[14] Abu Bakar Atiku, *Wathiqa to the people of Gwando* (Arabic Ms. Ibadan, uncatalogued.)

[15] See Al-Masʿudi, *Muruj al-dhahab*, Paris edition, vol. III, pp. 1–2.

[16] *Tarikh*, Beirut, 1960, vol. I, p. 193.

[17] Quoted by Oliver and Fage, 1962, p. 47.

Leo Africanus is probably referring to the Zaghawa when he speaks about 'Zingani':

> The king of Nubia maintaineth continual warre partly against the people of Goran (who being descended of the people called Zingani, inhabite the deserts and speak a kind of language that no nation understandeth) and partly against certaine other people.[18]

It may be reasonable to maintain, from the above quotations, that during the Middle Ages the Zaghawa dominated all the land from Lake Chad through Darfur northwards up to the desert. They controlled the caravan routes to Nubia, Tripoli, and Egypt, as the statement of Leo Africanus seems to suggest. What is important, however, is the fact that contacts and communications between the Niger–Chad region and the Sudan can be traced back to medieval times and probably farther back to classical antiquity. As late as the nineteenth century Darfur was considered, geographically, part of the Niger–Chad region, i.e. Sultan Bello includes Darfur among *Bilad al-Takrur*.[19] Denham and Clapperton, who visited Bornu between 1822 and 1824, reported a tradition that Darfur, as well as Wadai, had been 'at no very distant period, tributary to the Sultans of Bornu'.[20]

Islam became the official religion in Darfur in the sixteenth century during the reign of Sulayman Solong (1596–1637). It had a tradition of several centuries in Bornu by that time. If we therefore consider the long-standing connexion between the two regions we may say with some degree of probability that Islam came to Darfur from the West rather than from the East. It is highly probable that Islam was introduced to Darfur from the Lake Chad region through the annual traffic to Mecca. The road to Mecca through Darfur has been frequented by pilgrims from the Chad region from ancient times up to the present day. It appears that it had been much preferred to the Trans-Saharan route from the Chad region to Tripoli and Egypt. This latter route was taken only by those who could afford to buy or hire a camel for the long journey across the desert.

---

[18] *The History and Description of Africa*, bk. VII, p. 826.
[19] *Infaq al-maysur*, op. cit., fols. 3–4.
[20] 1826, vol. II, p. 178 (3rd ed.).

The majority of pilgrims, however, set out on foot through Darfur and the eastern Sudan, stopping from one place to another to earn by their labour the necessary provisions to continue the journey. Burckhardt, who made the journey from the Nile valley to Hijaz in 1814, gives a detailed description of the routes followed by these pilgrims through the Sudan.[21] The major ones were from Darfur through Kordofan to Sennar and then either through the interior of Abyssinia to Massawa or through Shandi to Suakin. He estimated the number of those who followed the Sennar–Massawa road as between 150 and 200 annually, and those who travelled from Sennar via Shandi to Suakin as 500 annually. A considerable number of the 'Takruri' pilgrims used to settle in the Sudan on their return from Mecca, with the result that at the present day there are large settlements, especially in the Gezira, Gadarif, and Kasala.[22]

With this rather long digression, we have endeavoured to establish the constant traffic between the Niger–Chad region and the Sudan from the distant past up to the present day. We can safely assume therefore that much of the Mahdist literature current in the Niger-Chad region in the nineteenth century found its way to the Sudan. There is also more direct evidence to show that the Sudanese Mahdi, Muhammad Ahmad, was influenced by ideas from the Niger–Chad region. In the first place, we know that Muhammad Ahmad did not declare himself the 'expected Mahdi' until his famous meeting with 'Abdullahi b. Muhammad (later the *Khalifa*) at Masallamiya in 1881. Before this meeting Muhammad Ahmad had already acquired some fame for his asceticism which enabled him to become head of the Sammaniyya order. But there is no evidence that he contemplated the idea of assuming the office of Mahdi until his meeting with 'Abdullahi. Tradition has it that at the first encounter 'Abdullahi 'twice swooning at the sight of Muhammad Ahmad, greeted the latter as the expected Mahdi'.[23] It was not long after this meeting before Muhammad Ahmad proclaimed his mission and declared a *jihad*.

[21] 1819, pp. 406–414.   [22] See, Isam Hassan, 1952, pp. 60–112.
[23] Holt, op. cit., p. 43.

Now 'Abdullahi, who soon became the Mahdi's right-hand man and later his successor, came from a family which originated somewhere in the Niger–Chad region. His great-grandfather, 'Ali al-Karrar, came from the Niger–Chad region on his way to Mecca. He, however, settled among the Ta'aisha in Southern Darfur and married a local woman. He soon acquired considerable reputation as a holyman, and his amulets and medicines were widely sought. 'Abdullahi's father, Muhammad Adam (nicknamed *Tawr Shayn*—'the ugly bull'), continued the tradition in the family with much success as well. When his father became old, 'Abdullahi succeeded him as soothsayer and diviner among the Ta'aisha people. On the authority of his divinations, Ta'aisha used to plan warfare and raids. In 1873, when fighting broke out between Al-Zubayr and the Rizaygat, 'Abdullahi went and gave his services to the latter. He was, however, captured and only escaped execution through the intervention of some holymen among Al-Zubayr's followers. Al-Zubayr granted him pardon, probably in the hope of making use of his services, and made him settle at al-Kalaka, south of Nyala. Then 'Abdullahi wrote to Al-Zubayr saying:

I saw in a dream that you are the expected Mahdi and I am one of your followers; so tell me if you are the Mahdi of the Age, so that I may follow you.[24]

Al-Zubayr rejected the offer and the correspondence ceased.

'Abdullahi then left Darfur, accompanied by his father intending to go to pilgrimage. When they reached the territory of the Jimi' people (on the white Nile, north-east of the Nuba mountains) they were persuaded by their chief, 'Asakir Abu Kalam to abandon the idea of pilgrimage and settle there. Here Muhammad Tawr Shayn died, not before advising his son to seek out the 'expected *Mahdi*' and help him. It was from here too that 'Abdullahi proceeded to Masallamiya, where he met Muhammad Ahmad and hailed him as the 'expected Mahdi', as described above.

We can hardly doubt therefore that Muhammad Ahmad assumed the role of the 'expected Mahdi' at the invitation of 'Ab-

[24] Holt, op. cit., p. 44.

dullahi. This explains why 'Abdullahi soon rose to pre-eminence in the Mahdi's retinue. He was appointed the *'Khalifa* designate' in spite of strong protest from the Mahdi's own kindred, the *Ashraf*. His supremacy was absolute, and when it was questioned the Mahdi issued a proclamation in his favour in the most emphatic words:

> He whom we have mentioned is our *Khalifa* and his *Khilafa* is by a command from the Prophet. Whoever of you believes in God and the last day and has faith in my Mahdiship, let him submit to the *Khalifa* 'Abdullahi, both outwardly and inwardly. If you see him apparently transgressing in a matter, leave it to be judged by the knowledge of God and a good interpretation—the *Khalifa* is the leader of the Muslims and our *Khalifa*, and our representative in all matters of Faith. Beware of murmuring against his right, thinking evil or failing to obey him. . . .[25]

Such, then, was the high position to which 'Abdullahi, the *faki*[26] of Darfur, was elevated under the Mahdia. His supremacy soon brought peoples from Kordofan and Darfur to a position of leadership, and so it was not long before the Mahdia came to be known as the régime of 'westerners' as distinct from the 'riverain' people of the Sudan. In fact, from the beginning the Mahdi sought support in the west by performing the *hijra* to Jabal Qadir in Kordofan. Later hordes of peoples were transported from Darfur to the capital, Omdurman, to guard the régime and protect the Faith. Taking into account the early career of the *Khalifa* 'Abdullahi, his first meeting with the *Mahdi*, and the subsequent role played by him and western peoples in the establishment of the Mahdist State, we can safely maintain therefore that the Sudanese Mahdia came as a fulfilment of current expectations prevailing in Darfur and the Niger–Chad region at large.

It is significant that immediately after the fall of El Obeid (January 1883) the Mahdi opened correspondence with the rulers of the Niger–Chad region demanding recognition and support.[27] This created a state of unrest, particularly within Bornu and the Sokoto Empire.

The Mahdi sent a letter to Shehu Bakr of Bornu (1881–84)

---

[25] Holt, op. cit., extract from pp. 106–7.
[26] *Faki* is the Sudanese version of *Faqih* (jurist).
[27] Holt, 1958b, pp. 276–90.

setting forth his claims.[28] The Shehu referred the letter to the local holymen, who pronounced against the Mahdi's pretensions, and consequently no reply was sent back. Mahdism, however, found its way to Bornu through the conquests of Rabih. This Rabih was by origin a slave brought up in the family of Al-Zubayr Pasha. At an early age he showed great military ability, which placed him as one of the commanders of Al-Zubayr's army. When, in 1879, Al-Zubayr was deported to Cairo his son Sulayman assisted by Rabih raised a revolt at Bahr al-Ghazal against the Egyptian régime. They were defeated by Gessi, and Sulayman was killed. Rabih collected the remnants of the army and proceeded towards Bornu through Dar Runga and Bagirmi. After a host of adventures and constant fighting he crossed the Shari river and sacked Kukawa, the capital, in 1894. He then established himself in Dikwa and ruled the whole of Bornu until 1900, when he was defeated and killed by the French.

During the early years of his régime (1882–85) the Mahdi sought unsuccessfully to communicate with Rabih. But although Rabih did not answer the Mahdi's letters, he carried his conquests in the name of the Mahdia. His army wore the Mahdist uniform, read the *Ratib*, and fought under a Mahdist flag. Yet he was more of a military adventurer than a genuine Mahdist. What is important, however, is that between 1894 and 1900 Bornu was to all appearances a Mahdist state.

In the Sokoto Empire the Mahdi found support in the person of Hayatu b. Sa'id, a grandson of Sultan Bello. From him the Mahdi received a letter of glowing devotion:

> I and my father and all that belong to me swore allegiance to you before your manifestation was perceived. . . . Shaikh Usuman dan Fodio, recommended us to emigrate to you, to assist you and to help you when you were made manifest.[29]

In recognition of this unqualified support, the Mahdi appointed Hayatu as his agent and ruler 'of all the people of Sokoto who were subjects of your great-grandfather, Usuman dan Fodio'.[30] Proclamations to this effect were sent to Hayatu to distribute to

[28] Tomlinson, and Lethem, pt. I, p. 8.   [29] Holt, 1958b, p. 286.
[30] MS., Sudan Government Archives, Khartoum, *Mahdiyya*, bk. V, p. 6.

all the ruling emirs of the Sokoto Empire. In the meantime a certain Muhammad al-Amin Ahmad was appointed as sub-agent of Melle under Hayatu b. Saʿid.

Armed with this authority, Hayatu declared a *jihad* and gained a large following in Adamawa and the Mandara region. When Rabih conquered Bornu, Hayatu thought it worthwhile to attach himself to him. He married Rabih's daughter, Hawwa, and the two men continued to wage a *jihad* in the name of the Mahdia. It appears, however, that Hayatu soon found himself completely overshadowed by Rabih, th emilitary man who was more interested in conquests than in the Mahdist cause. So, when Rabih was engaged against the French in 1900, Hayatu attempted to flee from Dikwa, but he was captured and killed by Rabih's son Fadlallah. Later, Fadlallah himself was killed by the French at Gujba.

Thus, Hayatu b. Saʿid, a member of the ruling Fulani aristocracy, had shaken the solidarity of the Sokoto Empire by accepting the Sudanese Mahdia and fighting for it. He argued that the *jihad* of Usuman dan Fodio had precipitated the Mahdia and that the Shehu's prophecy about the appearance of the Mahdi had been fulfilled.[31] The Sokoto Sultans, on the other hand, although recognizing the validity of the Shehu's prophecy, maintained that its manifestations had not yet appeared. They held that the Mahdi's appearance should be preceded by strife, general disorder, and complete anarchy, and the Sokoto Empire had not yet reached that stage of decay.

Later, however, the European occupation was interpreted as the expected crisis, and there was a general cry to evacuate the land to the 'infidels' and emigrate to the east. When the British approached Sokoto, Sultan Attahiru I (1902–3) left before their arrival, summoned whom he could, and marched eastwards on the pretext of going on pilgrimage. He was followed by numerous people, and they all assembled at Burmi, in Gombe emirate. The Burmi region was under the Mahdists, followers of Malam Jibrella, a Fulani of Katagum, who was admitted to Mahdism by Hayatu b. Saʿid. In 1902 Malam Jibrella was captured by the

[31] Sudan Government Archives, Khartoum, *MS. Nujumi*, pp. 58–59.

British and deported to Lokoja, where he died. His followers, however, continued to resist the British occupation, and when Sultan Attahiru arrived with his followers at Burmi they joined hands and resolved to fight. They were defeated and the Sultan himself was killed.

The Battle of Burmi (1903) was the climax of the British occupation of Hausaland. It was also a landmark in the history of the Fulani Empire. Its importance is indicated by the number of dignitaries who were present at the battle. Besides the Sultan and his sons, there were the Emir Bashir of the Melle Fulani, who evacuated his land for the French, Alfa Hashim, the well-known Tijani leader, Abu Bakr, emir of Nupe, Bello, brother of the emir of Kontagora, Ahmadu, the emir of Misau, and the Magaji of Keffi.[32] By many Fulani the whole affair is spoken of as the *jihad*, Sultan Attahiru as a *shahid* (martyr), and the exodus as the *hijra*.[33] After Burmi a large number of Fulani (estimated at 25,000) gathered round Attahiru's son, Mai Wurno, and Ahmadu of Misau and migrated to the Sudan. Both Mai Wurno and Ahmadu settled on the Blue Nile and provided a focus for Fallata settlement, which has continued to the present day.

The events related above give an indication that the spread of Mahdism in the Niger–Chad region was checked at the close of the nineteenth century by European intervention. This was almost simultaneous with the defeat of the Mahdists in the Sudan in 1898. When the Mahdists in the Sudan were again allowed to function under the leadership of the Mahdi's son, al-Sayyid 'Abd al-Rahman, there was almost an automatic revival of Mahdism in Nigeria under the leadership of Malam Sa'id, son of Hayatu. Malam Sa'id communicated with al-Sayyid 'Abd ar-Rahman and acted as his agent in Nigeria. By 1923 he had collected a large following from the Fulani of Bornu and Gombe regions. Unlike the Sudan Government, which worked in harmony with the Mahdists, the British Administration in Nigeria was alarmed and decided to 'nip the movement in the bud as soon as possible'.[34]

[32] Tomlinson and Lethem op. cit., pt. II, p. 28.   [33] Ibid., p. 29.
[34] The Governor of the Northern Provinces of Nigeria in his speech to the Governor-General-in-Council when the proposal for the deportation of Malam Sa'id was being discussed.

So Malam Sa'id was arrested in 1923 and deported to Buea in the Cameroons, where he remained until 1945. In 1945 he was removed to Kano, where he remained under house detention until 1959, when he finally regained his freedom. Now an old man, Malam Sa'id is still a devout Mahdist, but he can hardly claim any followers.

The story of Mahdism in Nigeria is but one example of the stream of Mahdist traditions which prevailed in the Niger–Chad region during the nineteenth century and the early years of the twentieth century. In Senegal the *jihads* of Seku Ahmadu (d. 1843) and al-Hajj 'Umar (d. 1864) were also considered preludes to the advent of the Mahdi.[35] In fact, throughout the French-speaking territories of the Savannahland of West Africa, Mahdist manifestations appeared here and there, and from time to time, causing much unrest and agitation.[36] Here again, the Imperial Government acted in a decisive manner and successfully checked the spread of Mahdism.

REFERENCES

Al-Masudi *Muruj al-dhahab*. Paris edition.
Al-Ya'qubi
    (1960) *Tarikh*. Beirut.
Burckhardt, J. L.
    (1819) *Travels in Nubia*. London.
Denham, D. and Clapperton, H.
    (1826) *Narrative of Travels and Discoveries in Northern and Central Africa, in the years 1822, 1823, and 1824*. London.
Encyclopaedia of Religion and Ethics.
Holt, P. M.
    (1958a) *The Mahdist State in the Sudan 1881–1898*. Oxford.
    (1958b) 'The Sudanese Mahdia and the Outside World', *Bulletin of the School of Oriental and African Studies*, pp. 276–90.
Ibn Khaldun
    (1958) *Muqaddima*. Cairo.
Isam Hassan
    (1952) 'Western Migration and Settlement in the Gezira', *Sudan Notes and Records*, vol. 33, pp. 60–112.
Le Grip, A.
    (1952) 'Le Mahdisme en Afrique Noire', *L'Afrique et L'Asie*, No. 18, pp. 3–16.

[35] Seku Ahmadu is described as the forerunner of the *Mahdi* (*Alladhi yalihu 'l-Mahdi*), Nuh b. al-Tahir b. Abu Bakr b. Musa, Arabic Ms., *Bibliotheque Nationale*, vol. 6759, fol. 31. Al-Hajj 'Umar is called 'the *Wazir* of the Mahdi', Martin, 1963, p. 53.   [36] See Le Grip, 1952, pp. 3–16.

Leo Africanus
(1896) *The History and Description of Africa*, ed. R. Brown. London: Hakluyt Society.

Martin, B. G.
(1963) 'A Mahdist document from Futa Jallon', *Bulletin de l'I.F.A.N.*, vol. XXV, Ser. B, nos. 1–2, pp. 47–65.

Oliver, R. and Fage, J. D.
(1962) *A Short History of Africa*. London.

Smith, H. F. C.
(1961) 'A neglected theme of West African History: the Islamic Revolutions of the 19th Century', *Journal of the Historical Society of Nigeria*, vol. II, no. 1, December.

Tomlinson, G. J. F. and Lethem, G. J.
(n.d.) *History of Islamic Propaganda in Nigeria*. Reports. London: Waterlow.

Arabic MS. Sources: cited in footnotes.

XI. CONFORMITY AND CONTRAST IN SOMALI ISLAM

I. M. LEWIS

I. INTRODUCTION

In discussion of social change in Africa it is often forgotten that some of the most pervasive and sociologically arresting examples of cultural adoption and adaptation have occurred under the impact of Islam. Like other world religions, and perhaps more than most, Islam indeed offers a particularly rich field—so far quite inadequately exploited—for the systematic study of the ways in which different social systems and cultures react to a common external stimulus. This field of research is all the more important, since it offers a unique opportunity for confirming and enhancing the synchronic sociological analysis of traditional institutions. For if traditional institutions have the forms and functions attributed to them by sociologists it must be possible to explain, at least in part, the patterns of assimilation which arise with the adoption of Islam. There must be some logical correspondence between the traditional structure of a society and the manner in which it interprets Islam. Here, surely, is a significant field for comparative sociological analysis.

With this in view, in this paper I seek to show how within the broadly integral Muslim culture area of the Somali of North-East Africa salient differences in traditional social organization are reflected in correspondingly different patterns of Islamic assimilation. The variations in this common culture area on which I wish to focus attention are those which distinguish the pattern of life and social system of the northern nomadic Somali from those of their southern and part-cultivating kinsmen. These differences are accompanied by and, as I shall argue, intimately connected with corresponding variations in Muslim religious organization.

II. THE GEOGRAPHICAL AND HISTORICAL SETTING

The northern nomadic Somali who make up the bulk of the total Somali population of about three million people extend southwards from French Somaliland, through the Somali Republic and Ogaden region of Ethiopia into the arid plains of Northern Kenya. In this relatively barren environment the nomadic husbandry of camels, sheep, and goats, and sometimes cattle, is the dominant pattern of life, with cultivation restricted to a few areas of high rainfall, mainly in the north-west. Within this overwhelmingly pastoral world, with its characteristic nomadic ethos, the southern Sab Somali, consisting of two main tribal confederacies (the Digil and Rahanweyn), occupy the wedge of relatively rich arable land between the Shebelle and Juba Rivers in the south of the Republic. Although the Sab still practice animal husbandry extensively, their main interests lie in their fields, where they grow sorghum and a variety of other crops. Unlike the pastoralists, they occupy stable village settlements set in the centre of their arable lands.

This difference in economy and way of life, keenly felt by both groups, is accompanied by a variety of cultural differences, of which the most immediately striking is the possession by the Sab of a separate and quite distinct Somali dialect which differs from the speech of the northern Somali to much the same extent as Spanish does from Portuguese. And in the genealogical idiom in which social relationships are phrased throughout the Somali culture area, this division between the northern nomads and southern cultivators is reflected in the national Somali pedigree, where each division is attributed to a separate founding ancestor.

These distinguishing features and others to be noted presently are the outcome of distinctive historical processes in the two regions. Over the last thousand years or so the Somali people as a whole have been engaged in a large-scale, but unco-ordinated movement of expansion from the north. In the course of this tide of migration, in which clans and lineages, often in conflict, jostled each other forward, a wide variety of groups settled in the arable lands between the Shebelle and Juba and mingled there with other ethnic groups, particularly with parties of Galla and North-East Coastal Bantu. Out of this amalgam—which is restricted to this area—the Sab clans emerged with their distinctive characteristics and with a sense of separate identity within Somali culture as a whole, which is matched by the northern nomads' traditional contempt for cultivation. This process is well reflected in the derivation 'large-crowd' popularly given to the Sab clan-name 'Rahanweyn'.

Both these areas appear to have been exposed to Islamic influence for a similar period, for both the northern and southern Somali coasts have unquestionably been in extensive contact with the Muslim world for almost a thousand years. The ancient trading stations, developed, if not founded, by Arab and Persian Muslims about the tenth century, along both coast-lines are a testimony to this. Moreover, from the little that is at present known of the history of Muslim contact, there appears to have been no salient difference in either the source or nature of Islamic penetration between north and south. Certainly, today all the Somali are Sunnis of the Shafi'i rite; and the two main *tariqas*, the Qadiriyya and Ahmadiyya, are similarly represented in both the north and south. Indeed, the Somali as a whole, and this should be emphasized, are highly orthodox and incline to a fervent and deep attachment to their faith. The introduction of Islam can thus, I think, be assumed to be a fairly constant factor rather than a crucial variable in the present situation, and certainly there are no wide or systematic doctrinal differences between north and south.

In interpreting the different patterns of Islamic assimilation which have arisen in the two areas, therefore, we are forced to consider the effect of the differences in social structure and culture which distinguish these two segments of the Somali nation. In the following sections I outline briefly what seem the most significant variations in relation to the different patterns of Muslim assimilation which have resulted. I concentrate particularly on structural features, because they seem the most significant in the present context.

III. NORTHERN SOMALI SOCIAL STRUCTURE

While the entire Somali nation is embraced within a single national genealogy and Somali society as a whole is divided into groups on a basis of agnatic descent, there are important differences in lineage organization between the north and the south. In the north the widest political units are clans with populations of the order of 100,000 individuals. As befits a nomadic people, these units are not strictly localized; and without reference to locality clans are highly segmented internally into a wide array of subsidiary lineage groups. Of these segments within a clan, the most stable political grouping is represented by the so-called 'dia-paying group'. This unit, with a male population rarely exceeding a few thousand persons—and sometimes considerably smaller—consists of closely related agnatic kinsmen united not only by the bond of descent but also by an explicit contractual treaty laying down the extent of their common obligations. The most characteristic assertion of common interests relates to homicide, the group as a whole being responsible for the security of its members' persons and property. Damages and indemnities for injury or death (*dia*, commonly 100 camels for a man's life) are paid and received collectively by the group, which, in default, is also responsible for pursuing the blood-feud.

Within the dia-paying group, which is the primary locus of the individual's jural and political allegiance, disputes are settled, forcibly if necessary, by the intervention of the group elders. Between dia-paying groups, however, there is traditionally no machinery in northern Somali society for enforcing settlements. Although acknowledging a common set of moral assumptions and a generally common tariff of damages for injuries, groups in the past could only resort to arbitration, and conciliation depended upon the willingness of the parties to a dispute to compose their differences. Failing this, self-help was the only resort. In such circumstances, as will be obvious, the respective numerical and fighting strengths of groups was, and to a certain extent under modern administration still is, all-important.

Despite the extent to which the loyalties of the individual

stock-herder are bound tightly to his dia-paying group, the group has no formal organization of authority. Generally, there is no single 'headman' with any authoritative functions, and all adult men have in principle an equal say in decision- and policy-making. Indeed, the situation is such that lack of formally instituted political authority is a key-note of northern pastoral society. Moreover, with the premium which naturally attaches to force as the ultimate sanction in group relations, strongly developed lineages are at a distinct advantage and enjoy a superior political status in relation to weaker collateral segments. Hence, the order of seniority by birth is not a factor of direct political significance in lineage relations, although first-born ('*urad*) lineage segments retain certain ceremonial duties in the veneration of common founding ancestors.

Although northern Somali political relations thus depend upon a combination of contractual with agnatic principles, and lineages provide the primary referents by which the individual identifies himself in relation to others, lineages are not normally corporate groups in a geographical sense. The pastures of northern Somaliland are regarded as a common gift to Somali nomads in general and are not conceived of as divided out among specific groups. Consequently, while lineages tend to exercise proprietary rights to specific wells and trading centres, pastoral movement is wide-ranging and it is only extremely rarely that agnatic kinsmen live for any length of time together in a circumscribed territory. Generally, in the pastures camps of nomads and livestock belonging to different and often potentially hostile lineages intermingle, and prescriptive rights to territory are not asserted. At the same time, with the widespread use which is made of contractual alliance as a basis for political and legal collaboration at all levels of lineage structure, and not merely at the level of the most stable political aggregate which I have called 'dia-paying group',[1] the combination of lineages by genealogical assimilation and manipulation which is so prominent a feature of

[1] For a fuller discussion of the role of dia-paying groups in northern Somali society and their highly relative and fluctuating character, see Lewis, 1961, pp. 161 ff.

other segmentary lineage societies is rare in northern Somaliland. The actual form of lineage pedigrees is thus apparently very largely a product of actual generation growth.[2] For the lineage identity which a person acquires at birth remains of vital significance throughout his life, and there is hardly any ambiguity about the genealogical (and hence social and political) placement of individuals or groups. And with the extreme emphasis which is thus given to agnatic descent as a basis for unfailing, though elastic and variable social bonds, marriage is viewed as a subsidiary source of social and quasi-political ties. Hence, ideally, one marries where one has already no strong agnatic ties, and marriage is preferentially directed outside the close circle of agnatic kin. Thus, marriage never takes place within the dia-paying groups; and the customary preferential Islamic patrilateral parallel cousin marriage is not practised by northern Arab nomads. In keeping with the social distance between affines, high bride-wealths and correspondingly high dowries are regularly exchanged. Nevertheless, marriage is unstable and divorce extremely frequent.[3]

The preceding is, of course, necessarily a very cursory summary of northern Somali social structure, but it will, I hope, serve to bring out the points of difference which I wish to emphasize in relation to the southern Sab, to whom I now turn.

IV. SOUTHERN SOMALI SOCIAL STRUCTURE

Southern Somali social structure exhibits a number of significant differences which can be summarized quickly, though inadequately, as follows. First, with their history of mixed origins, the southern Somali have a somewhat amorphous and certainly highly heterogeneous lineage structure. The maximum socio-political units here are essentially confederations of lineages—usually of disparate clan origin—united according to the stock explanation by a kind of act of union or 'promise' (*balan*) on the part of the original founding segments. These southern territorially based units, corresponding in size to the

---

[2] This is discussed in detail in Lewis, 1961 and 1962a.
[3] For a more detailed discussion of Somali marriage and the factors affecting its stability, see Lewis, 1962b.

'clans' of the north, differ again from the latter in also representing generally the standard locus of dia-paying solidarity in the south. They are not, as in the north, normally divided internally into a number of separate and autonomous dia-paying groups. These southern 'clans'[4] are, however, internally segmented on a putatively lineage pattern, and under the clan chief each internal section has a representative headman, the structure of authority paralleling that of internal subdivision. Externally, southern clans are loosely linked together, again on a putative genealogical basis, in wider federations, but these larger associations do not act as corporate political groups.

This southern equivalent to the northern Somali clan is essentially a land-based unit, and frequently the names in its shallow quasi-genealogical framework refer directly to territorial sections rather than to genealogical segments in a true sense. The clan's arable resources are clearly demarcated from those of other similar units and distributed internally among its sections. Acquisition of rights to arable land in the south thus requires, if a person is not already a member of a land-holding group, that he should seek admission as an adopted client in the clan of his choice. In return for receiving a grant of land for cultivation, the client has formally to undertake to accept joint responsibility with other members in the payment and receipt of all damages involving his clan of adoption. Normally clients are thus admitted after giving these undertakings and paying nominal gifts to the headman and clan chief.

Generally three classes of residents are distinguished: (*a*) descendants of the groups which were party to the original clan treaty; (*b*) long-standing accretions of diverse origin; and (*c*) recently adopted aliens. In addition, there were in the past often attached serfs of Galla and Bantu origin, who performed much of the actual labour of cultivation. These last, however, have in the last few generations been progressively assimilated and appear today to enjoy rights to land similar to those held by other

[4] For a number of reasons, particularly their territorial basis, it would be preferable to use the term 'tribe' here, but I have retained 'clan' to emphasize that the units under discussion represent the same level of grouping as northern Somali clans.

adopted clients, although a certain stigma still attaches to them. In practice, the present situation indeed is that although the dialect spoken by the southern Somali is that of the founding groups, it is virtually impossible to find any living Somali who can produce an authentic genealogy tracing descent from them. Thus, in reality, these cultivating clans consist of layer upon layer of adopted clients in varying degrees of assimilation to an original founding core, which, over the generations, has been swamped by subsequent accretions. So varied are these that there is no Somali clan or lineage of any size which is not represented among them. Some clans have something approaching what might be called a 'dominant lineage structure', but in general this is a very approximate and over-simplified way of characterizing the situation: and in keeping with this genealogies are of very shallow depth compared with the north.

Yet in every one of these mixed units there is one section putatively associated with the original founders and referred to like the first-born segments of northern lineages as *'urad*. These segments play a special part in clan ritual, usually having the task of slaughtering animals killed in sacrifice, and invariably are those containing the most authentic stocks in each clan. They are not, however, 'first-born' in a literal sense—as is generally recognized—and among the southern Somali in general the division of groups is not, as in the north, the outcome of lineage growth in a historical sense, but merely a putative idiom in terms of which people and groups are associated. And, apparently in keeping with this loose-form organization, with its lack of any firm fabric of agnatic kinship, marriage most frequently takes place within the bounds of dia-paying solidarity. Indeed, since marriage is here regarded as a means of strengthening weak existing ties, rather than as in the north of supplementing strong agnation, there is no objection to the characteristic pattern of Muslim patrilateral parallel-cousin marriage which, with matrilateral cross-cousin marriage, is practised preferentially. Bride-wealth and dowry, however, are small in comparison with the north, although there seems to be little difference in the high degree of marriage instability.

V. CULTIC VARIATIONS

A prominent aspect of Somali Islam generally is the power of intercession ascribed to Muslim saints as intermediaries between man and the Prophet and God. Here three main categories of saints are recognized. There are first those great saints of Islam, particularly the founders of the Qadiriyya and Ahmadiyya *tariqas*, who enjoy universal respect and veneration for the quality and strength of their *baraka* (mystical power) and *karamat* (miraculous works). Secondly, there are a large number of local Somali saints who are venerated for their own personal piety and works and the prominent part they have played in Somali Islam. The third and final group of saints consists of those Somalis who are venerated not, as in the previous category, for their known piety and blessing, but simply as the founders of lineage segments. These last are lineage ancestors who have in effect been canonized within Islam.[5]

Saints vary, of course, in the charismatic status accorded to them, and the most powerful, respected, and best-known saints in the lineage ancestor class are the founders of large groups of clans. Typical of these are Shaikhs Darod and Isaq, founders of the Darod and Isaq families of clans in the north; and Shaikh Digil, putative founder of the southern Digil and Rahanweyn Somali. Here the degree of mystical power attributed to these saints corresponds directly to the numerical size of the groups which they represent, but varies inversely with the extent of social and political cohesion, which, at this high level of grouping, is minimal.

At a lower level of grouping immediate differences are evident between the north and the south. In keeping with the strength of lineage ties among the northern nomads and the highly ramified character of their lineage system, every ancestor in the genealogies is in principle regarded as a saint and so venerated at periodical ceremonies in his honour. Among the southern Somali, however, where lineages have less vital functions, in place of the northern hierarchy of lineage saints one finds a proliferation of local saints honoured for their particular mystical

[5] This is dealt with more fully in Lewis, 1955/6 and 1962.

powers. Typical of, and outstanding among these is Shaikh Mumin, whom most of the Rahanweyn clans regard as the protector of their crops from attack by birds and other pests. Other similar saints, who also have no special lineage status, provide general security and blessing in all departments of life at the many shrines in the country occupied by the Sab.

Here, then, clearly a degree of selection as between north and south occurs in the categories of saints who are most widely venerated, a selection which conforms to the differences in lineage organization already noted. But the effect of the differences in social structure between the northern nomads and their southern kinsmen extends beyond this. Among the northern pastoralists the characteristic religious expression of social identity at the level of the clan takes the form of an annual celebration (*siyaro*) in praise of the clan ancestor. This is a typical memorial service performed regularly by other groups, larger and smaller, at other levels of lineage division.

In the south, however, the corresponding rite of clan identity is not a similar ceremony in honour of the putative group ancestor, but a collective rain-making ritual (*roobdoon*) held annually at a traditional sacred centre. Here petitions are addressed directly to God, through the Prophet, without the intermediacy of ancestors, and in a definite order the several main subsections of the clan make animal offerings, praying for rain and prosperity in the coming year. Characteristically, the privilege of making the first offerings belongs to the so-called '*urad* and genealogically most authentic clan section. Rain-making in the north, by contrast, is not a collective clan rite in which the several divisions of a clan assert their corporate identity, but a generally *ad hoc* affair in which small groups of nomads encamped in the pastures pray to God to bring them rain as they see the clouds massing before the onset of the wet seasons.

These differences in corporate cult life clearly reflect the prevailing distinctions in lineage structure and ecological concern between north and south. But to avoid misunderstanding, it must again be emphasized that these distinctions in the characteristic forms of religious activity associated with northern and southern Somali social structure are essentially variations which exist within a common framework of orthodox Muslim assumptions, beliefs and practices. In the south, as in the north, the same or similar saints in other categories are venerated in the same fashion, and neither region asks more of its saints or imputes more power to them, thus leaving in both areas the unique position of God and his Prophet unchallenged. And this overall assimilation of Islam seems, as I have suggested elsewhere, to accord with the common Cushitic pre-Islamic substratum of beliefs, for the former existence of which there is evidence in both the north and south.

But what is perhaps more striking, though less easy to characterize accurately, is a wider division of emphasis between the two groups of Somali which seems again to conform to the underlying differences of their socio-ecological circumstances. In the north especially there is a very clear-cut ideal distinction between the spiritual and secular order which assumes concrete expression in the division which is made between 'men of God' (*wadaad*, the Somali equivalent of the Arabic Shaikh) and 'men of the spear' or 'warriors' (*waranleh*). All those who devote their lives to religion and practise as priests, whatever other resources they depend upon for a livelihood, belong to the first category, while the remainder and larger part of mankind consists simply of 'warriors'. In practice, 'warriors' and priests rub shoulders together in the same lineages; and because of the exigencies of the nomadic life and social system, religious settlements of priests fully independent of the all-encompassing nomadic world have rarely been able to establish themselves. In reality, all men—men of God included, however reluctantly— remain finally subject to the bonds of common dia-paying group allegiance which afford the only sure source of security for person and property. In practice therefore, while the distinction between the two orders is theoretically maintained and is buttressed by the mystical power which is generally attributed to priests, the pastoral social system is in effect all-pervasive.[6]

[6] For more detailed consideration of the special features of northern Somali Islam and the distinction between 'priests' and 'warriors', see Lewis, 1963.

In the south the situation is rather different. Here separate and autonomous, and often powerful, religious communities of priests have been able to establish themselves in the arable regions and have played an important role in southern local politics. Here, moreover, even at an ideal level, the distinction between 'warriors' and priests is not so clearly defined, and priests are certainly allowed greater influence in clan politics than is the rule in the north. Indeed, some priestly sections have infiltrated into clan confederacies, where they have established themselves as priestly dynasties and the Arabic title 'Shaikh' is in some cases applied in the south with a political as well as religious connotation. This has led to the involvement of the mystical powers of shaikhs in the political life of the southern Somali, especially in wars between clans, to an extent which is foreign to northern Somali.

Southern Somali society thus conveys the impression that in secular affairs, and inter-clan politics particularly, Muslim influence is more pervasive than it is in the north. Hence, the possibilities of wider agricultural settlement and the accompanying distinctive features of social organization appear to offer more receptive conditions for Islamic assimilation, such at least as to make the social conditions of the south conform in some respects more closely to those in other African Muslim societies than is the case in the north. Here surely it is significant that in southern Somali society the favoured form of preferential parallel-cousin marriage is practised extensively in contrast to the position in the north. This tentative conclusion, however, is in no sense intended to suggest that the depth of Muslim piety is greater in the south than the north. This is something which is very hard to estimate objectively, and my own impression, for what it is worth, is that the northern Somali are as devoted and fervid adherents of Islam as their southern countrymen.

REFERENCES

Lewis, I. M.
  (1955/56) 'Sufism in Somaliland: a Study in Tribal Islam', *Bulletin School of Oriental and African Studies*, vol. XVII, pp. 581–602; vol. XVIII, pp. 145–60.

(1961) *A Pastoral Democracy*. London.
(1962a) 'Historical Aspects of Genealogies in Northern Somali Social Structure', *Journal of African History*, vol. III, no. 1, pp. 35–48.
(1962b) *Marriage and the Family in Northern Somaliland*. East African Studies, No. 15. Kampala.
(1963) 'Dualism in Somali Notions of Power', *Journal of the Royal Anthropological Institute*, vol. XCIII, pp. 113–15.

XII. THE JUMBE OF KOTA KOTA AND SOME ASPECTS OF THE HISTORY OF ISLAM IN MALAWI

GEORGE SHEPPERSON

I

The Arabs in central Africa, wrote David Livingstone on 10 August 1866, 'cannot form a state or independent kingdom: slavery and the slave trade are insuperable obstacles to any permanence inland . . . all therefore that the Arabs do is to collect as much money as they can . . . and then leave the country'.[1] Thirty years later, however, a British Officer in the employ of King Leopold's forces in the Eastern Congo, writing of the fierceness of the Arab campaign against the consolidation of European power in that area, claimed that if the attempt of the Arabs had succeeded, 'it is probable that the (Congo) Free State would have been replaced by a Muhammadan Empire analogous to that of the Khalifa in the Soudan'.[2] Unless, therefore, such statements are wild generalizations, profound changes must have taken place in the Arab attitude to central African politics during the period from the 1860s to the 1890s. Professor Roland Oliver, in noting that this occurred 'abruptly' between 1884 and 1888, concludes that 'the Arabs were now aiming at political power'. [3]

If this thesis is correct the destruction of Arab ambitions in British, Belgian, and German central Africa during the Scramble for Africa had important consequences for Islam in these parts—nothing less, in fact, than the overthrow of a potential Islamic State or States. Thought on the spread of Islam in central Africa in the last half of the nineteenth century is too often influenced by the observation that the Arab traders did not proselytize. Had they achieved political power, this would not have been necessary, if Ibn Khaldun's assertion that 'The vanquished always

[1] Livingstone, 1874, vol. I, p. 92.   [2] Hinde, 1897, p. 19.
[3] Oliver, 1951, p. 52.

seek to imitate their victors in their dress, insignia, belief, and other customs and usages'[4] is to be believed. Indeed this process had begun long before the threat of Arab political power in central Africa, as Livingstone noticed when, in 1866, he met the Yao chief, Mataka, to the east of Lake Nyasa, commented on his Arab dress, and noticed of the square house in which he was lodged that 'indeed most of the houses here are square, for the Arabs are imitated in everything'.[5]

To add to the complications of the study of the spread of Islam in central Africa—and leaving aside the complex and cryptic question of its existence there in the pre-European period[6]—one must note the levels at which, during the nineteenth century, it was introduced. 'In Central Africa,' noted a Scottish participant in the British battles against the Arabs at the northern end of Lake Nyasa in the mid-1880s, 'we meet with three classes of Arabs—first, the Muscat, or white Arab, who is the true species . . .; second, the Mswahili, or coast Arab, who is black, but is strictly Muhammadan in religion . . .; and third, any upcountry native who adopts the manners and customs of the Moslem.'[7]

Out of the shifting alliances of these groups (among themselves, with the indigenous central African peoples, and with European power, missionary as well as secular) came the first substantial patterns of Islamic penetration into the regions around Lake Nyasa.

II

In the nineteenth century the main agency of the spread of Islam into these parts was the Yao. Although this inland people, through their trade with the coast, appears to have entered into commercial competition with the Arabs of the littoral as early as the beginning of the century (if not earlier), one authority claims that they did not adopt Islam on any large scale until about the

---

[4] Issawi (ed.), 1950, p. 53.   [5] Livingstone, op. cit., p. 73.
[6] Cf. Ntara, p. 3; he speaks of one Hasan bin 'Ali who tried to make himself chief over the Malawi in the sixteenth century. I am grateful to Mr. T. Price for this reference; see also Price, 1954, pp. 31–37, for other stimulating speculations on Muslim influence in central Africa about this time.
[7] Fotheringham, 1891, p. 12.

1870s, when numbers of coastal Arabs came to live among the Yao or to trade in Yao country.[8] If this assertion is correct it suggests that, until a powerful foreign standard of comparison (the Arabs) was available in the interior, the Yao had no social incentive to follow Islamic practices.

According to the first African historian of this people, it was the Amasaninga Yao who were mainly responsible for the spread of Islam in the Nyasa regions.[9] Certainly, one of their chiefs, Makanjila, by the 1870s, impressed British observers as an established Muslim and the head of a well-ordered township. Visiting him in 1877, the consul from Mozambique noted that his court was 'better than many of the Zanzibar tumble-down mansions', remarked on his raiment of 'checked Muscat cloth of silk . . . with a gold fringe'; and observed that he had a ' "mwalimu" who teaches reading and the Koran'.[10] Eight years later the British consul for Nyasa added that 'Muhammad Makanjira' had a 'large school-house' and that the children were taught Swahili as well as the Quran.[11] A Christian missionary, however, who visited him in this same year claimed that Makanjila 'was a mere puppet of the Swahili and Arabs who were about his court'[12]—an impression which does not accord easily with the traditional picture of the fierce figure who stripped and whipped the British Vice-Consul in 1888.

This Yao chief's headquarters were on the other side of Lake Nyasa to Kota Kota (an Arab corruption of Ngotangota), with whose ruler, in spite of a common religion, Makanjila competed for the lion's share of the slave trade from the Congo to the east coast, and with whom he was in frequent armed conflict.

III

The rulers of Kota Kota, on the eve of the British occupation of Nyasaland (now Malawi), were a line of Jumbes, owing, as their name suggests,[13] an allegiance to the Sultan of Zanzibar.

---

[8] Rangeley, 1963, p. 25.   [9] Abdallah, 1919, p. 44.   [10] Elton, 1879, pp. 288–9.
[11] Public Record Office, London: F.O. 84, 1702, No. 2, 19 March 1885.
[12] *Nyasa News* (Likoma), August 1893, p. 31.
[13] Freeman-Grenville, 1962, p. 116.

The origins of the first Jumbe, Salim bin 'Abdallah, are obscure.[14] He probably came to Lake Nyasa from Zanzibar, after a spell at Tabora and Ujiji, in the mid-1840s; secured some political power over the peoples around Kota Kota not only through his possession of firearms but also by acting as a protector against the Ngoni; and built dhows to trade in ivory and slaves from west to east across Lake Nyasa. After his conquest of Marenga, chief of the Marimba country near Kota Kota, he set himself up as the 'Sultan of Marimba' and later assumed the title of Jumbe. Like the British after him, as his power increased, he employed a policy of indirect rule. Although Livingstone, when he visited the first Jumbe in 1863 and 1866, was not impressed by him as an agency for Islam among a pagan people, it is to Salim bin 'Abdallah that the effective beginnings of the faith in Kota Kota, traditionally the most important Islamic centre in Nyasaland, must be attributed.

He died in the 1860s and was succeeded by Mwinyi-Mguzo, who was also from the east coast. Like his predecessor, this Jumbe does not appear to have been noted for his proselytizing piety; although, when the Scottish missionary, Laws, met him, he saw that he was having three boys taught Arabic.[15] The British Consul from Mozambique, who visited the second Jumbe in 1877, noticed that he observed Ramadan himself, although he did not force it on others.[16] More important, the Consul saw that he was flying the Sultan of Zanzibar's flag.[17] If, when he died (about 1875–79), Mwinyi-Mguzo was not styled the *wali* of the Sultan of Zanzibar it is clear that his period as Jumbe of Kota Kota marks the transition to a complete representative of the Sultan on Lake Nyasa.

This was the third Jumbe: Mwinyi Kisutu, 'the scion of a good Zanzibar family'. It is this Jumbe whom the accounts of the final

[14] There is considerable confusion as to dates and names by various European witnesses of the Jumbes of Kota Kota. The dispatch by Major C. A. Edwards to Commissioner Johnston, Kota Kota, 17 July 1894, gives what is probably the most reliable short history (Confidential Print, North Zambezi, No. 2., in F.O. 2. 67 Africa, 1894). Unless otherwise stated, all references to the Jumbes are taken from this.

[15] W. P. Livingstone, pp. 126–7.

[16] Elton, op. cit., p. 298.   [17] Ibid., p. 294.

stages of the British occupation of Nyasaland call 'the Jumbe of Kota Kota'. He, indeed, of all the Jumbes, deserves the appelation of *wali* of the Sultan of Zanzibar.[18] An English visitor's impressions of 1876 indicate the growth of the Jumbe of Kota Kota's power: 'The town extends a considerable length along the shore. Many square houses, so closely packed one can scarcely make one's way through the place . . . Many oil palms'; and then, significantly, 'Jumbe has the red flag (of the Sultan of Zanzibar) flying over his house.'[19]

The third Jumbe's political importance was soon appreciated by the British Commissioner and Consul General for Central Africa, Harry Johnston. Johnston first heard of Mwinyi Kisutu (to whom he usually referred as 'Tawakali Sudi'[20]) in Zanzibar from the Sultan,[21] who gave him letters to the Jumbe of Kota Kota. Between 1889, when Johnston first visited him, and 1895, when Arab power in Nyasaland was finally broken, the British Commissioner had no doubt that the Jumbe, as representative of the Sultan of Zanzibar, had done more than any other to prevent the Arabs at the north end of the Lake, with their Yao and other African allies to the south, from combining successfully to drive the British from the region.[22] Johnston was qualified to speak of Muslim power, for he had been interested in Islam since he had first visited North Africa in 1879. He realized from the first that Jumbe, whose rule he described in terms of a 'Swahili merchant prince' with his 'feudatories',[23] was something more than a simple slave-trader—an impression which other Europeans in the area were prone to receive. At Kota Kota, said Johnston, there were to be seen 'real white Arabs, men with the complexions and features of Europeans and Persians' from Muscat or Aden: 'I found them very potent allies in enabling me to win Jumbe's friendship and confidence. They spoke

[18] Cf. F.O.2.88, C.A. No.57, 19 May 1895. Johnston.
[19] Cotterill, 1878, p. 239.
[20] Johnston, 1898, p. 92, and for photograph of Jumbe III.
[21] Johnston, 1923, p. 260.
[22] Cf. Ibid., pp. 260–5, Johnston, 1898, p. 76, etc.; F.O.84.1969, Africa, 26 October 1889; Swann, 1910, p.291; Fotheringham, op. cit., pp. 275–82, etc.
[23] F.O.84.2051, No. 14, Africa; Johnston, 17 March 1890, p. 131.

vauntingly of the power of the British at Aden and in the Persian Gulf.'[24]

Johnston went so far as to claim that Jumbe's support of the British cause 'turned the whole tide of Arab feeling in Nyasa and Tanganyika in our favour'.[25] Whatever is the truth of this assertion, there is no doubt that, after some wavering, the defection of the Jumbe of Kota from the Arab cause around Lake Nyasa prevented the emergence of any sort of Muslim political dominance in British Central Africa. And that the Arabs of Nyasa were threatening this, ideologically as well as militarily, is clear from such remarks attributed to a group of them at Bandawe in 1885 as 'Don't pray to the white man's god, but pray to the Arab's god. He is the God of all black men.'[26] Furthermore, as Johnston noted, there was no colour prejudice among the Nyasa Muslims: 'a black Mohammedan is thought quite as much of as a white one'.[27]

Although the Jumbe of Kota Kota was persuaded that political realities compelled him to throw in his lot with the British by accepting a subsidy from them, he seems to have determined not to be swallowed up ideologically by them. Johnson called him 'a very strict Mohammedan'.[28] More than once the Scots from Livingstonia tried to establish a Christian mission at Kota Kota. But 'Jumbe expressed his very decided wish *not* to have a Mission at his town. He said . . . that they (the Muhammadans) were not heathens, they had their own religion.'[29] It is not clear whether he read Arabic; but he certainly signed his name in it; and he could read and apparently write Swahili in Arabic script. Swahili, in fact, was something of a status symbol with him, as it doubtless was with the other Arabs in the Nyasa area. When, at last, he consented to have a teacher from a Christian mission at Kota Kota he accepted one from the Universities Mission to Central Africa (with its headquarters at Zanzibar) and not from the

[24] F.O.84.2051, No. 14, Africa; Johnston, 17 March 1890, p. 131.

[25] F.O.84.2061, Africa, No. 7, 1 February 1890.

[26] Livingstonia Papers: William Harkness, Katunga's, 12 January 1885.

[27] F.O.84.2051, No. 14, Africa; Johnston, 17 March 1890, p. 196.

[28] Johnston, 1898, p. 92.

[29] F.O.2.54. No.3 Central Africa, Sharpe, 2 January, 1893.

Livingstonia missionaries. It is possible that the Jumbe had some grudge against them for not intervening on his side in his battles with the Tonga and the Ngoni.[30] But it is more likely that his preference for the U.M.C.A. missionaries—he referred to their Bishop respectfully as 'Askaf'[31]—was because at least one of them (W. P. Johnson)[32] could read the Quran in Arabic and that all of them were more familiar with Swahili than the Scottish missionaries, who concentrated on the local African tongues—'the language of my slaves',[33] in the Jumbe's words. Of these local languages, however, he seems to have made an exception of Yao, probably because it was spoken by a partly Muslim people who were his trading intermediaries; certainly, when Johnston read to him in Yao a letter from Queen Victoria soliciting his friendship he appears to have understood it and to have given Johnston, in consequence, a cordial reception.[34]

In spite of the Jumbe's complicity in the slave-trade—and even after he had accepted a subsidy from the British and was aiding them against his co-religionists at Karonga at the north end of Lake Nyasa, he engaged in the trade—he was regarded with affection by white and black alike. Some of this may have been due, after his death on 8 July 1894, to the ineffectiveness of his successor. Most of it, however, was probably the result of his personal qualities and policy. He 'was very liberal with his revenues, dividing one-third amongst his Chiefs and Headmen and subjects. This action of his caused him to have much influence and to be liked by his people.' Even his U.M.C.A. critics, who had been very harsh in their judgement of his slave-trading, spoke of him with affection. One of them wrote a few months after his death that the Jumbe 'was never known to turn even a little child from his baraza (council) if he had any complaint to make'.[35] Another noted that he was spoken of as 'Jumbe Mare-

[30] 'Jumbe talks as if we were responsible for all the actions of the Atonga and the Angoni'; Livingstonia Papers: William Harkness, Cape Maclear, 11 September 1882.

[31] F.O.84.2051. No 14, Africa, Johnston, 17 March 1890, p. 131; cf. also Johnston, 1898, p. 93.

[32] Barnes, 1933, pp. 126–7.   [33] Hine, 1924, p. 152.

[34] F.O.84.2115, Central Africa, No. 12, 17 March 1891.

[35] *Nyasa News*, No. 6, November 1894, p. 202.

hemu, the Jumbe who found mercy'.[36] In spite of the unpopu-
larity and the subsequent deposition by the British of his successor, it seems to have been the reputation of Mwinyi Kisutu which
ensured that, as late as 1905, if not later, the graves of the Jumbes
at Kota Kota were being looked after in 'a rather better class of
house';[37] and that during the Second World War Nyasaland
soldiers included among their marching songs a nostalgic tune
about the Jumbes of Kota Kota, whose rule—apparently when
contrasted with the British—was not oppressive ('aJumbe tili
nawo; aJumbe akana kulemera').

Yet, in spite of the reputation and power of the third Jumbe
of Kota Kota, Commissioner Johnston, his greatest friend in the
new Administration, declared in his report for 1894 that the 'Arab
traders in Central Africa are far too much attached to the pleasure
of the life on the coast to look upon themselves as permanent
settlers in the interior'.[38] Indeed, shortly before his death it was
reported that Mwinyi Kisutu had sent his sons to Zanzibar and
was thinking of retiring himself. His reasons seem to have been
disputes with his *akida*. But even if he had not died before this
became possible, there is nothing to suggest that he contemplated the extinction of the office of the Jumbe of Kota Kota,
although, with the extension of British Protectorates over
Central and East Africa in 1891, the position of *wali* of the Sultan
of Zanzibar was no longer possible in anything more than a
ceremonial sense. Nevertheless, Jumbes could have continued
at Kota Kota, entering, on a smaller scale, into a similar relationship with the British to that provided for the emirates in northern
Nigeria.

When the fourth and final Jumbe, Mwinyi Kheiri (or Heri),
son of Jumbe's predecesser, was sworn in on 7 September 1894
his inauguration was conducted with appropriate Muslim ceremony.[39] The British representative at Kota Kota had reported
shortly after the old Jumbe's death that the people wanted

[36] *Central Africa* (London), vol. XIII, 1895, p. 52.
[37] Farrar, 1905.
[38] *Report . . . of the . . . first three years Administration of . . . British Central
Africa . . . 1894*, (c. 7504), vol. LVII, 741, p. 26.
[39] F.O.2.68, Africa, Nicoll to Johnston, 23 September 1894, pp. 310–11.

'Sheikh Mbwana, the coastman living at Ngombe, to come here to place the new Sultan on the throne, as he is a Mullah, or priest'. As was customary with the British at this time, when circumstances permitted, the religious feelings of their Muslim subjects were taken into consideration; and Shaikh Mbwana was brought across the Lake to officiate spiritually.

The presence of a British official representative at the installation of the new Jumbe indicates that the new Administration looked forward to some form of indirect rule. But Mwinyi Kheiri had other ideas. In spite of the old Jumbe's last words that they should obey the British, Mwinyi Kheiri, with a group of local Arabs and Yaos, plotted to kill all the headmen of the old Jumbe and to overthrow the new Administration. By May 1895 he was deposed and deported to Zanzibar.

The deposition of the fourth Jumbe brought to an end half a century of a unique experiment in the creation of a Muslim institution in central Africa. The Arabs, first from Karonga, then from Kota Kota, were driven from Nyasaland. But, as was reported in 1912, they had 'left Kota Kota and the surrounding district a heritage of Mohammedanism which stubbornly resists all the advances of Christian missionaries'.[40] By 1927 the Muslims of Kota Kota still numbered as many as an eleventh of its population.[41] And some followers of the Jumbe continued, as late as 1935, to oppose the Chief whom the British had set up in his place: first Chigwe and then Msusa. Religion added to political complexities in the area, as the Provincial Commissioner saw when he noted in his report that 'the visit of an Arab Sherifu who sided entirely with the Jumbe's followers did not help to increase Msusa's authority'.[42]

IV

In these words there is, perhaps, an echo of the old British fear that Islam would unite the peoples in central Africa against them; a fear which Sudanese and Somali Mahdism, German intrigues with Islamic elements in Africa during the 1914–18

---

[40] Hofmeyr, 1912, p. 3. [41] Hetherwick, 1927, p. 185.
[42] *Nyasaland, Annual Reports . . . 1935*, p. 58.

hostilities, and a vague but none the less real unease about an imagined Pan-Islamic movement kept alive until well after the First World War.[43] It was clearly expressed in 1912 by a South African missionary in Nyasaland when he wrote:

Islam may be particularly acceptable to the natives because it is a black man's religion and not one acquired from the whites. Undoubtedly there is already among the natives a dislike and distrust of the white man as such. And the more this feeling grows—as grow it will—the more will anything that is totally apart from the white man appeal to the native. Another cause may be the direct or indirect encouragement and assistance given to them (the Muslims) by Government officials and others who help them build their mosques, and show a preference for Mohammedan *askaris* and servants.[44] Apart from anything else this question has its serious political side which should cause such men to think twice before in any way encouraging Mohammedanism. When the time comes—and who that knows South African history will deny that it ever will come—that the blacks seek to drive the whites out of the country, it may be in Mohammedanism that they will find the common rallying point which at present they lack, and it may be in these Yao *askari* they will find the leaders they need to bring them to the point of facing the white man.[45]

Forty years later, however, an authority could state that Islam in Nyasaland is 'making little or no progress... and even among the Yao appears to be only skin-deep'.[46] If the existence, noted in the 1950s, of Islamic sectarianism as a distinguishing mark between different groups of Yao chiefdoms,[47] suggests that there may be some exaggeration in this statement its general tenor is undisputed. After the coming of the British Administration some Muslims in Nyasaland may have gone as far afield as Cairo to learn Arabic, but the major result appears to have been to turn them into clerks in the villages, writing the vernaculars in Arabic characters[48]—and even this practice was not widespread. And few, if any, African Muslims from Nyasaland have made the Pilgrimage to Mecca.

Islam, of course, claims the allegiance of sections of the Asian

[43] See Shepperson and Price, 1958, pp. 405–9.

[44] That this was also a fear of missionaries in German East Africa is clear from *Moslem World*, vol. II, 1912, pp. 409–10; cf. also pp. 221, 424, 439.

[45] Hofmeyr, op. cit., pp. 6–7. [46] Anderson, 1954, p. 170.

[47] Mitchell, 1956, p. 51. [48] Barnes, op. cit., pp. 126–7.

community in Malawi, but has never become a major force with them as with some of the Asians in East Africa. Thus, even here, it continues to maintain that epiphenomenal character it has always had in Malawi.

Its failure to achieve substantial roots among the African peoples of Malawi is not difficult to understand. The destruction of Arab and Yao political power by the British is probably the foremost reason. If Islam had been firmly based among these peoples, and if the different groups of Muslims in Nyasaland had not been divided against each other, Islam would doubtless have survived and probably increased in influence. But it was not securely rooted among them. Furthermore, its main adherents after the coming of the British administration were the Yao chiefs.[49] They were a group that looked nostalgically to the past—a past, for many of them, of the slave-trade and domination over the local peoples. At a time when the power of the chiefs was being threatened by literate and nationalistically conscious Africans, Islam had few attractions. Although during the period of the beginnings of African nationalism in Nyasaland (1900–16) the Turkish and Egyptian independence movements were in the air, and promised modern types of Islamic culture, for aspiring Africans who had seen something of the possibilities of the new ways of life, either at the technically conscious Scottish Christian missions or in the mines and industries of South Africa, Islam was identified with a non-industrial civilization which offered nothing of the power of the Christian West.

By the time Malawi became independent, the industrialization and autonomy of the States of the Middle East was so far advanced that this impression could no longer be maintained. Independent forms of African Christianity (in control or cult), the excitements and fresh allegiances of the new nationalism engendered by the struggle against the Federation of 1953, and sheer secularism made an Islamic revival impossible. Pan-Islamism had been replaced by Pan-Africanism. The Jumbe of Kota Kota, as a symbol of a new way of life and an alternative to European domination, was replaced by one of the Cewa, with

[49] Rangeley, op. cit., p. 25.

whose chief, Mwase of Kasungu, he was in continual friction. And that son of the Cewa was Dr. H. Kamuzu Banda.

REFERENCES

Abdallah, Yohanna B.
(1919) *The Yaos*. Zomba.
Anderson, J. N. D.
(1954) *Islamic Law in Africa*. London.
Barnes, Bertram H.
(1933) *Johnson of Nyasaland*. London.
Cotterill, H. B.
(1878) 'On the Nyassa and a Journey from the North End to Zanzibar', *Proceedings of the Royal Geographical Society* (London), Vol. XXII.
Elton, J. F.
(1879) *Travels and Researches . . . East and Central Africa*. London.
Farrar, N.
(1905) *Three Weeks Trip in British Central Africa, 1905*. (Copy in Commonwealth Relations Office Library, Central Africa Pamphlet No. 6.)
Fotheringham, L. Monteith
(1891) *Adventures in Nyasaland*. London.
Freeman-Grenville, G. S. P.
(1962) *The Medieval History of the Coast of Tanganyika*. Oxford.
Hetherwick, A.
(1927) 'Islam and Christianity in Nyasaland', *The Moslem World* (Hartford, Conn.), vol. XVII.
Hinde, Sidney L.
(1897) *Fall of the Congo Arabs*. London.
Hine, J. E.
(1924) *Days Gone By*. London.
Hofmeyr, A. L.
(1912) 'Islam in Nyasaland', *The Moslem World* (Hartford, Conn.), vol. II.
Issawi, Charles (ed.)
(1950) *An Arab Philosophy of History*. London.
Johnston, Sir Harry H.
(1898) *British Central Africa*. London.
(1923) *The Story of My Life*. London.
Livingstone, D.
(1874) *Last Journals*. London.
Livingstone, W. P.
(n.d.) *Laws of Livingstonia*. London.
Livingstonia Papers: National Library of Scotland.
Mitchell, J. Clyde
(1956) *The Yao Village*. Manchester.
Ntara, S. Y.
(n.d.) *Mbiri ya Acewa*. Lusaka (Publications Bureau of Rhodesia and Nyasaland, 2nd edition).
Nyasaland
(1935) *Annual Reports of the Provincial Commissioners*. Zomba.

Oliver, Roland
  (1951) 'Some Factors in the British Occupation of East Africa 1884–1894,'
    Uganda Journal (Kampala), vol. XV
Price, Thomas
  (1954) 'The "Arabs" of the Zambezi', *Muslim World* (Hartford, Conn.),
    vol. XLIV.
Rangeley, W. H. J.
  (1963) 'The aYao', *Nyasaland Journal* (Blantyre), vol. XV.
Shepperson, George, and Price, Thomas
  (1958) *Independent African*. Edinburgh.
Swann, Alfred J.
  (1910) *Fighting the Slave Hunters*. London.

XIII. SOCIOLOGICAL FACTORS IN THE CONTACT OF THE GOGO OF CENTRAL TANZANIA WITH ISLAM [1]

P. J. A. RIGBY

I. INTRODUCTION

Studies of the spread of Islam in many parts of Africa have concerned themselves mainly with the problems of 'culture contact' or 'acculturation', because the introduction of Islamic beliefs into a large number of African societies involved radical political and social changes, apart from the more personal aspects of conversion. It is by now a commonplace in the study of religion that it cannot be carried out satisfactorily without a full appreciation of the social institutions in which it is embedded, both as an observable aspect of social action and as an integral part of the sociological models arising from the structural analysis of societies.

In this paper I shall examine Islamic contact with the Gogo people and their non-acceptance of Islamic influences upon three levels. Firstly, a brief sketch of the historical evidence for contact will be presented, with reference to different kinds of interaction between societies in Africa and Islam. Then follows a discussion of the relevant structural aspects of Gogo society and their relation to the adoption of Islam, and I conclude with a brief comparison of Gogo religious, cosmological, and spirit beliefs with Islamic doctrines and the possibilities of their syncretism. It is not possible in a paper of this length to go into the details needed for careful comparison, but the broad outlines are drawn, from which some conclusions about Gogo social structure and

---

[1] The fieldwork on which this paper is based was carried out from September 1961 until the middle of 1963. The early part of fieldwork was supported by the then Colonial Social Science Research Council. I continued fieldwork as a Research Fellow of the East African Institute for Social Research. For this I am indebted to both these organizations. The conclusions and ideas expressed in this paper are, of course, entirely my responsibility.

the role of Islamic religion in other social structures may be adduced.

A considerable number of works on the traditional religions of African societies have included discussions of Islamic influence upon them, in varying degrees of length, detail, and theoretical insight. It is necessary to refer at least to some of these in order to set a background against which Gogo contact with Islam and its social and cultural associations can be explored. But first it must be established whether or not there *is* a problem to examine: that is, has there been sufficient contact between the Gogo people and Muslims so that the problem of the acceptance or rejection of Islam can be postulated? This is, of course, a primarily historical question, and it is therefore relevant to reiterate some fairly well-known facts about the penetration of Islam in East Africa generally and central Tanzania in particular.

II. HISTORICAL CONTACT WITH ISLAM

The country of the Gogo people lies some 300 miles from the coast of East Africa at Dar es Salaam and Bagamoyo. This part of the coast has been strongly influenced by Islam since the seventh century, when it came under the Caliph 'Omar ibn al-Khattab.[2] In fact, the port of Mogadishu and others on the Somali coast were Islamic soon after the *hijra* in 622;[3] but the coastal areas of Tanzania did not become an integral part of Islam until the thirteenth century, when Islam was a major element in the contact of the East African coast with the Indian Ocean trading area.[4] Islam was established on the coast not primarily by the emigration of Arabs but by the Islamization of African states. Mathew maintains that:[5]

African kingships which had become Mohammedan progressively acquired the techniques and organization of Islamic states.

I shall discuss the concepts of 'state' and 'kingships' in relation to Islam later. But there is no doubt that these coastal states, whether Arab or African, had very limited contact with the inland

[2] Mathew, in Oliver and Mathew (eds.), 1963, p. 102.
[3] Lewis, 1955/56, and discussion below; also Levy, 1957, p. 2.
[4] Mathew. op. cit, p. 110.   [5] Ibid.

areas of Tanzania, although in the fourteenth century Ibn Battuta found that Maldive cowries were used as currency throughout large parts of Africa, and beads had a continuous popularity in East Africa from medieval times on. There are suggestions that there may have been a trade route from Kilwa, on the coast south of Dar es Salaam, to the state of Mali in West Africa, and it is not known why the Islamic states on the East African coast had so little contact and influence farther inland during this period of several hundred years. In his analysis of Islam in Somaliland, Lewis emphasizes that the coastal sultanates had a profound influence upon the early spread of Islam in Somaliland.[6]

In the sixteenth and seventeenth centuries the trade from the interior to the coast was mainly in ivory and slaves, but the export of slaves did not become important until the nineteenth century.[7] Also until then it is fairly certain that caravans did not move westwards to the interior, but the peoples of inland Tanzania, mainly the Nyamwezi, who live to the west of the Gogo, came to the coast to trade. Some of the routes used by the Nyamwezi lay through Gogo country, and it is certain that the route used in the middle and late nineteenth century by Arabs, missionaries, and others to reach Uganda and the lakes lay through the centre of Ugogo. The earliest reference to this route is for just after 1763, when the King of Buganda (Kabaka Kyabagu) imported cups and plates from the coast and his son Semakokiro (who was Kabaka from 1797 to 1814) exchanged ivory for Indian *kaniki* cloth from the coast.[8] Hence it is fairly certain that Muslim traders and Arabs were operating on routes through Gogo country from the second half of the eighteenth century onwards. This was probably more a hand-to-hand trading through local contacts. The organization of caravans on the route through Ugogo belongs to the late eighteenth century and the early nineteenth century. Arab settlements in Nyamwezi to the west of Ugogo did not appear until the 1820s at the earliest,[9] and by 1870 there were

[6] Lewis, 1961, p. 209.

[7] Mathew, op. cit., p. 117. Freeman-Grenville, in Oliver and Mathew, op. cit., p. 152.   [8] Freeman-Grenville, op. cit., p. 153.

[9] R. G. Abrahams, personal communication.

Arab settlements at Kagei, Tabora, and Ujiji on Lake Tanganyika. But Arab penetration was even then very limited in size and concentrated in areas which would be immediately of political or economic advantage to them, as in Buganda when Kabaka Mutesa adopted Islam in 1867 and observed Ramadan for ten years. West of Lake Tanganyika, Tippo Tip (Muhammad bin Hamid) defeated the Bemba and established an ivory trade in 1867 and 1868. In order to transport his ivory to the coast, he made an alliance with the Nyamwezi leader Mirambo, and the route he used is almost certainly the one already described as lying through the heart of Ugogo. The number of Arabs in the interior, however, was very small; but most of the traders on the route through Ugogo from Tabora to the coast were probably Muslims.

It is fair to say, then, that considerable numbers of Gogo have had continuous contact with Arabs and other Muslims at least from the middle of the nineteenth century until the present day. The part of the caravan route which lay through Ugogo was considered hostile by all travellers, both from the point of view of its physical hardships (drought and lack of food supplies) and the hostility of the Gogo people. The Arabs did establish a post on the south-eastern boundary of Ugogo at Mpwapwa (Mhamvwa), and this later became more important under the Germans and by the siting of a mission station there. There were in fact Nyamwezi settlements along the trade route in Ugogo, as there were in Ukaguru to the east. But there appears to have been limited contact between them and the Gogo, and they had little influence upon the surrounding Gogo community, other than the adoption by the Gogo of certain names for places and people.[10] Ivory was not available in large quantities in Ugogo, and both Ugogo and Ukaguru to the east were politically too uncentralized to allow of large-scale slaving. Beidelman states in his history of Ukaguru:[11]

> The Arabs appear to have found the larger and more effective political systems of the Nyamwezi and the central lakes region to be admirably organized for the securing of . . . (slaves and ivory).

[10] See Beidelman, 1962, p. 18.   [11] Ibid., pp. 14 and 18 and 25.

Moffet[12] suggests a further historical reason for Nyamwezi acceptance and Gogo rejection of Islam:

> By virtue of Arab penetration, greatly assisted by the Nyamwezi capacity for porterage (at which work they excelled), Islamic religion has a firm hold in the west, whereas the still largely pagan Gogo were little affected.

Relations between the Muslim traders and the Gogo were mainly concerned with the right of passage through Ugogo and the provision of supplies for the caravans. Gogo taxed Arab (and later missionary and other) caravans very heavily.[13] There is no doubt that had it been possible the Muslim traders would have established more settlements in Ugogo and spread Islam as they had done in Nyamwezi country to the west. Nearly 150 miles of their most important inland trade route lay through Ugogo. We may then legitimately consider the question as to why Muslim settlements did not grow up to any extent in Ugogo and why the influence of Islam on the Gogo was not greater.

Admittedly, the time depth of contact was limited, as I have already described; but studies from West Africa have shown that time is not the major single factor in the Islamization of an African society. There are more important structural reasons why Islam (and later Christianity to some extent) did not penetrate Gogo society to a greater degree in spite of external political pressures and the built-in proselytizing nature of the faith itself.[14] Related to these are theological and cosmological discrepancies between animist religions and Islamic ideas. Gogo did profit to some extent from the Muslim-run trade through their country, and it is reasonable to assume that Islam would have

[12] Moffet, 1958 (ed.), p. 290.

[13] In the historical accounts of Gogo contact with caravans, both Muslim and Christian, no mention is made of the fact that Gogo have little surplus of food and water at the best of times during the dry season, the time chosen for most of the early journeys. Gogo must have suffered considerable difficulties in finding enough to supply caravans. The high taxes they extracted probably went towards buying food and livestock from surrounding areas. Caravans to Uganda used this route, rather than the northern route through Masailand, because they could obtain at least some food, water, and shelter, and not only because the Masai were militarily hostile.

[14] There is no evidence that Muslim traders *did* actually proselytize in Ugogo during this period.

spread if there had been a political and social basis for it to do so.[15]

I do not wish to suggest that the Gogo displayed any organized reaction to Islam or any other outside influence; this would not have been likely with their non-centralized political organization. Nevertheless it was the very form of their social system, and the fact that it is still intact, that inhibited the penetration of Islam in Ugogo. It is to some of these structural considerations that I now wish to turn.

III. SOCIAL STRUCTURE AND THE SPREAD OF ISLAM

The absorption of Islam in several African societies has been interpreted in terms of: (*a*) the theory of the Muslim military conquerors and the creation of Islamic states; (*b*) the peaceful absorption of Islam into pre-existing state structures where it has modified those structures and been modified by them; and (*c*) the theory of historical accident and cultural diffusion. For the purposes of this paper we shall ignore this last interpretation. Both theories (*a*) and (*b*), those of military expansion of Islam and its adoption by pre-Islamic African states, can, however, lead to facile 'structural' generalizations that Islam can only be absorbed within politically centralized systems and state structures, and that where traditional 'stateless' polities still exist, Islam is *ipso facto* excluded. The origin of this idea is most likely attributable to the fact that much of the work published on the influence of Islam in African societies has been concerned with West Africa, where centralized political systems are characteristic and date from very early times. The very important analysis by Lewis of Islam in Somaliland has corrected this error and shown that there are much more complex structural factors involved than this level of generalization permits of.[16]

[15] Greenberg, discussing the Islamization of the Hausa communities in Kano, emphasizes the role of trade in this process. He says: 'Here, as everywhere in the history of Islam, the avenue of trade was the avenue of the propagation of religion.' (Greenberg, 1946, p. 4.)

[16] Lewis, 1955/56. Also, Nadel, in his analysis of Islam in Nupe religion, discusses it, to some extent, in terms of its political functions in a state organization. But the real value of his analysis lies in the fact that he did not suggest this to be a condition of its assimilation. He takes the analysis much deeper and

Trimingham subscribes to the theory of the 'unifying' role of Islam, which is important, but goes on to assume that this automatically means that stateless societies cannot absorb Islamic elements without change. Speaking of the Galla of southern Ethiopia, he says:[17]

They remained nomadic herdsmen under their own republican form of government and because of this they remained pagan. . . . We can follow the evolution of many Galla tribes from the stage of pastoral nomadism to cultivation, with the parallel process in the political sphere of evolution from a democratic to an aristocratic system, and in the religious sphere from paganism to Islam or Christianity.

Islam, however, is much more flexible than this interpretation suggests, and Lewis has shown that among the nomadic, pastoral northern Somali, who are highly 'republican', the Sufi Islamic orders (*tariqa*) are more closely integrated in the segmentary lineage and non-centralized political structure than among the more sedentary, agricultural communities of the south, where state-like types of political organization appear.[18]

I have given this example to illustrate that superficial correlations between broad 'structural' generalizations and the absorption of Islam are misleading and unfruitful. What must be demonstrated is the compatibility (or incompatibility) of specific structural relations and the accompanying religious and cosmological ideas within a society, with the basic elements of Islamic religion and its cultural correlates. Careful analyses have been published which refer to these questions in relation to many West African states, such as the Nupe, Fulani, Hausa, and so on (see bibliography at the end of this paper for some). For example, the studies of Stenning and Smith[19] have described the role of war and political expansion in Fulani Islamic states, and Nadel has

---

examines the complex processes of the adaptation of Islam and social change and relates its assimilation to specific Nupe institutions. See Nadel, 1954.

[17] Trimingham, 1952, p. 189.

[18] Lewis also suggests that although the integration of Somali and Sufi genealogies is more effective in the north, where lineage organization is still the basis for political action, the Islamic law (*shari'a*) finds broader application in the southern settled communities, where territorial proximity no longer implies genealogical propinquity. (See Lewis, 1955/56, p. 587.)

[19] Stenning, 1959, and Smith, 1960.

demonstrated the peaceful assimilation and modification of Islam in the pre-existing Nupe state. These studies have not only demonstrated the detailed and logical 'fitting together' of Islamic and traditional institutions and ideas but also the frequency of the rejection of individual elements of Islamic culture and law, even where their adoption appeared logically acceptable at first sight. But as Gogo society in no way resembles these state structures and military conquest organizations, it is relevant to look in more detail at the analyses of Islam in non-centralized political systems for closer parallels.

In spite of my earlier criticism of applying too generally the theory of a correlation between stateless societies in contact with Islam and their non-acceptance of it, there is some evidence to show that pastoral or semi-pastoral peoples with non-centralized political organizations resist Islam (and other doctrines based upon mysticism) more than others. Thus, Stenning says of the Pastoral Fulani:[20]

(The Pastoral Fulani) . . . speak the purest Fulfulde, and in general have been least amenable to conversion to Islam.

This suggests that for such peoples to assimilate Islamic religion and cultural elements there must necessarily be other structural prerequisites, if I may use the term. Lewis points these out admirably in his analysis of Somali Sufism. He concedes that the close interdependence of social structure and religion is very clear in Muslim *states*, where the Islamic law can be widely applied, but goes on to say:[21]

. . . the conformity of social and religious structure is equally far-reaching in a tribal Muslim society although it may not at first sight appear so.

He shows how Sufi (Muslim) genealogies and Somali genealogies perform the same functions in the social structure and, as I have already mentioned, how the Islamic Orders are integrated with the Somali lineage system. The knowledge of these genealogies is confined to elders and religious men who have recorded, or can recite, the total genealogies. Lewis sums this up:[22]

[20] Stenning, op cit., p. 14.   [21] Lewis, 1955/56 and 1961.
[22] Lewis 1955, p. 602.

Sociologically it is apparent that this claim of descent from the Quraysh (Mohamed's lineage) is the necessary outcome of the application of the Somali lineage principle to the part played by Islam generally, and Sufism in particular, in the social structure. This consistency is made possible by the parallel functions of Sufi and Somali genealogies.

On the broader impact of Islam on Somali society, he concludes:[23]

. . . in a very real sense Islam is the mainspring of Somali culture. Thus in a religious context the Muslim profession of faith has almost the force of an initiation rite into their society.

The pre-Islamic conception of the Cushitic Sky God (*Waaq*) had many elements in common with the Islamic idea of Allah, so much so that Somali call Allah by the words formerly used for the Cushitic God, with the same connotations. The principal bases on which Islam became incorporated into Somali society were thus: (*a*) the parallel roles of Somali and Sufi genealogies resulting in (*b*) the genealogical canalization of divine grace (*baraka*) from the Qurayshitic lineage through the Somali lineage genealogies (*abtirsiinyo*), and (*c*) the underlying similarities of the Cushitic (pre-Islamic) and Sufi religious concepts associated with the lineage structure and genealogies. In this way the tombs formerly venerated for their Cushitic power now became shrines venerated for their Muslim *baraka*.[24] It may be said of the Somali absorption of Islam that all the features of Somali social structure whose interaction with Islam is important were related to pre-Islamic Cushitic religious institutions.[25]

A further organizational element was the Somali Islamic communities (*jama'a*), which produced wandering teachers (*wadaad*), who moved from camp to camp teaching Arabic and the Quran. They also acted as unofficial repositories of Islamic law (*qadi*), performing much the same functions as the mallams in West Africa,[26] or their equivalents. It is through the literacy in Arabic of these teachers that Islam propagates its juridical elements, although the Shari'a is not as widely applicable in Somali society as are many of the more purely religious aspects

---

[23] Lewis, 1961, p. 26.   [24] Lewis, 1955, p. 587.   [25] Lewis, 1955, p. 582.
[26] See Greenberg, op. cit., p. 10. Also Nadel, op. cit.

of Islam.[27] *Wadaad* also act as unofficial arbitrators in disputes between lineages, and this is their main structural role. They are admirably suited to this, as they stand for pan-Islamic values outside those of lineages and compensation-paying groups, although they cannot entirely free themselves from these ties. They have no authority, but act as mediators. Their importance, and that of literacy and communities which can produce religious specialists, is summed up by Lewis:[28]

> It is probably through the *wadaad* who issue from the *jama'a* communities that Sufism exerts its greatest influence in Somali social structure.

Greenberg also emphasizes the role of Islamic teachers and literacy in Arabic for the spread of Islam among the Kano Hausa in the Sudan.[29] In fact, he makes this aspect fundamental to the adoption of Islam by them, suggesting that the role of Arab traders and their contacts was very limited.[30]

I have dwelt rather on this material from other societies, as I wish to suggest in what follows that this kind of analysis delimits the structural prerequisites for the acceptance of Islam in semi-pastoral non-centralized societies. I shall now discuss some aspects of Gogo social structure, religious and cosmological beliefs in their relations to external influences, in particular, Islam.

IV. GOGO SOCIAL STRUCTURE AND ISLAM

As I have already hinted, traditional Gogo political organization was not that of a centralized state structure. Neither did they have, as I shall demonstrate, a segmentary lineage organization in which agnatic descent combined them into 'tribes' or other local and political units.

The Gogo are a patrilineal 'Bantu' people who inhabit that part of the eastern Rift Valley where it spreads out to form part of the dry plains of central Tanzania. They subsist mainly upon agriculture, and may be said to be a sedentary population, but the area is economically marginal and subject to frequent

---

[27] Nadel also makes this point for the Nupe acceptance of Islam.
[28] Lewis, 1955, p. 594.
[29] Greenberg, op. cit., pp. 10 and 69.   [30] Ibid., p. 10.

droughts and famine. The population is comparatively mobile spatially for agriculturalists, and many Gogo have large herds of cattle, sheep, and goats, about which most of their values are centred. Gogo do not inherit land, and it would be true to say that in spite of present-day changes, decisions about cattle and livestock generally are more important to Gogo than those concerning crops and land.

Gogo live in large homesteads (*kaya*) spread out across the thorn-scrub plain, which comprises most of their country, and although there are scarcely any geographically discrete units which may be called villages, homesteads are grouped into sociologically defined neighbourhoods called *matumbi*. These fall within the boundaries of small ritual areas which we may call 'countries' (*yisi*). These units have definite boundaries, but lack secular political significance for reasons which will appear. During the period I was in the field the population of one of these ritual areas (which are not known or considered significant by government in local administration) rarely exceeded four to five thousand people.

Every person belongs to one of well over a hundred patrilineal clans (*mbeyu*), some of which are exogamous and others not, although the norm is that they should be so. These categories of people are again subdivided into sub-clans with praise-names (*milongo*) which are associated with avoidance objects (*miẓilo*). These may not be touched, killed, or eaten. Each ritual area is linked with one clan by the latter's possession of the rain-stones, stool, and other ritual objects used in rain-making and fertility rites for the country. These are inherited theoretically within the clan by the rule of patrilineal primogeniture. But these clans have little more than statistical preponderances in their own ritual areas, and there has always been a great deal of mobility between them. The member of the clan who is the current possessor of the rainstones is called the *mutemi* (or *munyaligoda*: literally, 'the owner of the stool'), and he controls ritual activity, agricultural phases, rain, and fertility in the area. Any homestead owner and his dependants coming to live within the boundaries (*mimbi*) of this area must accept the ritual leadership and precedence of the *mutemi* and other members of his clan. But the secular, political, military, and judicial powers of the ritual leaders are severely limited, and the office hardly resembles that of a chieftainship. Even in ritual matters the *mutemi* is to some extent dependent upon a diviner who usually lives in another ritual area, often at some considerable distance. He must be consulted before the initiation of most ceremonies and rituals and provides medicines for fertility and protection.

The Gogo have an ideology of patrilineal descent which is usually adhered to in inheritance and succession, but genealogies are not remembered to any depth, except in the case of the clans with ritual power. There are no localized lineages of any size, and they are not corporate. The heads of adjacent homesteads are often father and sons (the latter living with their mothers) at one stage of the family cycle, and by groups of full brothers with their mothers after the death of the father. Sets of full brothers may live within easy reach of each other due to the necessity for communal rituals at the gravestone (*citenjelo*) of their father, but the composition of homesteads is far from being based upon groups of agnatic relatives and their spouses and offspring. At funerals and other ritual occasions agnatic ties are used to group people and clan and sub-clan membership becomes important; but in most situations a great variety of individual kin and affinal ties on a 'network' basis are in operation.

Gogo clans are not linked to each other by any comprehensive genealogy or mythology, and each traces its origins to one of a large number of neighbouring peoples, including the Hehe, Nyamwezi, Masai, Kaguru, Sagara, Sandawi, Burungi, and so on. The remembered generations to this derivative origin are usually very few, seldom more than three or four; and there are historical and mythological tales of the reasons for which the clans' founders left their people and areas of origin, and came to settle in Ugogo. Each clan is, however, linked with one or more other clans in a complex of joking-relationship ties (*wutani*) whose origin is remembered in the clan histories. Some of these joking relationship links explicitly have their origin in a theory of a remote kinship relationship, but in no way do Gogo trace genealogies to a common origin and historical migration which could in any way link them with Islamic or Arabian origins.

Political power and status were largely associated with wealth in livestock, personal ability, and witchcraft power, and there was no hierarchy of secular political offices to which one could attach oneself. By virtue of their control of ritual and fertility, ritual leaders exercised a measure of control also over the natural products of their countries, in the sense that they could prohibit ritually the exploitation of any one of them if it became necessary to do so; but there was no form of tribute (except in the case of the hunting of some animals, notably the pangolin: *nyamung'umi*), and the ritual leader did not allocate the usufruct of land or any other resources. His ritual authority also enabled him to arbitrate in cases of witchcraft accusation and homicide, but he had no more judicial authority in the settlement of disputes than any other elder, and no military power. Some *watemi* accumulated large herds, many wives and dependants, and had a monopoly over slaves taken in war, but the prestige and status thus attained could equally be acquired by anyone with a large herd and homestead. There are no provisions in Gogo society for the legitimate exercise of greater political power or administrative authority.

In some ways the Gogo ritual leaders do resemble the Somali 'chiefs' (called *sultans*), who also had rain-making functions and to whom religious powers attached. But in Somaliland a chief was the head of a kinship group (a 'tribe') tracing common agnatic descent, and although he did not wield authority over a centralized state, his most important function was to preside at ceremonies held at the tombs of the eponymous tribal ancestors. He was thus the closest living person to God within that kinship group, and with God he had a special relationship. The chief, in a sense, was sacred. The ritual leader in Ugogo was not the head of a kinship group which was also a congregation; he simply held ritual precedence in a particular geographical area inhabited by members of a great many kinship affiliations. He was in no sense closer to a divine power than anyone else.

In Ugogo contact with Arabs and other Muslim traders in

the early days of Islamic penetration was usually on the basis of individual initiative, and in fact the ritual leaders deliberately kept away from strangers lest some physical harm be done them and the ritual peace of the country be endangered. They had no monopoly over the limited sources of ivory or other tradable goods, and no military power which would have enabled them to enter the business of slaving.[31] Even if political power could have been gained by association with the Muslim traders and Islam, there was no legitimate means of exercising this power within the limits of the structure of Gogo society.[32] In fact, it is clear that the role of the ritual leader and the premises upon which it rested were entirely incompatible with conversion to Islam and genealogical connexions with Arabian or any Muslim groups. For the justification of the ritual authority of certain Gogo clans does not rest upon their association with the areas from which they came, or the people there from whom they are descended. Rather it rests upon that part of the history which tells how they gained ritual control of their specific area, either by coming with the rain-stones to a virtually empty place or by the acquisition of the rain-stones from a group already there by some 'justifiable' method.

Gogo clans thus had no means or reasons for linking themselves historically with any powerful group of outsiders, Muslim or otherwise, and there was no basis for a fictional genealogy supporting lineage authority. Clans or individuals could thus not be invested with divine grace by rules of descent, except in relation to the areas in which they had ritual leadership. That is, it was the locality in association with the clan that conferred ritual authority; not descent from an ultimate source of divine grace.

[31] Gogo had age groups of warriors which cut across ritual boundaries and which were mobilized in defence against enemies, including the Masai and the Hehe. But these groups seldom embraced large parts of Ugogo in their actual organization, and ritual leaders were not in control of them.

[32] It will be shown in a forthcoming paper that the creation of government chiefs in Ugogo by the British administration, in keeping with the policy of indirect rule, did not have the effect intended of fully integrating roles of secular political authority with Gogo social structure. They always remained external; an addition, an imposition from outside. (See my paper, 'Politics and Modern Leadership Roles in Ugogo', in V. Turner (ed.), *Colonialism in Africa*, vol. III, 1970.)

We have seen, then, that in Ugogo there were no politically dominant groups or clans which could take over Islam to their own political advantage as there were in the West African States.[33] Neither could Gogo clans or kin groups adapt to a new myth of origin which would bind them to the Prophet's lineage and so ensure the flow of divine grace which was so important among the Somali.[34] The very concept of divine grace is foreign to Gogo cosmology and, in keeping with their kinship organization and non-segmentary lineage system, Gogo religious and cosmological concepts bear no relation to Islamic theological doctrine. Gogo do not think of the spirits of the dead as being in any hierarchy of proximity to God, as I have already mentioned; nor do they think of living senior kin as any more endowed with spiritual power. The elders are simply closer to the spirits of the dead because they knew most of them when alive, and their age seniority gives them more wisdom, both secular and religious.

But before I examine in more detail Gogo religious ideas and cosmology and their significance to the non-acceptance of Islam, I shall consider one more structural problem: the lack of any group or community of specialists in Gogo society who could have taken on the functions of religious teachers, the agents of the spread of Islamic religion and culture. The importance of this role in the spread of Islam in West Africa and Somaliland has already been mentioned. In the West African states there was often sufficient specialization to allow the growth of such a group; in Somaliland they emanated from the religious communities and had a very definite function outside of the purveying of

[33] Nadel says of Islam in Nupe, 'The King first adopted Islam. . . . From the beginning, then, Islamization in Nupe was bound up with political interests and represented a "change from above" ' (op. cit., p. 233).

[34] The importance of a theory of descent from origins close to the Prophet is shown in many Islamic African societies. Trimingham (1952, op. cit., p. 193) says of a group of Islamic Galla, 'The ruling families of the Wallo (Galla) were the only Muslim Galla who have ever made any pretensions of Arab descent.' Greenberg, op. cit., p. 12, says of the Hausa Muslims, 'All the Islamized tribes of the Sudan seek to establish a traditional connection with Mecca—or, if their history does not take them back to the time of the Prophet—with Baghdad, the seat in later times of the Abbasid Caliphate.' It is likely that many other Islamized groups in East and North-East Africa trace descent ultimately to Muhammad's lineage or other Arabian lineages. Trimingham (1962, p. 19) confirms this for the Bajun people of the north Kenya coast.

Islamic doctrine and law. There was no group or category of people within Gogo society which could take on these functions, and I have already shown that the small Muslim communities which did grow up along the trade routes through Ugogo had little influence upon the Gogo themselves. All Gogo specialists, such as smiths, diviners, potters, and basket-makers and others, continue to participate in the basic economic, social, and political activities of the community common to all. Only a few diviners specialize and are successful to the extent that they take part in no other economic activities, and this is the only role internal to Gogo society which could have taken on novel functions.[35] But again there is no community or cult-group of diviners, and the skill of divination is passed down through dreams, thus ensuring the choice of the spirits of the dead, and not through apprenticeship and 'learning the trade'.[36] However, literacy and the literary dissemination of doctrine, though important, have not always been essential for the spread of Islam. There is evidence that the majority of the population of the medieval Islamic states on the East African coast were not literate, as there is a conspicuous lack of inscriptions in the remains of their towns.[37]

In concluding this section it should be noted that there are a number of cultural elements in Gogo society which could in some respects be said to correspond with some aspects of Islamic culture. Among these are circumcision and initiation into adult society, which have been absorbed from local institutions in many parts of West Africa and accepted as a part of Muslim

[35] Nadel has shown how Islamic ideas influenced divination techniques in Nupe. One Gogo diviner I came across used the novel method of 'reading' a book during a consultation and flipping the pages rapidly. Whether he could actually read or not was considered irrelevant, however, as he 'saw' what he wanted through his powers as a diviner, not as a reader. But I have seen no evidence of Islamic influence on Gogo divination, and Gogo do not use Islamic texts as charms or medicine. Rather, Gogo divination techniques and the social context in which they operate are entirely bound up with Gogo values. If there is influence from external sources it is from the Nilo-Hamitic Masai and Baraguyu peoples, and sometimes from the Taturu (Tatoga) in the north-west of Gogo country.

[36] This is equally true of the skill of smithing (*wutyani*).

[37] Mathew, in Oliver and Mathew (eds.), 1963, p. 116.

doctrine. The importance of initiation into Islamic orders in Somaliland has been discussed by Lewis. But circumcision in Gogo thought does not involve initiation into a religious community and a setting out on the path to God. There could be no Islamic influence upon Gogo circumcision in any of its religious, cultural, or functional aspects without radical change in the premises upon which it is based; and it is still entirely bound up with Gogo religious ideas and the fertility of the country, under the influence of the ritual leaders.

V. GOGO RELIGION AND ISLAM

Gogo believe in the spirits of the dead (*milungu*) and their power to influence the living. A great number of occurrences, good and bad, are attributed to the intervention of the spirits of the dead, but death is never caused by them and is always the result of witchcraft. The spirits of the dead are propitiated in a number of ways and at fairly frequent intervals. But the only regular rites of propitiation are connected with the spirits of the ritual leaders of the country, at yearly rituals for fertility, rain, and protection from sickness and natural catastrophe. Most family spirits are propitiated only irregularly, upon the instigation of a diviner.

The spirits which can and do affect a person and interfere in his affairs are not only those of his lineal ancestors. They are of a wide range of paternal and maternal kin, and even close affines and other kin of one's wife. It is up to a diviner to decide which spirits should be approached upon specific occasions, but the participants in the ritual usually call out the names of all the dead kin they can remember at the particular moment. Any of the spirits can be approached through the gravestone of one's father, for all the spirits are in the same 'place'. It is seldom necessary to know where the graves of one's grandfathers are, and indeed they are often very far away. Some minor rites of propitiation can be performed in the house about one of the roof poles of the outer room.

Gogo draw strong, if only implicit, associations between cattle and the spirits of the dead, and the best way to propitiate the latter is the sacrifice of a beast. It is also essential that all propitiatory rituals must take place early in the morning, before the herd has gone out to pasture, or 'the spirits will disperse and not come to listen when you call'. Another indication of this association is that at beer sacrifices or libations (*misambwa*) a ring of mud or beer lees is made around the correct roof pole and beer poured into it. This trough is called *mulambo*, which is also the drinking trough made for cattle at the wells during the dry season. At the end of the ceremony a breach is made in the ritual trough and the beer allowed to flow out in the direction from which the clan came. This opening is called *ideha*, which is the gate to the cattle byre (and thus also to the homestead).

Although in serious cases cattle must be sacrificed to the spirits of the dead, showing their considerable power, this is the case usually only for the communal rituals for the country, to the spirits of the ritual head. But the spirits of the dead are in no way held in awe and are in fact addressed in everyday tones during the ceremony, and sometimes positively rudely.[38] Although the oldest male member of the family should be present, a great variety of people participate and address the spirits during most rites, and a person is chosen to do this as much because of generation position and age as any association with spiritual power. Members of the senior generation 'remember the names of the dead' and so can perform the ceremony more adequately than others.

There is another manner in which the spirits of the dead may contact the living, and vice versa. This is through spirit possession (*kutowa macisi*); but anyone may be possessed by the spirits and there is no cult group associated with spirit possession. Mediums do not form a specialized group with specifically religious functions.

Thus, although there is the conception that the dead can interfere with the living, there is no idea that they are in closer association with any other source of supernatural power, and they are not, as I have said, held in any particular awe. They may

[38] I know of one elderly lady who was said to address the spirits in the most abusive tones and language and gain excellent results every time.

be offended if neglected, but are not intermediaries for any other divinity. In fact, the name of the clan founder is seldom mentioned in propitiation. Gogo say that he is included in the term *wakuku ʒetu* (our 'ancestors' of all kinds), and that is as far as one should go. There is no hierarchy of spirits, and no necessity for the spirits to intercede on behalf of the living. There are no eponymous lineage ancestors whose spirits must be approached, although maximal lineage groups (who can trace their patrilineal descent) may be named in some contexts after the apical ancestor. But he is not specially approached and has no more spiritual power than any other spirits. Usually his grave would probably be unknown. The only exception to this is again in the case of the ritual leaders' clans, who claim to know the graves of all their 'lineal' ancestors from the founding of the country.

It is apparent that although Gogo have religious leaders with considerable ritual power, they are not in any way the heads of religious groups and do not have links with a specific set of spiritual beings whom only they may approach. They simply hold ritual sway over an area and the people within it at any point in time, who are not a kin group tied in a congregation to one set of ancestor spirits. And even within these limits, religious leaders in Ugogo have little power to enforce their authority. Neither are they particularly powerful when they die, except in so far as the dichotomy exists between the spirits of the clan with ritual precedence, and others in the one area. The gravestones of the *watemi* religious leaders have no communal group reference outside their local context, within which they may be said to have more ritual influence than those of individuals of other clans in that area. This is not, however, because they are in any way genealogically senior to others; I have already shown that they do not have to be the spirits of lineal ancestors, but may be those of a great variety of dead kin. The Muslim concept of *baraka* and its inheritance could thus not be integrated into the role of Gogo religious leaders and the spirit world they have to deal with.

Before concluding with a brief exploration of Gogo ideas of a high god, I must make some mention of one more category of spirits in Gogo belief which are wholly evil to all except those who control them. These evil spirits are called *masoce* (singular *isoce*) and are acquired by people who dig up the bodies of those recently buried and 'resuscitate' them. Some of these evil spirits live in the bush, others are controlled by people who use them to their own (mainly economic) advantage. Into this concept could possibly be absorbed the Islamic one of malignant spirits or *jinn*. But in Gogo thought these evil spirits do not have wills and a domain of their own; they do not possess people. Instead people possess them as an adjunct to their evil and avaricious designs. They are essentially a part of human activity.

Gogo do talk of a remote female being (*Maduwo*) who is sometimes credited with creation in general but is more often associated with dust-devils (*mankhundi*). The word is used to frighten children, and there is a story of how Maduwo comes and snatches away bad and disobedient children. The power of Maduwo is considerable but not specified, and she is not so interested in human affairs as to be held responsible for death or other misfortune. She is said to make appearances, always in some other part of the country, and Gogo cynically say that the reported appearances are always elsewhere: you never meet a person who has actually seen or experienced Maduwo. Otherwise the concept is of a vague and evil power, otiose and unapproachable. It would be inconceivable to address prayers to this power, and adults stand in no fear of it.

It can be seen from this brief sketch of Gogo spirit beliefs and religious ideas that they do not conceive of religious activity as an approach to a final all-powerful divinity, or even a remote ancestor near to a divinity. And neither is there any logical reason that there should be such a concept in Gogo belief when Gogo religious ideas are viewed in terms of their ideology of descent and kinship, and their concepts of history. There is no structural hierarchy of segmentary lineages which could be subsumed eventually under one major genealogical myth linking all to a common set of spirits and, through them, to a source of divine grace and power. If Gogo clans are linked at all it is through historical accident or remote non-lineal kinship links. In terms of Gogo society and belief then, there is no room for a concept of divine authority and power into which it would be advantageous to be finally absorbed, parallel with the Islamic concept of final absorption in God (*gnosis*). Consequently, no external or internal *group* can claim any more divine authority than any other and provide for its justification in terms of Gogo social institutions and religious beliefs. As a result of this, most external religious influences are absorbed by individuals as a way out of their society and cannot be internalized. This applies also to Christian conversion. Until recently, when there are other motivations, Gogo did not easily accept any external or novel religious affiliation; although not because of the strength of Gogo religious beliefs, which are very tolerant and amorphous. But conversion, meant a complete break with Gogo social values and institutions and a move to the outside of them. If Islam could have provided some Gogo with reasons for accepting conversion, it would have had also to provide somewhere for the faithful to go; not physically, but as a social category. Their new way of life and religious belief could in no way be integrated with Gogo society itself.

VI. CONCLUSIONS

In a paper of this scope it is obviously not possible to give a systematic analysis of Gogo religion and social structure and their incompatibility with Islamic religion and culture. This would entail a detailed examination of Gogo cosmology, witch beliefs, divination, and so on, and a wide range of cultural elements, relating each to the processes of the absorption of Islam as seen in other societies. What I have tried to do is demonstrate in general terms why, although the historical circumstances existed for the peaceful assimilation of Islam into Gogo society, this did not occur. I have suggested that this is at least partly a result of the existence of certain structural elements in Gogo society unfavourable to such assimilation, and the lack of certain other structural prerequisites for the absorption of Islam into non-centralized tribal societies. In spite of the flexibility of Islam in adaptation to local conditions (amply demonstrated for many parts of Africa), in all Islamic communities there is a basic unity of religious practice and theological belief, and these common elements demand certain structural prerequisites, depending upon the form of the pre-Islamic society.[39] In Ugogo these prerequisites were not present, and instead there were others of a negative nature.

Consistent with the structural incompatibilities of Gogo society for Islamic syncretism, I have tried to show that Gogo concepts of spirits of the dead, spiritual power, and divinity are also incompatible with the main Islamic theological notions; or, for that matter, with those of any religion based upon mystical concepts. This interpretation may have served to highlight some of the conditions for the acceptance of Islam in African societies.

REFERENCES

Beidelman, T. O.
    (1962) 'A History of Ukaguru: 1887–1916', *Tanganyika Notes and Records*. vol. 58, pp. 11–39.
Greenberg, J.
    (1946) *The Influence of Islam on a Sudanese Religion*, Monographs of the American Ethnological Society, No. X.
Hailey, M.
    (1956) *An African Survey*, London.
Levy, R.
    (1957) *The Social Structure of Islam*, Cambridge U.P.
Lewis, I. M.
    (1955/56) 'Sufism in Somaliland—A Study in Tribal Islam', *Bulletin of the School of Oriental and African Studies*, vol. XVII, no. 3, pp. 581–602; vol. XVIII, no. 1, pp. 146–60.
    (1961) *A Pastoral Democracy*, O.U.P. for I.A.I., London.
Little, K. L.
    (1951) *The Mende of Sierra Leone*, Routledge and Kegan Paul, London.
Moffet, J. P. (ed.)
    (1958) *Handbook of Tanganyika*, Government of Tanganyika, Dar es Salaam.
Nadel, S. F.
    (1954) *Nupe Religion*, Routledge and Kegan Paul, London.
Oliver, R. and Mathew, G. (eds.)
    (1963) *History of East Africa*, Vol. I, O.U.P., London.

[39] Greenberg (1946, p. 11) describes this basic underlying unity of Islamic culture and says that although Islam reached the Hausa '. . . through such diverse media as the Negroes of Mali and Songhai, Tuaregs and Arab traders, it is still possible to speak of the effect of Islam on the Hausa people as a single coherent process.'

Smith, M. G.
  (1960) *Government in Zazzau: 1800–1950*, O.U.P. for I.A.I., London.
Smith, W. Robertson:
  (1889) *The Religion of the Semites*, 3rd ed. 1927, A. E. Black, London.
Stenning, D. J.
  (1959) *Savannah Nomads*, O.U.P. for I.A.I., London.
Trimingham, J. S.
  (1949) *Islam in the Sudan*, O.U.P., London.
  (1952) *Islam in Ethiopia*, O.U.P., London.
  (1962) *Islam in East Africa*, C.W.M.E. Research Pamphlet, Edinburgh House
    Press.

XIV. A CONTROVERSY OVER ISLAMIC CUSTOM IN KILWA KIVINJE, TANZANIA

PETER LIENHARDT

Under the names '*adah* and '*urf*, Islamic legal authorities have long recognized the existence of local custom which can sometimes run counter to details of the *Shari'a* . Traditional customs hallowed with age in particular Muslim communities may be at variance with what members of these communities find recommended in the Arabic legal text-books if and when they learn to read them. The divergence between the strict prescriptions of the scholars and the custom of the community is not, however, to be attributed simply to difficulties of acquiring the books and reading them. Customary procedures have their own positive content, and even in Arab communities and the centres of Arab civilization local custom has continued to assert itself side by side with the scholarly law. But where Arabic is not the daily language of the community one may expect to find more people doubtful of the ways in which their own popular Islam differs from the prescriptions of the *Shari'a*, and here arise differences of opinion within one and the same community.

What is a man to do if his studies suggest that the custom of his community is at variance with what the text-books say? In an Arabic phrase, 'Religious learning is like the sea': there may exist other books he does not know of that give authoritative support to local practices. Not all would copy those of the extremist *ikhwan* of the Wahhabi movement, who, with a passion for reform greater than their learning, held as forbidden or disapproved local practices which the consensus of learned opinion allowed. Even if a man is convinced that some of his people's customs are unsupported by scholarly authority, he may decide that there is little he can do about it. What if they are supported by local men whose reputation for holiness is greater than his own? Or what if taking action would involve a change in the society which most would think out of proportion to the seriousness of the issue involved? I remember one religious leader in Tanganyika commenting regretfully on women in a particular village who, with all good intentions, would pick up and suckle any infant they saw crying if they had the milk to give it. Strictly speaking, all the children so suckled by the same woman probably entered into the prohibited degrees of kinship with one another as a result of this solicitude, and no one knew who as a child had been suckled at one time or another by whom. This cast some doubt on the strict validity of marriages in the village when the children grew up, but the man who knew this could scarcely suggest that the whole village should avoid the dangers of this anomaly by becoming exogamous.

This case, however, was simply one of neglecting the strict law. In other instances the action is positive, and it is argued that since the community is traditionally Muslim, its customs must be so likewise. Thus, there exist customs which, though unsupported in the books, are still for particular communities their own religious orthodoxy. They have been handed down, it is said, from the great men of the past; and were not the people of olden times more pious and more learned than the backsliders and opportunists of nowadays? Nevertheless, the improvement of communications and the increase of literacy in recent years have produced various influences working upon the local scene and modifying the system of values in which local custom operates. There has been contact with the Christianity, the agnosticism, and the social doctrines which have spread out from the west, and also contact with Islamic thought from other Muslim countries which have been less isolated before.

In East Africa changes brought about through the introduction of missions and colonial rule have also altered the situation by modifying the relative status of the people of the interior and the coast. Not very long ago the coastal people could look upon themselves as the truly cultured and civilized people of East Africa, for those were days when the only literate education was an Islamic one and the only religion with claims to universality was Islam. Colonial rule brought with it a slow change. Many pagans of the interior were converted to Christianity, a religion which also carried with it a claim to universality and a body of learning, while the Muslims of the coast naturally resisted any change of faith. The Christian mission schools, largely rejected on religious grounds by the coastal people, provided an education more in tune with the forces of the European society from which they came than did the old teaching of the Quran schools and the mosques, and it was these European forces that were changing the political and economic organization of the country. Pupils of such schools acquired better qualifications for government and commercial employment than could be obtained under the existing Islamic system. This disadvantage of the coastal people was not easily made up by government schools: many of the religious leaders and ordinary Muslims of the coast for long distrusted government schools, because even if they were not specifically Christian neither were they Muslim in the traditional sense. It was feared that Muslims attending them might receive teaching that conflicted with their faith. Following from this state of affairs, many people of the coast, by experience, are now made conscious that disadvantages have followed from conservatism. Some look for progress to a more modern organization within the Islamic system. In this roundabout way the reformers of local custom come to have a number of extraneous forces on their side.

The controversy I speak of here was closely connected with these matters, though it has little directly to do with education. It arose over the question of how to pray for rain. This confrontation between local orthodoxy and the orthodoxy of the religious text-books took place in the little town of Kilwa Kivinje in 1959. Kilwa Kivinje lies on the coast of southern Tanganyika and has a population of just under three thousand, almost all of whom are born Muslims adhering to the Shafi'i school of law. Most of them fast Ramadan and many pray the five daily prayers, though apart from those who are unwilling to do this, there are some who do not know the words and once they have grown up are embarrassed to admit it, so cannot ask to be taught. Many of the people have attended Quran schools and so learned to read the Arabic letters and to write their own language, Swahili, in Arabic script. But as for the Arabic language, although Arabic is the language of prayers, of sermons, and of law books, there are not many people in Kilwa who have any knowledge of it.

In the early months of 1959 there was general distress in Kilwa because of the lack of rain. The situation was not so bad as in the year before, but the rain that had fallen had come inconveniently in heavy showers, with periods of hot sun from a clear sky in between. The sun had killed the rice before it could get established. This was before the time of independence, and some of the people remarked that the German colonial government and the earlier government of the Sultans of Zanzibar had been much more effective in matters of rain than were the British. The earlier governments used to give an animal to be slaughtered in a ceremony called *ʒinguo mji*, 'ridding the town of evil', a ceremony used in praying for rain and also in times of war and epidemic. It was said that when the Ngoni were threatening Kilwa during the period just before the Germans came, the people had consulted an augury to find out what they could do and had learned that they should 'rid the town of evil' according to custom. So they had taken a black bull round the town in procession—the word *ʒinguo*, which occurs in the name of the ceremony, is connected with the idea of going around or unwrapping. But on that occasion they simply released the bull into the bush like a scapegoat instead of sacrificing it. It was said that when freed this bull had become very ferocious and had come to the outskirts of the town digging up and eating corpses in the graveyard (a kind of behaviour attributed to sorcerers). The ceremony had succeeded. The Ngoni approaching Kilwa saw the shadows of palm trees and thought they were shadows of a great army which they dared not face. They left Kilwa in search of easier game.

It is not, of course, possible to know everything that was said about the lack of rain at the time of the dispute in 1959: I can only report what was said to me and what I overheard. One opinion I heard attributed the lack of rain to God's displeasure with the people for having left off their pious and wholesome old ways. In the past, it was said, they were generous with each other and used to share out their harvests among their families and neighbours. Thus, they acquired blessing (*baraka*). Now the blessing was withdrawn, for every man was filled with self-interest, eager to cultivate for himself and sell his produce in the market for money. Some of the personal misgivings which followed from social change and the moving of a subsistence towards a cash economy were thus expressed in relation to the divine control of weather.

There was no widespread certainty that anything done would necessarily produce more rain. It was said that rain might or might not come as a result of prayers, but that there was no point in people's thinking that they could just pray once and get what they wanted. Only constant perseverance made prayers fruitful. The example of the Prophet was quoted in this connexion, for God had at first laid down that the set prayers must be prayed fifty times a day. The Prophet had interceded on behalf of mankind and asked God to reduce the obligation to five, but even he had had to beg God three times to do this before the favour was granted. (According to the religious commentators, the Prophet Muhammad was advised by the Prophet Moses to ask for this mercy during his visit to heaven.)

Many people in Kilwa are adherents of the Qadiriyya religious order, whose Shaikh there has a high reputation for holiness. (At the time of the 1959 elections, when there was a slight doubt about the relations of Muslims and Christians in Tanganyika, the now President made his first visit during his election tour to Kilwa to this remarkable man.) One of the members of the Qadiriyya order said that the best way to bring rain was to fast for one to three days and make a vow to the saint who founded the Qadiriyya, Shaikh 'Abd al-Qadir al-Jilani. To him many miracles were attributed. One of the Qadiriyya songs sung at funerals refers to how Shaikh 'Abd al-Qadir used to preach sitting on a dead palm trunk, and how, when he departed, this dead trunk went on repeating his sermons—*Gogo limesema maneno yake*: 'The tree trunk spoke his words.'

The opinion that was to prevail, in as far as any did, since in the long run it was largely ignored, was that of a man who was probably the most learned in religious books in Kilwa. In spite of this superior learning, he did not hold the highest position there in religious precedence, since religious appointments tend to go in families and there were others from families longer established in the town who were closer to these mosque livings. At a meeting called to discuss the question of praying for rain he stated that the religious authorities said nothing about making sacrifices in this connexion: what the people should do was to fast for four days and then to gather with their flocks and herds outside the town and pray for rain. The meeting agreed to do this, but with little enthusiasm. Most people still seemed inclined to think that if anything was to be done effectively it was by the *ʒinguo mji*, the ceremony that had proved successful in the past.

The *ʒinguo mji* is a ceremony that has been very widespread in the East African coastal area, though it now seems to be passing out of use. It has been performed in slightly different forms, to my knowledge, from Lamu to the Kilwa area, beyond which points my inquiries did not reach. Some said in Kilwa that the *ʒinguo mji* should begin with a three-day fast. Others said fasting had nothing to do with it. Since it did not occur on this occasion, I cannot say which opinion corresponded better to the actual performance of the ceremony, but I have not heard of a fast preceding the *ʒinguo mji* elsewhere, and so am inclined to think that the talk of fasting may have followed from the other opinions about fasting expressed on this occasion. The victim, it was said, should be a black he goat or a black bull which was led round the town in procession before being sacrificed, the banner of the Qadiriyya order being carried along with it in Kilwa. Three rounds of bread made from millet flour and called *mofa* were contributed by each household. This is a special sort of bread used for ceremonies and has the alternative name of *mikate ya sadaqa*, 'charity loaves'. The meal is made up of the flesh of a sacrificial victim, and this bread is spoken of here and in other places as fulfilling the Islamic duty of dispensing charity.

After taking it round the town the men led the victim out to a place in the bush called *Kwa Bwana Fundi*, where there was a little spring. *Bwana Fundi*—'Mr. Technician'—was a German of the colonial period who lived near the place. The word *kwa* usually occurs in names of places associated with spirits. The men kept the bull there in the bush with them for the night. Meanwhile the women were spending the night just outside the town at a place where there are two baobab trees. The older of them has fallen on its side and is called *mbuyu kiwete*, 'the lame baobab', while the younger is *mbuyu mkuta*, 'the skipping-rope baobab'. Both of them have a great many ship's nails hammered into them where people have tried to return sorcery to those they suspected of directing it against them. Here the women spent the night skipping with a rope tied to one of the baobab trees. Before the skipping-rope baobab grew to full size they used the other baobab, and in those days they used to wear plain clothes, as in mourning, but on changing over to the skipping-rope baobab they altered their custom and began to dress in their best clothes for the ceremony.

The next day the bull was sacrificed in the bush. There was a particular man whose job it was to kill it, and his two assistants helped him to cook it later, but this was not a matter of any great significance in Kilwa, and the jobs were not hereditary. In the village of Pande, about twenty miles from Kilwa, where the *zinguo mji* has been performed more frequently in recent years (the headman there said it had taken place three times within the last twelve years) any man might kill the bull, and of course in Islam in general it is not significant who actually performs a sacrifice so long as it is a Muslim man. Before the bull was slaughtered there were little Arabic prayers in rhyme, each repeated seven times over. The men, or such as could, wore two white cloths, one round the waist and the other over the shoulders (a style of dress reminiscent of the *ihram* costume of the pilgrimage when the pilgrims are in a state of purification). At each repetition of the prayer they would invert the cloth that lay over the shoulders and bring it over the forehead. The first prayer ran:

> *Marhaba bi-'l-nabi, al-nabi wa-'l-sahabah*
> *Wa aminna bihi wa bima jabah.*

Welcome to the Prophet, the Prophet and his Companions,
We believe in him and in what he brought (i.e. the revelation).

The second prayer was:

*Ya Allaha jid (sc. Allahumma jud) amtara
Ghaithan wa-'l-mann min dirarah.*

O God bring copious rain
In the clouds, favour lies in heavy rainclouds.

Men laid their hands on the back of the bull (so one informant said) and then it was slaughtered with the usual Islamic expression, *Allah akbar*, 'God is most great'. The skin of the victim was cut up to make it useless and was left in the bush, where it would be eaten by hyenas. The meat was taken back into the town to be cooked and was eaten at the Friday mosque with the charity bread. (In this respect the ceremony at Kilwa Kivinje was unlike that at Kilwa Kisiwani seventeen miles away, where the meat could on no account be brought back into the village.) The bones were carefully collected to be taken back into the bush with the hooves and other inedible parts and buried there under a particular kapock tree, a sort of tree much associated with spirits. The food at the mosque was set out on mats, and at the end of the meal the people inverted the mats and repeated the prayers. This inversion of the mats and earlier of the cloths that were on the men's shoulders is clearly a symbolical expression of the desire to change circumstances. Connected with the same word *zinguo* is also another ceremony, this time a personal one, to perform which is called *kuringuliwa*. It is adopted by some people who find themselves suffering from a run of personal misfortune.

As I have said, the *zinguo mji* was not carried out. A meeting attended by the District Commissioner and the Liwali of Kilwa decided to take the advice of the religious teachers who proposed fasting and prayer according to the recommendations of the books. But the decision was a half-hearted one, the more so because Ramadan and the six days of super-rogatory fasting that follow it had only just ended. People were tired of fasting and began making excuses for avoiding it. At the meeting which discussed the question of a special fast the District Commissioner had acted with circumspection: immediately after the meeting began he had announced that the subject was a religious one and that he would hand over the conduct of business to the Muslim officers. This was a rather touchy time. Independence was approaching, but the people did not yet know when or how it would come.

In spite of the tact of the District Commissioner, many people were ready to take up any attitude to excuse themselves from standing by the decision of the meeting. A number continued to say that a question of religion such as this should have been discussed by the Muslims in the mosque, and it was not for the District Commissioner to teach people their religion. (In fact, the District Commissioner had only been there at all because he had specially been asked to come, presumably with the idea in some quarters that the Government might be prepared to contribute a bull to the *zinguo mji* ceremony, though when it came to the point it was never asked to do so.) Others, in rather similar vein, said that if any fasting was to be done the Government officials should do it—were they not in charge of the welfare of the country? Many just did not expect any quantity of rain in any case. There was no idea of praying for a miracle in their idea of praying for rain. The rainy season was near its end, and they said that any rain that came now would be of little use— were they to fast for drinking water? And there were quite a number who expressed annoyance at having a change in the customs of the past introduced. It was asked rhetorically whether the people of the past could not be assumed to have been more learned than those of the present day. It seemed to me that there was some suggestion that because the men of the past were born earlier, even though they had died, they were much older and wiser people, fitting in with the idea of wisdom's being associated with seniority among the living. But probably the main cause of lack of co-operation in the fast was what was often said too: that Ramadan and the six super-rogatory days were enough and the people could not face any more fasting.

I do not know how many people fasted at the time agreed, but there were not many. Some with high religious reputations were to be seen eating and smoking in public. Others who would have followed their example in fasting and had even begun the fast also followed their example in not fasting when this became plain. And there were some who drank their tea in private until they were quite sure that it was respectable to drink it in public. The rain did not noticably increase, and the rainy season was soon at an end. Nothing had happened to justify any earlier point of view, nor had the confrontation of tradition by book learning reached any clear conclusion in favour of either.

The material relevant to such a dispute as I have here described is naturally extensive and varied, but out of it I will select only one conversation, also from Kilwa. Among those present were a Matumbi, a Yao, a reformer of custom, a religious Shaikh, and a Muslim stranger from Mombasa. Both the Matumbi and the Yao have shrines for ancestral spirits, and the reformer was criticizing them for this. He announced provocatively that to maintain these shrines was forbidden (*haramu*) in just the same way as eating pork. The Yao replied that his tribe was accustomed to this old traditional way of maintaining shrines dedicated to ancestors whom they asked to help them in their difficulties. The reformer told him: 'You are all unbelievers and neither full Muslims nor full pagans. You are just giving foreigners the opportunity to criticize us.' The Yao said that theirs was simply a harmless custom; it was just a matter of remembering the ancestors and was simply like saying the *fatihah*. The stranger, playfully encouraging the controversy, asked why, if this was forbidden, the Muslims used a prayer calling by name on those who had fought on the Prophet's side at the Battle of Badr: were they not all dead people? The religious shaikh announced that Muslims read this prayer in order to ask the people it mentioned to pray to God for them in accordance with their wishes. The Matumbi and the Yao then said that if this was so, surely they had the right to ask their ancestors to pray for them? Another Matumbi finished off the conversation by saying that praying to the ancestors was effective, but it was still wrong. This was because when people went to pray at ancestral shrines there were evil spirits there. These spirits repeated the prayers, and when they opened their mouths towards heaven their breath stank so abominably that the angels could not endure it and asked God to grant the prayer quickly to stop the smell. This sort of praying was wrong therefore because it amounted to a molestation of the angels.

The details of this controversy over rain provide a glimpse of one small Islamic community undergoing the complex process of social change. This process includes the questioning and modification of values. Communications, so important in producing social change, bring not one but manifold influences to bear upon the values of the small locality. Here indirect influences are just as important as the direct ones. In Kilwa, Westernization and the more fully *Shari'a* form of Islam enter together upon the local scene. At the same time there are movements towards a more fully cash economy, to wage labour, and to a resultant increase in the economic independence of the young.

Because of the improvement of communications the society changes its scale. People have wider and more frequent contacts outside their traditional localities. They have more to compare themselves with. This is particularly the case while the change of scale is going on, for the more obvious differences within the new, wider area have yet to be ironed out. It is found that what is taken for granted in one place does not necessarily command sympathy in another. In the comparison of values which arises, change has already occurred in the larger centres, and there are aspects of life there, whether of comfort or sophistication, which excite admiration. They carry a higher prestige than the people of the small locality can credit to themselves. The attitudes of their inhabitants cannot be ignored. Self-consciousness increases among the people of the small locality, particularly among the young. The values of the local community are questioned.

Reason and will play an important part in change, for being less satisfied with their position when they have more to compare it with, the people want to produce change while it is producing them, to direct themselves towards improvement, and to control it. In the wider sphere in which they move they also wish to guard themselves against criticisms of themselves which they either know or suspect to be made by relative strangers, people whose opinions they cannot disregard because they seem in some ways to be leading a superior kind of life. One finds, for example, younger Mawiha living away from home who congratulate themselves on having escaped receiving the conspicuous facial markings of that people. They find that the significance attached to these markings at home does not apply when Mawiha are away from home, and the markings single them out in ways they find embarrassing.

In the general questioning of values those of religion do not escape scrutiny. The prestige of religious practice and leadership suffers some decline. Here those religious leaders who are ill-equipped to justify religious practice on a basis of scholarship are at a loss. Those who are better educated make some progress in having their views accepted and in advancing in prestige relative to the rest, for though they may lack the strength of hereditary position, this disadvantage is of less account when hereditary position itself is being questioned too. As the social world of the small community is broadened, corporate folk customs decline, since customs which people find difficult to explain rationally need something more than local and personal authority to justify them. On the other hand, it is difficult to replace them with more orthodox and rigorous practices which are new to the local community. This would demand an authority which even the educated cannot easily achieve in a period of doubt.

INDEX